GAVIN GOODFELLOW

The Lure of Burnt Swamp

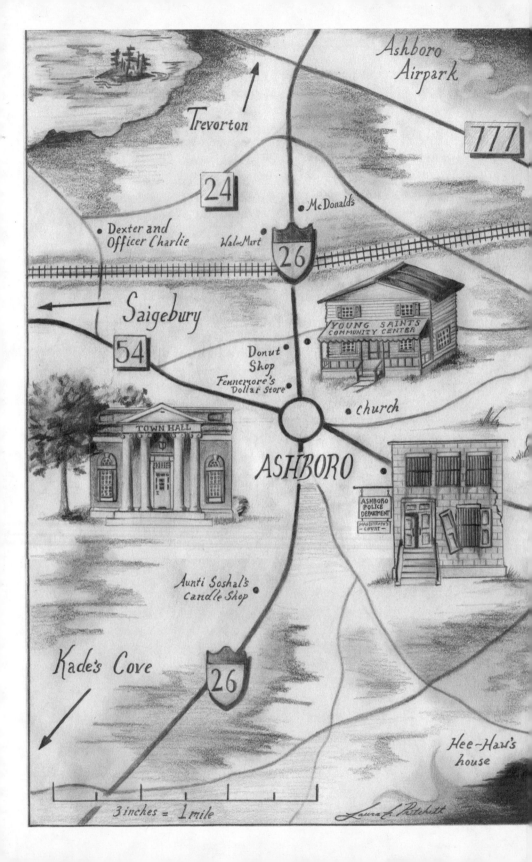

GAVIN GOODFELLOW
The Lure of Burnt Swamp

by

CANDY ABBOTT

GAVIN GOODFELLOW
THE LURE OF BURNT SWAMP
Copyright © 2007 Candace F. Abbott

ISBN 978-1-886068-02-5 hardbound
Library of Congress Control Number: 2006940792

ISBN 978-1-886068-03-2 soft cover
Library of Congress Control Number: 2006911216

Fiction · Fantasy · Faith · Religious and Inspirational · Young Adult

Published by Fruitbearer Publishing
P.O. Box 777, Georgetown, DE 19947
(302) 856-6649 · FAX (302) 856-7742
www.fruitbearer.com

www.GavinGoodfellow.com

Graphic design by Candy Abbott

Editorial Team: Diane Cook, Managing Editor;
Marlene Bagnull, Litt.D.; Joyce Moccero; Linda Windsor

TOLL FREE ORDERS: 1-800-247-6553
www.AtlasBooks.com

Scripture is taken from:

The Message (MSG), copyright © 1993, used by permission of NavPress Publishing Group.

The King James Version of the Holy Bible (KJV), public domain.

The *HOLY BIBLE NEW INTERNATIONAL VERSION* (NIV), Copyright © 1973, 1978, 1984 International Bible Society. Used by permission of Zondervan Bible Publishers.

Printed in the United States of America

For Natalie and Trevor,
Kade and Saige

Godly grandchildren—
praise the Lord!

Reader, Be Warned!

You are about to engage in genuine
spiritual warfare.

Keep a cool head.
Stay alert.
The Devil is poised to pounce,
and would like nothing better
than to catch you napping.
Keep your guard up.

1 Peter 5:8 (The Message)

Contents

GAVIN GOODFELLOW

The Lure of Burnt Swamp

Preface

Forces of evil or natural disaster?

Fire remains mystery after ten years

By Di Cook
Senior Staff Reporter
dcook@thedailyencounter.com

ASHBORO – The ultimate fireworks display, triggered by a freak fire that assaulted Burnt Swamp nearly ten years ago, continues to baffle state environmentalists. No Fourth of July man-made fireworks can compare to the mysterious Halloween blaze that still smolders and flares in a swamp east of the town limits of this Eastern Shore community.

The four-alarmer struck just before midnight on October 31, 1997, bringing volunteer firefighters from the neighboring communities of Trevorton, Natsville, Kade's Cove, and Saigebury to fight the inferno. Twelve men were injured, one critically, as they struggled to bring the flames under control.

"This is the most unusual fire we've encountered in my lifetime," says Wesley Wyatt, assistant state fire marshal. "Even now, it shows no sign of burning itself out. The state has invested more time and money than we can justify, so we're putting it on the back burner—no pun intended."

Though there is no evidence of arson, Wyatt says he believes mischief makers started the blaze, but local residents don't agree. Some attribute it to a freak storm they say appeared out of nowhere and hovered over the cypress swamp. Officials from the National Weather Service at Mount Holly, NJ, say that no storm appeared on their radar that night.

Warnard Elijah Stokes, 84, who lives in the swamp, says the fires are evil. "Them fools at the weather service don't know what they're talkin' about. I saw them lightnin' bolts myself, and they weren't from no trick-or-treaters. They came straight from the talons of them fallen angels that were cast out of heaven. You can scoff about ghosts and goblins if ya want, but I know evil when I see it. And that was pure evil, clean through."

When asked to confirm a rumor that he inherited a diary that holds the key to extinguishing the current blaze where modern technology has failed, Stokes refused to comment.

According to Ashboro mayor Bruce Goodfellow, "Stokes is an eccentric with no clear grasp of reality." Right or wrong, the good people of Ashboro still clean Burnt Swamp's debris off their porches and sidewalks every day, endure the slight "rotten egg" odor, and have grown accustomed to a perpetual cloudy haze that blocks the afternoon sun.

"We can live with a little inconvenience," Goodfellow says. "After all, no place on earth is perfect."

CHAPTER ONE

GAVIN

Dumbfounded

"Dragon breath!" Gavin wrinkled his nose at the smoke that hung above the woods.

"Who you calling dragon breath?" Eric frowned. "I've been brushing. See?" He pulled his lips back and bared his teeth so the wire of his silver retainer glinted.

"Not *your* breath, Eric—Burnt Swamp. I've been trying to figure out what it smells like."

"Dragon breath, hmm?" Molly twirled the walnut-brown curls at the end of her waist-length braid. "I like that." She dug into her backpack for her ever-ready notebook.

Gavin watched the smoke's feelers slither up the path as it had for ten of his twelve years. But today the wispy tongues flicked at him and his cousins as if to say, *Back off. The road to Uncle Warney's is off-limits.*

"Why would you want to describe swamp stink anyway?" Eric raised an eyebrow. "A su u-u-mmer scho-o-o-l assignment from Woebe?"

"That's not funny." Gavin's good mood faded. His cousin's summer school dig expanded the gap between them that labeled Gavin a dunce. *What's the deal? Eric used to be my best buddy. Now he's Mr. Cooler-Than-You-Could-Ever-Hope-To-Be.*

"Why can't you be more like Eric? Sometimes he feels more like my son than you." His dad's words at breakfast struck a bitter chord in Gavin's tender heart. He was tired of competing with his not-so-perfect cousin.

"You want funny? How about this?" Molly assumed her favorite radio announcer voice and pinched her nose so hard it looked like her freckles would pop off. "Burnt Swamp smells like a fireplace burning cheap cigars and Billy Bragg's sneakers."

"The ones that got soaked when the boys' toilets overflowed." Gavin chuckled. At least she got them off the subject of summer school. He didn't feel like discussing his reading problems today. Or ever.

"Good one, Molly!" Eric slapped his sister on the back. "Billy Bragg's sneakers are smellier than dragon's breath any day."

Gavin smiled to see Molly and Eric goofing around together. He couldn't remember the last time he felt like they were a "family."

No one would guess those two were twins. They'd been at odds with each other for two years and didn't even live in the same house! Molly was so upset when her dad remarried, she begged her stepfather to adopt her. Since they had different last names, Eric told Gavin it was easier to forget they were brother and sister. Gavin thought they were both being stupid.

"Maybe dragon's breath doesn't smell so bad, after all." Gavin grinned, trying to keep the happy momentum going. He raked his fingers through his hair, pushing back stubborn red locks that tickled his eyebrows.

"You know what else is funny?" A puzzled expression clouded Molly's face. "The ground seems spongy. And it feels like we're going in the wrong direction. Shouldn't we be closer to the edge of the swamp by now?"

Eric kicked a twig that would be cinder by nightfall. "Nah, you've just lost your bearings." With that, he slipped, slid into an awkward sprawl, then straightened up. "Good save, if I do say so myself." He flexed his muscles and grinned. "When you're a jock, you're a jock."

"Shouldn't a jock know how to walk without tripping?" Molly punched him in the arm.

Eric scowled back at the twig. "*Harrumpf*. First the ground turns to spongy moss and trips me up, and then you try to push me down."

Gavin offered a humorless laugh, but his gut continued to churn. *Yeah. Eric's turned into a jock—or is it a jerk? And Molly's got brains. What have I got to show for my stinking life? Summer school.* The oppressive guilt weighed him down, agitating him more than ever. And the ground *did* seem weird and spongy. There were no chattering birds or scampering squirrels in this place—only the mournful sound of a hoot owl.

"*Hoo-hoo, hoo-WAAAHH, hoo-WAAAHHH.*"

As the threesome rounded a bend, heading deeper into the woods, the underbrush seized Gavin's ankle. *Eeeee-rie!* If Gavin didn't know better, he'd think the scraggly forest wanted him to feel alone and friendless.

With his next step, a dark-green patch of moss gave way beneath his sneaker. Dropping to one knee, Gavin pushed with his hands on ground that felt squishy and warm, then shoved himself upright and took a deep breath. Big mistake. The air smelled of spores, and the smoke made him gag as though a hand grabbed him by the throat.

A sudden, prickly sensation numbed his arms and legs. When the feeling reached his brain, he grew light-headed, and his ears rang. Gavin closed his eyes. A thousand pinpoints of white light sparkled, spun, and swirled, then disappeared into a pitch-black vortex. A strange thought rippled through his fear. *Round and round they go; where they stop nobody knows.*

As soon as the stars vanished, the vortex unleashed a hot, moist, hideous odor. Gavin opened his eyes and stared into—the yawning jaws of a dragon! Gooey drool stretched like rubber bands between razor sharp teeth and dripped from nostrils at the end of a long, bony-crested snout.

Gavin screamed, or at least he thought he did, but he couldn't hear the sound of his own voice. In what seemed like slow motion, the dragon disappeared. *What was that? This is too weird.*

Blinking his eyes open, Gavin caught a glimpse of Molly and Eric's alarmed faces before again closing his eyes and doubling over.

So this must be what it feels like to faint . . . or die.

Gavin caught his breath. But instead of fear, he felt wrapped in something so safe he thought it must be his down feather sleeping bag. Reaching out for it, his arms touched only air. His body felt buoyant. Flashing his eyes open, all security vanished. One huge, purple dragon eye glared at him . . . then the monstrous head slowly vanished, as before.

It *was* a dragon, wasn't it? *Couldn't be.* The Burnt Swamp dragon was only a legend.

Where am I? What day is this? He tried to picture the kitchen wall calendar and decided it must be Wednesday. July. *Yeah, July 20th. The 20th? Oh, no! I'm supposed to be getting a haircut! Dad's going to kill me—if something else doesn't get me first.*

"Molly? Eric?" Silence.

Gavin was alone in the mist. In all the years the swamp had been burning, it had never looked like this. Gavin had stepped into a land of fog, glittering with flashes of white light.

He could see *through* everything, including the human figure that glided toward him. Gavin swallowed hard, taking in the man's features. It looked like his great-uncle Warney. As the image floated closer, Gavin decided this was definitely not another daydream.

The man had the same unnaturally straight posture, the same sincere smile, even the same gnarled wooden cane and bald head as his great-uncle.

"Uncle Warney?" Gavin coaxed out a whisper that echoed in reverse with each syllable getting louder than the first before cresting and fading into the mist.

"Yep, Gavin, it's me, all right." Warney's ghost-like lips moved, while his hazel eyes stared straight through Gavin.

"If you're Uncle Warney," Gavin's insides writhed, "then what's with the robes?" *Shouldn't he be wearing his worn-out jeans and faded T-shirt?*

Warney chuckled. "Robes? You're one to be talkin' what with your wearin' the same striped shirt three days in a row."

Only the real Uncle Warney could come back at him like that. "But how can you be here? You're supposed to be in your shack—I mean your *house*. Molly and Eric and I are—" Gavin swiveled around— "I mean *were* on our way to see you. Where in the world are we, anyway?"

Gavin felt the old man peer into his soul, drawing him into the unthinkable.

"Did I . . . die? Did you die? Did we die together? Is this heaven?"

Uncle Warney's eyes crinkled into a smile. "Nah, ya didn't die. I didn't die. Not yet, anyway. Yer havin' a vision."

"A vision? You mean I'm . . . No! I don't have visions. Maybe daydreams, but they never talk back. No! *Visions are too weird.* People think I'm stupid now. If they see me having visions . . ." Gavin's knees buckled. "No! I *can't* have visions."

"T'aint yer choice, Gavin. At least not yet, anyways. God has some revelatin' he wants to do, so pay attention." The moment Uncle Warney spoke of God, he glowed brighter.

"G-G-God?" Tears pooled in Gavin's eyes as he slowly turned around in this ethereal realm, searching the swirling mist for a hint of Molly or Eric or anything *normal*. Completing his circle, his eyes again rested on Uncle Warney who stood there, but was not there—seen, but unseen. Gavin reached out. His hand passed right through the old man's belly.

Ohmigosh! Gavin jumped back.

"Whoa thar, young feller. Some things are fer touchin', some not."

His uncle's nearness made Gavin feel almost at home and, for an instant, he longed to feel the roughness of the old man's unshaven face upon his cheek.

Uncle Warney opened his fist and revealed an object about the size of a Fig Newton. On closer inspection, Gavin could see that it wasn't a square cookie at all but a book. Bound with cracked leather straps, the miniature object looked even more ancient than its owner.

When Uncle Warney moved closer to Gavin, a whiff of the book's musty smell assaulted his nose.

"Phew! What is that? It stinks."

Uncle Warney didn't answer. Instead, in slow motion, he placed his bony hand on Gavin's shoulder.

Gavin jumped back. "How'd you do that? How come I can't touch you but you can touch me?"

Again, no answer. Whatever that thing was, Uncle Warney handled it with deep reverence. Maybe it was a shrunk-up version of the New Testaments that preachers handed out on the streets.

The old man stepped closer. "Here, Gavin. Eat."

"Eat what? That?" Gavin gagged at the thought. "No way! I can't eat a book, especially not that grubby-looking thing!"

"It's no worse than them textbooks ya nibble on." Warney raised an eyebrow.

How could Uncle Warney know that? "Yeah, but I only do that when I'm nervous. Besides, it's just the corners. And that's chewing, not swallowing whole books."

Warney nodded toward the book. "Have it your way."

"My way? Well then, *my* way is *no* way."

"Hear me, Gavin." The old man spoke with authority. "This private meetin's fer yer good and fer the good o' others. God wants ya to eat this book. It don't come from me but from the Holy One." He seemed to glow even brighter than before. "The Lord'll never force ya to do nothin' yer not willin' to do."

Gavin's heart raced.

"I know this is hard for ya. Jest 'member this—things ain't always what they seem. I know this book looks a mite unappetizin', but it'll be nourishin' to ya, I promise." Warney smiled. "More nourishin' than them cookies ya snuck from your mother's bakin' table after she told ya not to touch 'em'."

Guilt tracked a telltale red blush on Gavin's face and bore itself deep within his soul as surely as those chocolate chips had singed the roof of his mouth that morning. How'd Uncle Warney know *that*?

His uncle still offered the tiny book to Gavin. *Huh?* Were his wrinkles fading? Was his face getting brighter? Gavin looked over his shoulder, wishing Molly and Eric were there to tell him if he was going nuts-o or not. But all he saw was misty vapor in a world that appeared to have no beginning and no end.

"Do ya think God would ask anything of ya that wasn't good fer ya?" Warney's patient voice drew Gavin back to the real question.

Gavin trembled. Part of him wanted to run while another part needed to hear more. Besides, this place had no floor. How could he run with no floor? "I know God's supposed to do what's good, but none of this makes sense."

Uncle Warney nodded, and a slow grin spread across his face. "Ain't it yer heart's desire to do somethin' that makes a difference—somethin' that really *matters*?"

Gavin hesitated.

"This is yer chance, son."

Chewing on books, stolen cookies, his heart's desire . . . what else *does Uncle Warney know?*

"Nah, it's more than jest a chance," Warney said. "This book is yer destiny. Like I told ya, you can refuse to eat it if ya want. God don't force nobody to do His will. It's up to you. Fact is, He's got someone else standin' on the sidelines just waitin' fer the call ta action. But if ya refuse, you'll be losin' the blessin'. Yep, and I shore don't wantcha ta lose yer blessin'. That'll be somethin' you'll regret the rest of yer life."

Gavin closed his eyes. He didn't know what to do.

I don't understand anything that's going on here, but Uncle Warney's never steered me wrong before.

Gavin opened one eye just enough to peek at the Uncle Warney who appeared to grow younger by the minute. He was starting to look like he did in Grandma Jibbers' photo album before he got old—back when he had hair and his moccasins were new.

Pictures, smictures, a sarcastic voice taunted from the dark recesses of Gavin's mind. *Don't do it. That old codger can't be trusted, and you know it.*

It was the same voice that borrowed his father's favorite saying, "seize the moment," and told him no one would ever know about those cookies when he sneaked them and ran. The same voice that said he might as well forget the idea of playing ball or getting straight A's. The same voice that reminded him a hundred times a day that he was less than pond scum.

If you eat that book, you're going to wake up in bed with a mouthful of pillow, feeling stupid as ever. Or worse yet, a mouth full of swamp moss.

Molly and Eric would never let him live it down if he woke up prying swamp slime from his mouth. He squeezed his eyes tighter.

"Gavin, what will it be?" Uncle Warney's voice blocked the taunter's words. Love and approval flowed through Gavin's mind and soul. Better to make a fool out of himself in front of his cousins than to disappoint Uncle Warney. Sometimes a fella just had to hope with his heart.

With his eyes still closed, Gavin dropped his jaw to open his mouth, but his lips wouldn't part. *Come on, you can do this.* The harder he tried, opening his jaw as wide as he could several times, the tighter his lips pursed. Finally, in an incredible force of his will, Gavin's mouth flew open with a loud kissing sound.

Gavin heard Uncle Warney chuckle but didn't dare look at him or he would change his mind for sure.

"Taste and see," Uncle Warney said as he placed the tiny book on Gavin's tongue. "The Lord, He is good."

Whoa! It tasted sweet like honey. But, the instant Gavin closed his lips, the book swelled up like a roasted marshmallow, stuck to the roof of his mouth, and made him gag. He didn't dare spit it out, so he chewed. And he chewed.

His eyes flashed open in stunned surprise when bursts of flavor filled his mouth. It was delicious—better than chocolate. Chewing the book apart, his tongue discovered three textures. One part felt rough and tasted tangy like dried apricots. Another felt crisp and tasted like Granny Smith apple slices. The third was fizzy liquid that bounced on his tongue like 7-Up. The spray that filled every crevice of his mouth made him giddy. He managed to get the book down in three swallows.

A giggle party splashed in the middle of his stomach. Bubbling and tumbling, it worked its way up his throat, through his nose, and into his head. Woozy and off balance, Gavin suddenly wanted to dance. Just when he was about to jump for joy, the book turned sour in his stomach and made him feel like throwing up.

Gavin saw a mix of concern and pride in Uncle Warney's face.

So tell me . . . . But Gavin couldn't make his mouth work to voice the words aloud. *What's going on here?*

Uncle Warney answered as if he'd heard Gavin's every thought. "Them three textures and flavors is like the three parts of God—the Father's justice is sometimes tough to swallow; what Jesus done fer us on the cross, why, that's bittersweet and tender like them Granny Smith apples; and the living water of the Holy Spirit is refreshin' and energizin' like 7-Up, only it don't never run out or go flat. Ya conquered yer first hurdle by eatin' it. Yer on yer way."

In that fleeting moment, Gavin saw himself sprinting over the hurdles at school, just as Eric would. But the image fled as quickly as it came.

"This ain't no daydream, Gavin. It's fer real, fer keeps." Uncle Warney started to vanish, too. "Never fergit what the Good Book says:

'Neither death nor life . . .

neither angels nor demons . . .

shall separate you from the love of God . . .'"

"Where are you go—" Gavin's concern for Uncle Warney's fading image was interrupted by a sensation that someone who didn't belong in the mist was leering at him. Gavin knew it. Out of the fog, he heard a donkey braying. Then a loud buzz, like a thousand bumble bees, replaced the abrasive braying sound.

There *were* a thousand bumblebees! Gavin shook his head, convinced the insects were headed straight for him. Just as they raised their stingers to dive in, Gavin heard Molly say, "Lord Jesus!" At least it sounded like Molly. When she spoke, the bees formed into a long and steady stream that exploded into a trillion confetti-like fragments. Gavin opened his eyes. No trace of the phantom bumblebees. His skin felt cold and clammy, and he gulped a mouthful of air that threw him into another coughing fit.

All that remained of the vision was a stale aftertaste. Someone was bending over him. At first, all he could see was a blob with a brown rope dangling from it. Forcing his eyes to focus, he recognized Molly's freckled, panic-stricken face. Glancing around, he saw that he was back on the path that ran the perimeter of Burnt Swamp.

"Are you okay?" Molly stopped shaking his shoulder to help Gavin sit up. "You look awful. You're white—chalk-white and splotchy!"

Gavin's face felt cold. His eyes watered. "I'm okay. Where's Eric?"

"Oh, he walked on ahead," Molly said. "He's totally oblivious to the fact that you just about choked to death. What brought that on?"

"I don't know. Maybe I swallowed my spit the wrong way. Maybe it's this stupid air." How could he explain something he couldn't comprehend?

"You wait here," Molly said. "I'll go get Eric."

At first, Gavin felt relieved to be sitting on the wooded path, alone with his thoughts. But, when a cloud passed over the sun, accompanied by a faint but shrill braying sound, a shudder ran through him from his gut to his armpits.

CHAPTER TWO

Hee-Haw

Sneak Peek

Hee Haw Downes savored the braying sound of his laughter as he propelled it into the spirit realm and followed along in his stellar light body. *Astral projection. Remote viewing. Cool. Yeah, very cool.*

Alone, just the way he liked it. Looking behind, then ahead, the sixteen-year-old saw no trace of intrusion in the leaves that surrounded him. He glanced at his feet and smiled at the six inches of air between him and the forest floor. *I will never get tired of this.*

Willing himself upward, he soared through the treetops, slowing to a stop over his favorite haunt in Burnt Swamp. *Guess this is as far as I go for now.* A thin, almost invisible silver cord tethered his essence here in the woods from his belly button to the body that lay behind his locked bedroom door.

Nobody bothered Hee-Haw when he was in barricade mode. It took years of conditioning to get his parents to leave him alone, and now the payoff. Uninvited guests could mean serious repercussions if they discovered him zoned out like a zombie. Hee-Haw knew there was little chance of intruders. At least this weekend he wouldn't have to listen to his step-mother nag, "Nem, do this; Nem, do that."

He hated his name and the way she said it. At least he didn't have to hear her mouth since she was visiting friends out west. *And Pop's no threat.* Hee-Haw's father hadn't spoken to him in weeks. *Suits me fine.*

His cynical snort gave way to a round of harsh laughter that erupted from the core of his being as he relished his bird's-eye view of Burnt Swamp. Every time out, he tried going farther. This was the farthest he had ever gone in his spirit-body. No one had his talents. How he wished he could rub that revelation in the faces of those fogheads at school.

The ectoplasmic form of his spirit guide, Ooziss Naturus, whispered into Hee-Haw's ear. "Soon, very soon, they will come under your power and strength, but not now. Not today. Keep your mind on why you are here. And today's focus is?"

"Auras. It's fun discovering new auras, like yesterday and the day before and the day before that," Hee-Haw droned. "Ooziss, when will you teach me something new?"

"Patience, little human. Content yourself with the study of auras."

"I'm not little. I'm taller than . . . than anybody in school. Besides, I've been projecting for three years, and I know what I'm doing. I thought you were supposed to be my *guide*, not my *boss*." He stared straight into the intimidating eyes that glowered back at him. "I'm the boss of me, and I can go *wherever* I want, *whenever* I want."

Instead of his usual unpleasant response, Ooziss faded into the haze without a word, leaving the teen alone in the swamp.

"Suit yourself." Hee-Haw resumed his aura hunt by scouting the thicket below. *Who'd have thought I'd be flying so soon after getting my driver's license? The geeks think I'm dumb but, hey, if they only knew. Yeah, dumb like a fox. Who needs good grades when you can have this?*

"E-e-e-e haw, e-e-e-e haw!" Hee-Haw's throaty signature laugh echoed off the spiritual plain as he spied the golden halo emitted by a mouse scurrying along the smoldering ground.

"Gotcha, critter." He nose-dived for a closer look and hovered within an inch of the unsuspecting rodent.

Studying the auras of living creatures was not science to Hee-Haw—it was more like instinct. Drawn to auras as naturally as a reflection to a mirror, his vaporous fingers cradled the mouse's hue. Its life force coursed through him strong enough to rock Hee-Haw against his tether. "Whoa, baby. That was wicked!" If he could get a power surge like that from a mouse, what would bigger game do for him?

Thank you, Auntie Soshal. His mind's eye recalled her bouncy curls swaying in time to gentle music as her nimble fingers polished crystals. It was Auntie Soshal who nurtured his special gifts, who listened to his wants and needs, who gave him a key to her New Age candle shop so he could come and go after hours. He entertained the notion of popping in on her in his spirit form but decided he'd rather see her in person.

Auntie Soshal often rewarded him with trinkets. So far, his favorite was the set of aura goggles with "pinacyanole bromide" filters that he wore now. With them, he found it child's play to see auras. So what if Ooziss says I'm moving too fast. He marveled at how he could take material possessions with him on his journeys. Just as his clothes had followed his spirit body into the woods, the goggles he had been toying with in his bedroom came along, too.

Auntie Soshal labeled Hee-Haw a "metaphysical practitioner," but he didn't care a whit about titles. What he cared about was that he was gaining power, and it would only be a matter of time before he gained influence.

A flash of light radiated through the forest, jolting Hee-Haw to the core and slamming his form backwards. *What was that?* Hee-Haw forced his spirit body to swing around. Peering through his goggles, he stared at a reddish-orange vapor as intense as any F-4 funnel cloud he'd ever seen on TV. It appeared to be several miles away. *Now, that's what I call bigger game!* Maybe the swamp was stirring up and the rise of the all-powerful one had begun. It wouldn't be long before the gateway to the abyss was open and operational.

As fast as it flared up, the glow shrank to the size of a single human aura.

Hee-Haw willed his frame toward the glow to see what—or who—it was. *Gotta touch it. Gotta have it.*

Ha! It was just a scrawny-looking boy sitting there in the dirt, dazed. *A kid?* Hee-Haw drifted closer for a better look.

The ethereal sound of his spirit guide's voice slithered out of the mist. "That one is Gavin. Gavin Goodfellow."

"You mean to tell me that aura belongs to some wannabe? Isn't that the same foghead I've seen around school? Can't be. Nuh uh. No way could he qualify for a power force like that." Hee-Haw stretched out his hand in the direction of the glowing boy.

"Noooooooooooooooooo!" Ooziss' screech reverberated throughout the swamp. "Don't touch him. He is protected. Besides, you're not ready."

"You've *got* to be kidding." Hee-Haw couldn't bring himself to pull his hand back from Gavin.

Fissszzzack! A cosmic shock slammed into his spirit body and sucked him into a spinning funnel that twisted Hee-Haw's mind, will, and emotions into knots. Everything in him screamed from fear and pain. Objects appeared in the whirlwind and floated past: a flipping police car with flashing red and blue lights, a shield that twisted and turned. Other things banged into him—loose pages, yellowed with age, and a voodoo doll that stared at him with button eyes, then flew away after one of its hat pins grazed his head. As quickly as Hee-Haw's spirit body was sucked into the vortex, it was yanked out, leaving him face-to-face with his bearded spirit guide.

"I told you, not now!" Ooziss screamed.

Hee-Haw felt weak all over as he pulled off his goggles. Stretching his long frame out flat on his back, he hovered a fraction of an inch above the forest floor, confused.

"When are you going to start listening? You fool."

"Hey, who are you calling a fool?" Hee-Haw bolted upright.

"The one who thinks he knows better than his spirit guide and can do as he pleases. The one who disregards the rules. The one who tries the patience of the Order of Laddrach."

Hee-Haw hung his head in fake remorse, still jazzed about the walloping ride he'd just felt. "Uh, what's going on with this Gavin kid? His aura and the vortex thing—they're flukes, right?"

"If there is a fluke, it is you—you poor excuse for a human. Goodfellow is a serious threat. His aura is proof of that."

The image of *His Ooziness*, as Hee-Haw secretly called him, came into clearer focus. The long beard of the spirit guide dripped with green swamp slime. He watched as a dewy glob dropped off.

"Laddrach is closer than we know to freeing Shimera from the swamp. We are about to experience the end of time as we know it. The battle is almost upon us. Our adversary is equipping the lad, so do not be deceived by his meek countenance."

"Hey, what about me? Haven't you been equipping me?" Hee-Haw tried to spit in the weeds, but nothing came out.

"To be sure, you are gifted. But the truth is, you are weak."

Hee-Haw braced himself.

"I see the way you look at that picture on your bureau." Ooziss glared. "Until you stop moping and use your loss as a catalyst to sharpen your anger and revenge, you cannot be ready."

Hee-Haw's insides quivered, ever stronger, until his whole spirit-body shook with the force of an oncoming train—like the Amtrak that carried his mother and younger brother away three years ago. His stomach pinched and twisted, leaving him light-headed. *What's going on?* Was the vortex coming back? Panic pricked every nerve ending. It wasn't cool anymore. "Ooziss, help me!" he cried.

The spirit guide floated close to Hee-Haw's face. "Your discomfort is necessary until you take seriously what I am about to tell you. Do you think I am a fool? You are mistaken to think yourself better than I. When you are ready to heed my words, your tension will cease, and not before. Then, and only then, will I impart the vital information."

Hee-Haw continued to float and shake violently. "I'm . . . tr-tr-trying," he stuttered. The image of a tall blonde girl in a purple cloak invaded his inner vision.

"Who's that?" His shaking stopped.

"That," Ooziss said, "is your new ally, Bea Daark. She and her mother are about to arrive in Ashboro."

"Ally? I don't need any allies, especially no girl and her mommy. I'm supposed to be the boss, remember?"

Ooziss expanded to ten times his usual size. Hadn't Auntie Soshal warned Hee-Haw to "be careful"—that it was rare for someone to be placed with this particular spirit guide? Everyone knew Ooziss Naturus despised humans.

"Okay, forget I said that." Hee-Haw lowered his gaze. "But this Bea girl will have to understand I was here first."

The squeal of a jet engine battered Hee-Haw's super-sensitive hearing. Pulling himself upright, he floated behind a nearby sumac where he cupped his hands over his ears and dangled the goggles from one finger.

"Ah, your partners arrive," Ooziss announced. "Take your hands from your ears. You know your hearing in this realm cannot be muffled. Follow my instructions *to the letter* in your dealings with the Daarks. Their Old World witcheries will—"

"Old World? You mean they aren't New Age?"

"You dare to interrupt me?"

Hee-Haw began to tremble again. A loud rumble coursed through him. "But, but . . . sorry." The rumbling and trembling passed. "Just curious about their training."

"Their training is no business of yours. What you need to know is that they have at their disposal all the resources you need. Money

multiplies at Madam's slightest whim. And it is yours for the taking
. . . provided you can manage to make yourself indispensable to them."

Yeah. Hee-Haw grinned like a mule eating brambles. *Mine for the
taking. Make them need me. Auntie Soshal will have ideas for that.* His
laughter erupted as Ooziss faded away.

Giving Gavin another glance, Hee-Haw saw him still sitting there
alone on the dirt path with a dazed look on his face. "Stupid kid," he said
with a sneer. "There's no way that dork can stop what the Order had put
in motion so long ago. Try, Gavin Goodfellow. Try and fail. I don't care
what kind of aura you've got going for you—everyone knows you're a
loser. Once a loser, always a loser."

Hee-Haw's thoughts shifted back to the girl and her mother. He'd
show them a thing or two.

With a shake of his head and a jolt, he willed himself back to his
bedroom where he stared at the water-stained ceiling. Fits of hammering
above, as his dad fixed a leak on the roof, replaced the tension of Ooziss
and the vortex. So what if people appreciated his handyman dad's "quick
service and cheap prices"—as long as he stayed out of Hee-Haw's hair.

*So . . . money multiplies at this woman's whim, and it's mine for the
taking, eh? Maybe there's a way out of this dump after all.*

Hee-Haw looked down at his faded orange muscle shirt and denim
shorts. How much time had passed he didn't know or care. Giving his
goggles a careless twirl, he tossed them aside. A menacing laugh welled
up in his chest, forcing him to sit up. He never could laugh while lying on
his back. Despising the weakness he felt, he gave into the exhaustion that
engulfed him and flopped back down. *How dare that punk Gavin drain
me like this?*

Hee-Haw decided to have a little fun exercising his mental powers. *If I do this right, I'll be able to view the swamp from here.* Images of shifting mounds of earth, tangled undergrowth, and fallen trees formed in his mind. In the midst of it, he saw Ooziss making broad, sweeping gestures. *What's he doing? Manipulating those paths?* From the look of sheer amusement on Ooziss' face, whatever he was doing gave his spirit guide immense pleasure.

An annoying mosquito buzzed above his head. Instead of swatting it, Hee-Haw allowed the distraction to turn his attention from the woods to the pest. He concentrated on communicating with it. Within a few seconds, a swarm of his blood-sucking pals joined the lone mosquito. The buzzing black cloud circled above Hee-Haw's sleeveless left arm.

"Not me, you idiots—the kid in the woods." He jumped off the bed, grabbed the splintered wood of the window frame, and shoved it open. "Go!"

The black cloud hesitated briefly and then flew out the window.

He watched to be sure the mosquitoes headed in the right direction, then turned his eyes to the clouds where he saw a jet plane. *So, the Daarks have an agenda? Well, we'll see about that.* He thought he might float over to the airstrip and surprise them, but he was too tired, so he shuffled back to his rumpled bed.

Stretching out, the springs creaked under his weight. He closed his eyes and smiled. *Wonder how long it will be 'til the mosquitoes find their mark.* With every successive breath he exhaled, the mattress sagged lower, as if to match his level of fatigue.

CHAPTER THREE

GAVIN
Shifting Paths

Gavin sat on the wooded path and stared at the hardened ruts while he tried to get his bearings. Those ruts must have come from Uncle Warney's horse-drawn carriage. There was Uncle Warney again, in the forefront of Gavin's thoughts, making it more difficult to shake the vision of the ghost-book thing from his brain.

"Found him." Molly's voice sounded strange, like it was digitized with a soft buzzing sound.

Eric knelt beside Gavin. "Aw, did the poor Doofus fall down, go boom?"

"Always the compassionate one," Molly said, but the buzzing sound seemed louder to Gavin than her words. It grew in volume until he thought he might faint again.

More bumblebees?

It wasn't the vision returning. It was a very real, very huge black cloud—heading straight for him. He threw his arms over his head. "Mosquitoes!"

Swatting madly at the back of his neck, Gavin jumped up and started to run, but the cloud of mosquitoes latched on. He covered his face with his palms; the pesky insects plunged their stingers into the back of his hands and sucked blood from his fingers. When Gavin ran in circles, ducking under a low-hanging branch, they stayed right with him, pricking his ankles, stabbing his arms, raising itchy red welts all over his body.

"Stand still!" Molly's stern command caught Gavin's attention in the midst of his wailing and running and swatting. Turning wildly, he caught a glimpse of Eric's alarmed face. A spritz of repellent in Gavin's mouth revealed Molly's location the hard way. Spitting his way toward her, he quivered to a halt, not knowing whether to laugh or cry.

"I can't spray you if you're jumping around!" She redirected her aim toward the gyrating cloud and sprayed a steady blast that parted the swarm smack down the middle. Moments later, the mosquitoes zigzagged to the ground.

"Hey!" Eric jumped out of the way as Molly aimed the can at him.

Spraying another quick spritz over herself, Molly stuffed the can back into her bag.

"That was too weird," she said, looking around. "It was like they came from nowhere."

A thunderous roar drew their attention skyward.

Eric extended his arm and pointed. "You see that?"

Gavin couldn't see anything but swamp smoke. "See what?"

"Sleek." Eric gawked.

"What?" Gavin wondered why he always had to miss everything.

Molly squinted. "An eight-passenger Citation Ten—spelled with a Roman numeral X—the largest, longest-range, mid-size civil aircraft ever."

There she goes again. Miss Know-it-all. As if I give a frog's croak how it's spelled. Gavin tried to concentrate on the path before him. His knees felt weak again. "So what?"

"Looks out of place around here, don't you think?" Molly gave an unlady-like snort.

"Whatever you do, don't mention airplanes to Uncle Warney or he'll start telling his World War II stories," Eric said.

"Yeah." Molly smiled. "But Uncle Warney's stories are just what I need to spice up my article for *The Daily Voice*. Not only did he have a ringside seat the night the fire started, but he knows more than any other living soul about Burnt Swamp." Molly's hands were as animated as her lips.

Gavin's laughter faded when he saw a lone buzzard settle on a cypress branch above his head. Could a place get any more eerie? "I think we'd better keep moving or we'll never get to Uncle Warney's." The strength in his voice surprised him.

"Does he know we're coming?" Molly asked.

"How could he?" Eric said. "He doesn't have a phone."

"I know *that*." Molly twirled her braid. "I just thought maybe Aunt Louise might have seen him lately."

Mention of Gavin's mother reminded him of the haircut he was missing, which triggered thoughts of his father's temper. "Dad doesn't like me hanging around Uncle Warney, so don't go putting my name in your story."

"No problem. But I don't understand why your dad gets so bent out of shape about Uncle Warney."

Eric ran in place a few times, then sprinted ahead. "Why? 'Cause Uncle Warney's a religious nut," he said in an almost-perfect imitation of

Gavin's dad. "Talks to himself and preaches whether anybody's around to hear him or not. Everybody knows he's got a screw loose and the rest of them fell out a long time ago."

Gavin felt a knot in his throat as anger threatened to boil over. Uncle Warney was the only one who ever made him feel good about himself— like he was something more than a dummy. "Take that back," Gavin shouted.

"Screw loose." Eric skipped backwards. "Uncle Warney's got a screw loose."

"Take it back, right now!"

"Screw loose."

Gavin started advancing on his more athletic cousin. "I mean it, Eric. Take it back!"

"Stop it, both of you! You're acting like—"

Before Molly could finish, Eric sprawled backward on the dirt path with a vine of briars wrapped about his left ankle.

"That's what you get. Act like the devil, and the next thing you know, you're tangled up in Devil's Walking Stick." Molly stepped over her brother. "You know what they say, don't you? Kick the devil, and he'll bite you back with those thorns."

Gavin couldn't help but laugh. "Ha! The devil bit you!"

Eric flopped backward and moaned, "I'm bit. I'm bit."

"Stop horsing around." Molly pulled a neatly typed page from her denim shoulder bag. "Let's get back to my story for the school paper. How's this sound?

"Ten years ago, a violent thunderstorm tore through the region and struck a match under Burnt Swamp that started a fire no one could extinguish. Porous soil and air pockets, coupled with the weight of nature's mulch, sucked decaying matter under the ground's surface, creating a mother lode of kindling. A well-positioned lightning bolt set the stage for a fire that, even after ten years, has not yet run its course." Molly glanced up, took a quick breath, and continued reading. "What we don't want is another conflagration like the Great Fire of 1782 when—"

"Hold it right there." Eric propped himself up, tugged the vine free, and stood. "Con-flag-ration? What's that?"

Molly lowered her head and leveled her none-too-patient gaze at her brother. "It's the perfect word, that's what. A conflagration is an intense, uncontrolled fire."

Gavin groaned. Listening to Molly's essay all the way to Uncle Warney's wasn't his idea of a fun summer day.

"Bor-ring." Eric's words mirrored Gavin's thoughts. "Why don't you write about something cool—like swamp critters and prehistoric dinosaurs."

A gust of smoke-filled wind cut Eric's sarcasm short, parting his thick, black hair down the center. Cypress branches swayed above their heads. Eric tripped over a rock, then stumbled three steps on lanky legs before he landed in a pile of soggy, wet leaves. "Ugh," he grunted.

"Second down, Jock," Gavin said. But his smile vanished when the ground quaked and grew hot and spongy. "Whoa!" He stomped his feet only to find that the hard-packed earth looked normal. "That's weird. If I didn't know better, I'd think the swamp was creeping closer."

"Swamps may be creepy, but they don't creep," Molly said. "Next you'll be telling us that prehistoric creatures are out to get you. Come on, Gavin. Grow up."

Gavin started to sweat. It felt like somebody turned up the heat a gazillion degrees. The ground reeled again. Oh no, was the vision coming back?

Molly lowered her chin and gave him one of her what-ails-you looks.

What? Gavin was sure the earth beneath his feet was quicksand-slimy again. Didn't Molly feel that? Was the swamp following him?

"Gavin, aren't you going to help Eric up?"

"Like *he* needs *my* help?" Gavin groused while regaining his own footing. Though shorter than Eric and not as strong, Gavin grabbed his cousin's hands and pulled him up. When the ground lurched again, they both lost their footing and rolled into a ditch. Scrambling to gain a foothold on the mossy soil, Gavin slipped, and down he went once more. *But we don't have earthquakes around here!*

"Thanks for the help, klutzo." Eric, first to get up, offered Gavin a hand.

"Did you feel that?" Gavin's elbows propped his torso into a forty-five degree angle.

"Feel what?" Eric squinted and flipped the bangs out of his eyes.

"What's happening?" Molly asked. "I thought I saw a sign for the Lodge right through there a minute ago, and now it's . . . gone! How could we possibly be near the old hunting lodge?"

"The Lodge? Cool. I hear it's up for sale." Eric sprinted ahead toward a cluster of trees.

Gavin twisted from left to right, trying his best to get his bearings. "I don't know. This is really weird. It's like the paths shifted." He lagged behind with Molly. The sun-drenched path at the beginning of their journey now looked like a foreboding tunnel. Treetops merged together and intertwined overhead to block the sunlight that, only moments before, felt warm on Gavin's back and face. The shadows chilled his bones.

"We're lost!" Molly moaned.

"No, we're not." Eric loped back to them. "Come on, you whiny babies. I've been wanting to explore the Lodge a long time, and there that sucker is, right under our noses. How often do we get a chance to check out a house that's been vacant for years?"

Molly's face morphed into her I-could-be-your-teacher look. "We shouldn't be doing this, you know. Vacant houses are off-limits. Besides, people say this place is the main entrance to Burnt Swamp."

In spite of what she was saying, Gavin noticed Molly kept a steady pace as they walked single file on the narrow path.

Eric flashed a bracey grin at Gavin. "Besides, it's a free country. If somebody catches us, we can say we're scoutin' for potential buyers. It's now or never, buddy boy."

Molly shook her head. "Double trouble. That's what you two are. All I want is to get to Uncle Warney's and back home again where trees stay where they're planted."

Gavin figured Molly was exaggerating about the trees staying put, but what if the paths really did shift and that's why they wound up here instead of at Uncle Warney's? He didn't dare say a word. Most of all, he didn't want Eric to catch a hint of the fear that made his hands so clammy.

"Uh-oh." Gavin stopped so fast he kicked up a dust cloud. "It really *is* off-limits. Look!" He pointed to a rotting FOR SALE sign now plastered with big red letters that read SOLD. A smaller black-and-white poster was nailed to a nearby tree: NO TRESPASSING UNDER THE PENALTY OF THE LAW.

Eric ducked beneath a limb and came up with a bounce, shooting an invisible basketball into a hoop. "So what? Nobody's gonna know."

Molly shook her head so strong her braid swayed from side to side. "We'll know, and God knows."

"How good of you to keep tabs on what God is thinking." Eric's brows flickered a little.

Yeah, God knows. Gavin's thoughts scattered like the dirt he kicked up. For a minute, all he could think about was Uncle Warney and the vision swimming around in his head. He winced when a sharp stone poked through the sole of his shoe, and he thought about turning back and running home.

Instead, he took a deep breath and walked faster. His stomach churned and gurgled. The gurgle rumbled long and loud, like distant thunder. Out of him came the grandest belch of his life.

"Way to go! Good one, Gavin!" Eric hopped around and pumped his fist in the air.

Molly laughed so hard she had to stop and hug herself. "Now that's an *e-ruc-ta-tion* if I ever heard one. I've been looking for an occasion to use that word."

Gavin laughed with them at first. "And that's a *Mollyism* I'll have to remember." A puzzled frown crossed his brow as the burp left an oddly familiar taste in his mouth of . . . what?

Dried apricots?

Juicy apples?

7-Up?

While his cousins continued to laugh and dance along the dirt path, Gavin stewed. *Maybe it's not a daydream, after all.* That thought, coupled with an awareness that every step brought him closer to the forbidden Lodge, made his heart thump against his ribs.

A twig snapped above his head, causing a branch to careen downward like a spear, barely missing Gavin's neck. He lunged forward and glimpsed the form of a black buzzard flapping lazily into the sky. It gave him double shivers.

That was close. Safety in numbers, he thought as he caught up with Molly and Eric. As they approached the train tracks and stepped into the clearing, the sun burned through the smoke and beat down on Gavin full force. Perspiration gathered on his forehead in a matter of minutes.

Train tracks? Here? Stepping across the rails, Gavin couldn't imagine how they had gotten so turned around. But Eric seemed to know where he was going, so he kept following.

When the three cousins rounded the bend, the Lodge came into view. Instantly, Gavin felt cold all over. What if Molly was right and they were approaching the "main entrance" into Burnt Swamp where who-knows-what awaited them? Warning bells rang in Gavin's ears cautioning him to stay away. But the urge that lured him closer to the Lodge and to Burnt Swamp was even stronger. Surrendering to it step by step, he felt a seed of rebellion take root. *Hey, don't I deserve to have a little fun?*

Eric rushed ahead, cheering at the top of his lungs and shoving tangled underbrush out of the way. "Push 'em back, push 'em back, waaaay back."

Gavin shook his head. "Nothing like making a little noise. If anybody's within a mile, they'll know we're messing around where we don't belong."

"Just having a little fun," Eric called over his shoulder as he jogged out of sight.

"Looks like I'll have to postpone my interview with Uncle Warney," Molly said. "How in the world did we end up here?"

There, high on a mound in the clearing, sat the sprawling Lodge. While the pathway beckoned Gavin closer, the high-pitched scream of the jet returned. Assaulting his ears worse than last time, the message rumbled loud and clear in Gavin's chest—"Beware."

CHAPTER FOUR

Staking Claim

V aguely aware of the low hum of their Cessna Citation X, Bea grabbed a handful of her blonde hair and started twisting it absentmindedly.

"Bea, stop that!" Her mother's command exploded like a call to arms. The tension between them had been building for days.

Bea sighed and released her barely spiraled lock which fell into soft waves over her shoulder. Ever since their London departure at 6:45 that morning, Bea had tried to mind her manners, but seven hours of suspense was about all she could stand. This time, she wouldn't take no for an answer.

"Mum, why *won't* you let me see the blueprints? After all, Dragon's Lair Theme Park is as much my idea as yours. And you've never withheld anything from me before."

Madam Daark raised a finely arched eyebrow, lowered her chin, and leveled her eyes at her daughter. "Because."

Bea stared back with all the intensity her thirteen years could muster. *One thousand one, one thousand two . . . one thousand eight.*

Feeling her bottom lip pudge into a pout, Bea bit the tender flesh inside to contain the snide remarks brewing in her mind. She studied her mother's olive complexion and perfect posture and wondered for the umpteenth time if she really knew this Englishwoman at all.

Sitting side-by-side, Bea was struck once again by the lack of family resemblance. *Her complexion is dark; mine's creamy. She's big-boned; I'm petite. Her hair's black and white; mine's light. Even our personalities are opposite.* Aware, once again, that she and her mum were about as alike as pickles and pudding, she tried to picture her father. *Maybe he's Scandinavian, German, or Swiss.*

At last, her mother replied. "The Order has incorporated elements that are not to be revealed to anyone—least of all, you."

"Least of all, me? What's that supposed to mean?"

"And stop slouching, for Shimera's sake."

"I don't slouch. What did you mean, least of all me?" Realizing her mother had no intention of answering, Bea repositioned herself in the leather cushions.

The closer they got to Burnt Swamp, the more agitated her mother became. Why, she was even biting her nails! All her life, Mum had been rock solid, the personification of poise and confidence—always knowing the right modeling agency to contract, the perfect dress for any occasion, who to rub elbows with. She was more than a mother. She was her mentor and role model, the one who taught her to never let herself be shaken. And now *she* appeared to be falling apart.

Bea's thoughts wandered to their destination. Burnt Swamp and its forlorn community stood in stark contrast with her standard of living.

Maybe that was it—Mum just couldn't tolerate the idea of leaving all things cultural behind.

But no, that couldn't be why she was so distraught. When the Order had cautioned the Daarks about Burnt Swamp's lack of ambiance, hadn't Mum been the one to claim Ashboro as "a nothing little town ripe for the picking," especially if they flaunted their wealth? Hadn't she been absolutely gleeful that Burnt Swamp as well as Ashboro and its citizens would soon be under the Order's control?

Gazing out the window, Bea tried to survey the landscape below. Instead of the typical green and brown patchwork quilt she'd seen since reaching the continent, a dense gray cloud blocked her view. Unfastening her seat belt, she relocated to a window seat on the other side of the plane where she pressed her forehead against the glass.

"I can't see blinking much with that sooty cloud in the way."

"Vulgarity doesn't become you." Madam smoothed some wayward strands of hair. "We haven't even landed, and you're acting like a colonial. This will never do."

Ignoring her mother, Bea strained to see beyond the curtain of smoke. Elongated finger-like wisps of gray smoke covered the swamp below. The more she looked, the more a distinctive shape presented itself. "Is that the outline of the dragon? Or maybe his cave?"

Madam Daark unbuckled her seat belt, relocated, leaned over Bea at the window, and spoke under her breath. "That may or may not be Shimera's abode, so don't go jumping to conclusions. The 'pet' we seek is not likely to reveal its hiding place, especially at first glance."

Right on cue, the dense smoke parted for an instant. Like sparkling jewels, the faint glow of embers throbbed like misplaced runway lights on the surface of the swamp.

Bea leaned against the thick glass and let her gaze linger on the smoldering wasteland below.

"Look, Mum, you can see it! The swamp is smashing!"

Spread out below were ten square miles—*64,000 acres*—of mushy wetlands filled with smoldering cypress trunks and barren branches that looked like charcoal dolls with outstretched arms begging for help. Suddenly, the fog closed around the swamp, once again shrouding it from view.

Convinced that the thick fog lingering above the surface was seething dragon breath, Bea let her imagination run. *Not likely to reveal his hiding place? We'll see about that. Just you wait. We'll see who's ready for this and who's not.*

The plane banked to the right, throwing Madam against Bea.

"Why, of all the—" Madam Daark gasped, dropped into the seat, and fastened her safety belt.

Bea clicked hers, too. "You'd have thought that blooming bloke would warn us when he was ready to turn the plane."

"Bea, watch your language!" Madam Daark, usually appalled at anyone who pointed, extended her finger in front of Bea's nose. "There, look! See that spacious estate? That's our new home, the Lodge!"

In her whole life, Bea couldn't remember seeing her mother the slightest bit excited. But the enthusiasm was short-lived as Mum closed her eyes and perched her perfectly coiffed hair against the headrest. *How can she rest at a time like this?*

Madam Daark spoke in a monotone. "The pilot will be taking aerial photos." Opening her eyelids ever so slowly, she looked blankly at the ceiling or the air vent, Bea couldn't tell which. Her mother sighed. "And then he will put down on the new landing strip."

Ashboro Airpark was in ghastly condition, and Bea had no desire to hear her mother launch into yet another spiel about how much money she had poured into resurfacing the runway.

"As soon as we get to the Lodge, the first thing I'm going to do is find that bronze plaque." Bea trembled in anticipation. "It's supposed to be over the fireplace in the great room, right?"

Madam Daark heaved another, even deeper, sigh. "It's a *crest*, not a plaque. How many times do I have to tell you? The *crest* of the Order of the Knights of Laddrach."

"I know, I know. And we'll have to go on a treasure hunt to find the missing icons."

"Don't be impudent, young lady. The last time . . ."

Hearing her mother slip into lecture mode, Bea tuned her out, preferring the privacy of her own thoughts. For a fleeting moment, she imagined herself placing icons into the molded sections she'd only read about. What would it be like to activate the crest by placing the final talisman? Would she be instrumental in making history?

Seat belt in place, she turned her face to the window again, hoping for another look at the dragon's shadow, but they had flown out of range. *Soon!* The prehistoric beast, Laddrach's pet, would be released, and all power would be endowed on those who watched, who waited, who longed for the opening of the gateway.

The aircraft's wheels touched the tarmac, jolting Bea from her reverie. As soon as the Cessna came to a stop and the door opened, heavy smoke-filled air hit her in the face. Bea winced but recovered quickly by scanning the scene of a flawless black runway fringed with cattails, bent reeds, and tall grassy plants.

"Oh, Mum!" She danced down the steps and pirouetted. "It's perfectly *dreadful*." She squinted with delight and mischief.

"Quite so." Her mother's polished dialect seemed out of place under the smoky veil of Burnt Swamp. With muddled admiration, Bea watched the woman descend with the regal bearing of a queen. Her tightly knotted braid, secured at the nape of her neck, had not one strand of salt-and-pepper hair out of place.

As fine gray ash swirled around Bea, she had fleeting reservations about her mother's ability to make the adjustment, especially with this putrid air.

"And just where is our driver?" Madam snapped. Her eyes scanned the empty parking lot. Patience was never one of her mother's finer traits.

"Mum, did the Order consider Georgia's cypress swamps or the Florida Everglades? They would have been more pleasing to the nose."

"But they lacked one crucial element." Madam Daark retrieved her cell phone from her bag and pushed a few buttons.

"Ah, yes. Shimera," Bea cooed.

Raising a long slender finger to her cheek, Madam Daark turned toward the rising smoke and an occasional leaping flame. "If only the listless townsfolk of Ashboro knew. Soon the prophecies will be fulfilled."

Bea's eyebrows raised a notch. "Has anyone ever seen more than the dragon's shadow?"

Donalda Daark wiped the back of her hand across her brow in a look of exasperation. "I don't believe there's ever been an actual sighting."

Bea felt a strange, irresistible urge drawing her to the swamp, as though Shimera had called her by name. Feeling the presence of something truly powerful and old, very old, a tremor ran up her spine.

"Mum, can we go there? After dark? Can we drive through the swamp and see the fire for ourselves? Maybe even feel Shimera's presence?" Bea wanted to jump up and down like a child but contained herself by pressing her hands tightly together. Even so, her whole body shivered with expectancy.

A cloud of disapproval passed over Madam Daark's face. "Not now. Not even soon. We have to be back in the air before dark. Besides, you are far from ready to enter the swamp. An encounter with Shimera is out of the question at this time. It would behoove you to develop a healthy respect for the dragon and its abode. Now, where is our driver?"

Madam Daark stepped away from her daughter and muttered as she dialed her cell phone. After a brief conversation, she returned it to her bag. "Only one limousine service."

Bea nodded, but her thoughts were elsewhere. *I have a healthy respect for Shimera, Mum. Perhaps it will behoove you to begin to understand the power that has been entrusted to me.*

A daughter of the Craft, Bea felt proud of her Old World heritage that blended so nicely with New Age philosophies. Sometimes her mother could be such a snooty stick-in-the-mud. So what if Bea had experimented a bit prematurely with some incantations back home? This place promised a fresh start and a new life, far away from those finger-pointing wags.

Bea smiled as she touched the most recent charm on her tastefully cluttered 18-karat gold bracelet, the one engraved with her initials:

B.A.D. Madam Daark had known what she was doing when she named her daughter Beatrice Abernathy Daark. After all, nothing was what it seemed. Bad was good, and good was bad. *And I'm so good at being B.A.D.*, she thought as she looked around. *Surely, my name will shake up this wretched region and Mum will be proud of me.* She reflected on the mission she had come to execute: enlightening young commoners to the peace, prosperity, and power within their grasp—theirs for the taking if only they had a leader to show them the way.

And I'll soon be here to help you. A warm rush bathed her from the inside out. She relaxed and let it wash over her. *Yes, the field of souls is ripe for the picking. Before long, I'll be known as the chief harvester.* Hope soared within her as she speculated, once again, how the plan would unfold. *When word of my accomplishments gets back to the high priest, then he will take notice of me.*

"Come along." Madam Daark's voice gave Bea a start. "Our car has *finally* arrived."

The black stretch limo rolled to a stop. A tall, crisply-dressed driver jumped out and rushed to open the rear door.

"To the Town Hall," Madam Daark ordered. "We have an appointment at four."

"They'll wait for us, Mum," Bea said, gracefully taking her seat in the limo. "They want your money."

CHAPTER FIVE

GAVIN

Forbidden Lodge

avin gasped at the immensity of the building that loomed before him. "It's huge!"

"The word 'primitive' comes to mind," Molly said.

The two-and-a-half-story building seemed like it belonged there in the woods, smack dab in the middle of two narrow dirt roads. Built on an unnatural-looking rise, the structure was covered with aged cypress shingles, now a reddish-brown, with three stone chimneys poking through the roof.

"Intimidating, huh?" Molly inched closer to Gavin.

"Yeah," Gavin breathed. "And fancy. Look at that front porch."

Gavin's red and black Nikes crunched on the gravel leading to the Lodge. He couldn't believe the size of the place. The central section, like the rest of the building, was trimmed with overhanging eaves and rafter ends. Heavy timbers supported the hooded front stoop. Two dark green benches on the sides of the stoop looked inviting and repelling at the same time.

In one instant Gavin wanted to march right up and sit on a bench and in the next he felt the urge to run away. But Molly kept moving forward, so he scuffed along next to her. The front door looked heavy and old, not only because of its design but also from the multi-layers of peeling forest green paint. The old-fashioned doorknob was dented and black with age.

Knowing how Molly loved old things, he wasn't surprised when she climbed up the front steps for a closer look. Maybe he would sit on one of those benches, after all. Nah. Tired legs or not, Gavin didn't like the looks of them.

"Check this out." Molly touched engraved markings on the door panel and then yanked her fingers back as if they'd been burned.

"What's wrong?" Gavin asked from his safe vantage point at the bottom of the steps.

Molly didn't look as brave as when she'd first stepped on the porch. "Come up here. I want you to see this."

Gavin heard Molly quietly counting as he climbed the steps. He took a quick look at the artwork and stepped back.

"Twenty-two, twenty-three . . ." Molly lowered her voice and leaned closer to eyeball the markings. "Twenty-four slices of wood with slivers of clay—or is it pewter? I might be mistaken, but they look like runes."

A distant, donkey-like sound wafted through the woods, making Gavin shiver. The sound alone would have given him the heebie-jeebies, but considering where they were and the stuff Molly was inspecting, it really rattled him. "What's a rune?" he whispered.

"Witches use runes as a magical language to cast spells. I studied the occult last year for extra credit in Art Alternatives. I didn't know it was about pagan religion until we were well into it." She grabbed the curls at the end of her braid and chewed on them while she talked. "See how each has an emblem etched into it?"

Gavin shuffled closer to the door. "They look like harmless stick figures. This one's shaped like a bow tie."

"Well, yes, it is. If I'm right and these *are* runes, that's a Dagaz. It means attainment or wealth."

Gavin's shoulders shook from the creepy feeling that ran up his backbone. "You think witches lived here?"

"Maybe, maybe not. I'll do a pencil rubbing and study the symbols later. Do you have any paper?"

Gavin gave her a blank look.

"Silly me. *I'm* the journalist." Molly pulled a sheet of paper from her bag and went to work. "It's probably nothing more than the creative genius of whoever crafted the door. Wasn't this place built back in the late 1800s as a hunting lodge for Pennsylvania Railroad tycoons?"

She folded the paper as she stood. "Oh, no! I thought this was blank, but it's my Burnt Swamp story."

"So?"

She turned the paper from front to back and spoke in a whisper. "So, it might be a sign."

"You're talking over my head. Enough with the paperwork. I'll bet Eric's already inside snooping around. Let's check this place out." Gavin reached for the doorknob.

It's probably locked, Gavin figured. "Ouch," he yelled, jumping back. "That thing shocked me!"

"Shh, I think I hear something." Molly stiffened.

Gavin wheeled around and glanced in the direction of the woods. There, padding its way toward them, was Uncle Warney's cat—the ugliest, stockiest cat anywhere.

"Gross," Molly winced. "He looks wose than usual."

"Yeah," he said. From the looks of the matted fur and yellow scabs covering its head, neck, and back, he'd been in a bad fight. "Looks like he's gained weight, though. I'll bet he's thirty pounds of muscle."

"Look at that tail," Molly said, pointing. Long and thick with a stubby tip covered in grime, it stood in the air like an exclamation point, either begging to be rubbed or sending a signal to keep back. "I've always wished he didn't have that empty eye socket."

"Uncle Warney says that's his badge of courage," Gavin said, even though he didn't have a clue what that meant. When he reached down to pet it, Molly grabbed his arm, slapping her hand on top of his and squeezing so tight he thought she would cut off circulation.

"Stop that." He pried her fingers loose. "I love Ugly. And he loves me, see?" A loud noise filled the air as Ugly Cat began to purr, rubbing against his leg.

He reached down to pet it, and Molly screamed. "He's filthy! Don't you *dare* touch that thing!"

Gavin squatted in front of the cat for a closer look. "Ugly and I don't care about dirt, do we boy?"

Molly tossed her braid over her shoulder. "Ugly's ugly, but he's never been *this* ugly. Are you sure it's Uncle Warney's? Ugly Cat's white."

"This one's white—under all that soot and stuff."

Molly frowned. "Maybe so, but don't touch it. It could have rabies or Lyme disease."

"Or maybe he just lost its way like we did."

With that, the cat meowed a sickening gravelly sound and scampered back into the woods.

Yeah, that's Ugly, all right. Gavin never could figure out why Ugly came and went like he did, but the cat always made Gavin feel like he'd been caught red-handed.

"Good riddance." Molly turned her back to the woods and resumed her inspection. "Look at those windows. Somebody has covered or painted some of them black."

"So?" Gavin stared at the underbrush. He had more important things to worry about. "What if Ugly tips off Uncle Warney that we're here?"

"Don't be silly." Molly frowned. "Cats can't tip off people. We'll get to Uncle Warney's later. Right now, we'd better see what Eric's up to."

Gavin and Molly stole their way around the side of the Lodge. Stepping around broken glass and overgrown bushes, they found Eric on the back porch fiddling with the screen door.

"What do you think you're doing?" Molly asked.

"What's it look like? Trying to get in!" Eric barked.

Feeling guiltier by the minute, Gavin chewed his bottom lip. "Well, let's not break anything. We're in enough trouble as it is."

"For what?" Eric stopped what he was doing to stare at Gavin.

"For trespassing! Remember that sign?"

"Oh, that." Eric hopped off the porch and bolted around the corner of the house. "Hey," he yelled, "looks like this window over here isn't latched."

"Shh, be *quiet*." Molly whispered so loud she might as well have shouted, too.

"Good going, Cuz." Gavin bounded toward Eric, tripped, and stooped to tie his shoelaces.

Eric stretched his body toward the window sill, unable to reach it. "Gimme a boost," he called. "If anybody's gonna tumble in there, might as well be me."

Gavin crouched on all fours, becoming a wobbly human step stool.

Standing on Gavin's back, Eric hoisted himself up high enough to push the window open. He stuck one leg over the window sill, gave a silly grin, and flung the other leg over. No sooner had he disappeared into the building than Gavin and Molly heard a loud thud, a yelp, and a whole lot of hollering and thrashing around.

"Get off-a me!" Eric screamed.

Snapping, popping, thrashing sounds and shrieks of pain poured through the window. Gavin placed his hand on the outer wall and could feel movement. "The whole building's shaking." There were several clomp-clomp-clomping sounds and more snap-snap-snapping.

Molly grabbed Gavin by the shoulders and looked him in the eyes. "Somebody else is in there. What are we going to do?"

Before Gavin could panic or answer, the commotion stopped.

"They *killed* him." Gavin gasped and stared at Molly, whose eyes were as wide as the gaping window above them.

"Over here." Eric's words broke the spell. He had unlocked the screen door and stood in the doorway with the strangest look on his face—a mixture of pain and triumph and a dozen—mousetraps?

"We're in!" he shouted.

Gavin stared. Mousetraps dangled from every conceivable part of Eric's body—from his hair to the hem of his T-shirt to his shoelaces. "What on earth?" Sweat streamed down Gavin's back.

"You mean these pesky little things?" Eric said. Wincing, he held up his hand, slung off a sprung mousetrap, and sucked on his index finger. "Decrepit old traps."

"Eric!" Molly's hand flew to her mouth. "It's a good thing these old mousetraps don't have much spring left in them. If they were new, you could really be hurt." She screwed up her face and pointed. "Eeeww, there's mouse fur and blood on that. And you put your finger in your mouth." She gagged. "They're rusty, too. Did they break your skin? You might need a tetanus shot."

"Nah." Eric grinned. "Not to worry, Nurse Molly. I'm good."

It was beyond Gavin how Eric could rub his rear end with one hand, pull off mousetraps with the other, and carry on about being a trap-snapper while holding the door open so they could step inside.

"They're set up all over the place—watch out where you—" SNAP! Eric jumped as another trap latched onto his pant leg.

The soft padding of Gavin's sneakers squeaked on the hardwood floor as he and his cousins moved around the dark-paneled room. They were in what appeared to be a great room with two gigantic stone fireplaces.

"Whoa!" Gavin pointed. "Check out the head of that goat mounted on the wall."

"That's not a goat. It's a ram's head."

Molly was such a stickler.

"Look at the size of those horns." She scrunched up her face. "Who would want to stuff a ram's head?"

Gavin turned around and clutched his throat at what he saw mounted on the other wall.

"Gross. Who would want to stuff—a buzzard?"

All three backed away a few steps.

"Feels like that ram-goat thing is watching my every move." Gavin couldn't believe he'd said that out loud.

"You've been watching too many horror movies," Eric said. "But those eyes do sorta look like security cameras."

"Oh, my." Molly's voice was barely audible as she scrutinized the nearest fireplace. "I'll bet this thing is nine feet wide. And the hearth can't be any less than six."

Eric ventured around the corner and called to them through one of the fireplaces. "Yo, check this out—it goes all the way through."

Gavin and Molly rounded the corner to join Eric. A huge iron cauldron hung on the left side of the hearth.

"This must be the dining room." Molly drew in a long breath. "The paneling smells good. Clean and old, like furniture polish and antiques."

Gavin stared past the open beams and gawked at the wagon wheel chandelier. The shadow it cast looked exactly like a hangman's noose. A feeling of dread gripped Gavin's gut, and he instinctively touched his neck.

Molly scooted past him and disappeared down a dark hallway. A few moments later, she called out, "Hey, guys, you gotta see this!"

Glad to get away from the chandelier, Gavin dashed down the hallway ahead of Eric and found Molly in a small room where she was crouching by a claw-foot tub.

"It's just a bathroom," Eric said.

"Yeah," Molly agreed. "But check out this pull-chain toilet. The bedrooms are down there."

Gavin strolled along, counting. "Four, five, six. Six bedrooms? Guess the former owners had lots of company."

The cousins stepped up their pace, sprinting from one room to the next. Gavin paused every few steps to scrutinize doorknobs with hand-forged latches which he couldn't resist turning. He found one odd-shaped closet after another, all empty . . . except for the thing that swooped down and bumped him on the head.

"Bats!" he screamed and raced down the hall.

"No need to get excited," Molly said when he found her in a room with chunky wooden couches and chairs—bolted to the floor. "Bats are to be expected in a place like this that's been vacant so long. They won't hurt you." She ran her hand over a red leather cushion. "I've never seen mission-style furniture before."

"Bats can *too* hurt me—one bombarded my head back there!" Gavin banged on the nearest wall. The sound of mice skittering and scurrying away only made his heart race faster.

"Hey, guys," Eric called from the south end of the Lodge. "Here's the kitchen. It's a shame there's no food in the fridge."

The place where Gavin and Molly found Eric seemed friendlier than the rest of the house. Beyond the huge, modern, industrial-sized kitchen was another whole section that looked brand-new.

Gavin had never seen a place like this. "Here's a big rec room." He jogged to the left and down the hall. "And more bedrooms over here. And a couple of bathrooms with—hey, check out these shower stalls—there's enough room for your whole football team, Eric."

"Do you think the water's on?" Eric crossed his legs. "I gotta go."

"Don't you dare." Molly scowled at him. "You're not touching or flushing anything in this place."

Gavin skipped back to the recreation room, laughing, until he noticed something in the center of the floor. "What's this stuff?"

Molly and Eric joined him.

Molly scowled. "Looks like candle wax. And I don't mean birthday candles."

Gavin stared at the small mounds and dribbles by his feet. "There must be twelve or thirteen wax puddles."

"Yeah, a whole circle of drips." Eric nodded. He walked slowly around the circumference of the nine-foot circle etched into the floor and pointed to some faint markings. "Look."

Edging closer, Gavin leaned in for a better look. "Is that a . . .?"

"Oh, noooo." Molly's face contorted. "A pentagram. I'll bet this is where a coven meets. Let's get out of here!"

"Yeah, let's!" Gavin yelped. Maybe it was his imagination, but he was sure he felt a ghost breathing cold air on his neck. Another layer of goose bumps raised on his arms. "Eeewww," he wailed. Backing toward the door, he bumped into Eric. "Move it, Cuz."

Eric flipped the bangs out of his eyes and leaned closer to the pentagram. "Nah. I think it's kinda cool." Molly glared at him until he blurted out, "Okay, okay. If you two sissies insist."

"What time is it?" Molly asked. "I left my watch at home."

"I don't know." Gavin chewed on his bottom lip again. "Hope I make it home by supper time. One more missed meal and I'm gonna be grounded for life." Another twinge of fear stabbed Gavin's gut.

What am I afraid of? Getting grounded? No. It wasn't that kind of fear. It was creepier than that, like something other-worldly watching his every move.

A cold draft brushed his arm accompanied by a loud whooshing sound.

"You feel that?" he asked.

"You hear that?" Molly whispered at the same time.

"Yeah, cool." Eric said, already on the move. "Sounds like it's coming from those twin fireplaces." Molly grabbed hold of her brother's shirt and followed.

Gavin felt like he had iron weights attached to each foot as he crept along behind Eric and Molly. Retracing their steps to the oldest part of the Lodge, Gavin's heart inched its way into his throat. The noise at the gigantic fireplace was incredible, like a roaring tornado which spun chunks of charred wood around and around, thumping them into each other, and banging them against the fireplace wall.

Whoever heard of an indoor tornado? Dust, ashes, and powdery grit swirled up in gusts that pressed against Gavin's body and nudged him toward the opening.

"Yo-ho, baby!" Eric drop-rolled and stopped within reach of a couch. "Take a gander at that." He clung to the couch and nodded in the direction of the writhing chair legs about to come loose.

"Look out!" Gavin yelled and pushed Molly back. The bronze crest above the mantel rocked and thumped so hard Gavin was sure the thing would come crashing down.

Eric exaggerated his wobbling. But the moment he let go of the couch, the force pulled him toward the fireplace and dragged him along the floor. Struggling to stand, he said, "Nifty way to dust a house."

"If you're so cool with this," Gavin fixed his eyes on the twisting crest, "how come your voice sounds so shaky?" With that, one of the oak pegs that held the crest to the stone fireplace gave way.

"Enough!" Molly shouted. "Let's get out of here. Now!"

Adrenalin pumping, Gavin struggled to move forward. A mousetrap sprang open and rose to eye level where it danced and spun in the air in slow motion, bringing him to a hypnotic halt. Pinpoints of light danced around the spinning slab of wood and wire, and Gavin felt himself swaying. A strange desire came over him to yield to the pull of the air currents, and he felt himself beginning to relax.

"Gavin," Molly barked. "What ails you?"

The mousetrap clamored to the floor, and Gavin skittered away. He raced toward the window, but Molly and Eric beat him to it.

Molly leaned forward against the wind, arms wrapped around her head for protection, until she had to let go to swing herself through the opening.

Eric stopped halfway through, wiggling his rear end in Gavin's face.

"Move it!" Gavin couldn't believe Eric would fool around at a time like this. He gave Eric's backside a wallop and out he fell.

Gavin reached for the sill, but a gust of wind slammed the window down, fast and hard, barely missing his fingers. The noise was deafening. The suction tugged at Gavin's clothes, harder than before, pulling him closer to the fireplace. His feet left the floor.

No way! Gavin fought back with all his might. *I'm not going up any chimney today. God, help—*

A dozen mousetraps snapped and spun around his ankles as he felt himself being pulled across the room by invisible hands.

CHAPTER SIX

BEA *Settlement*

Snippets of small-town life assaulted Bea's sensibilities. Peering through the limo window, she didn't know which disgusted her more—the layer of gray cinders accumulating on the glass or the obvious lack of culture Ashboro had to offer. After miles of nothing to look at but a two-lane road with scraggly woods, they were approaching civilization, but the only retail establishments so far were a McDonald's and Wal-Mart.

Bea cringed as they drove past an old woman who shuffled between stray carts, clutching a plastic bag to her breast as if it contained her life's possessions. "Gives new meaning to the term *bag lady*, don't you think?"

"Umm hmm . . ." Madam Daark flipped a page of her tablet and nodded without looking.

The limo sped by a residential area with a string of plain-Jane houses where Bea caught a glimpse of children playing baseball in a vacant lot. A few streets beyond, two girls under a tree laughed as one pushed the other in a homemade swing fashioned from a tire and rope. Bea's heart twinged, not with embarrassment but with . . . *envy? Certainly not.* What was this longing in her, then? *At least those little girls are allowed to play.*

Bruce Goodfellow, attorney-at-law, grinned like he owned the town. "Welcome to Ashboro." His booming voice bounced off the walls of the reception area, a good match for his basketball-sized belly. "My office is right this way." He extended his arm, indicating a knotty pine door at the end of a dark-paneled hallway. "We'll speed you through settlement on the Lodge and, in no time, have you meeting with the Council about that project of yours."

Bea sat at the lopsided table that was dented and scarred, watching papers shuffle and pens scribble with astounding efficiency as they passed from attorney, to seller, to Madam Daark, and back. A spark of excitement skittered through Bea as her mother casually handed over a check for $666,000—a small price to pay for something that would soon change the world. They were now the proud owners of the Lodge—66.6 acres of overgrown farmlands and woods with some junky outbuildings, all surrounded by a burning swamp.

Goodfellow's chair scraped the wood floor as he stood up to dismiss the executor of the estate, a mousy little man of few words who had mumbled his way through the affair.

He's probably never seen this much money in his life, Bea thought.

"And now," the attorney smiled warmly at Bea and her mother, "I switch hats. You can call me *Mayor* Goodfellow. We'll slip next door to the conference room. The Council should all be here by now." He bent at the waist in an awkward bow and, with great flourish, extended his arm to show the way.

As the Daarks and Mayor Goodfellow approached the room, Bea heard the buzz of conversation behind the door, but it stopped the second she and her mother entered. Her first impression was that the rusty air conditioner in the window wasn't doing its job.

Mayor Goodfellow cleared his throat with a choking sound that made Bea want to gag. "Councilmen—and, uh, councilwoman—I'd like to introduce Madam Donalda Daark and her daughter, Beatrice. They're here, as you know, to discuss the feasibility of the theme park they want to build."

Three of the five council members stood, grinning, to shake hands with them.

A Humpty-Dumpty man, with popped shirt buttons and a protruding belly, leaned back in his chair. "Since when do we invite teenage girls to Council meetings?" Nobody acknowledged his question, so Bea mentally dismissed him.

The councilman who interested her most was the man who wore a clerical collar. Pastor Fred Bailey also wore what looked like a permanent frown. *Right. I thought things were going too smoothly. That one has trouble written all over him.*

With everyone seated and properly introduced, the mayor directed Madam Daark toward a laptop computer on a podium. "As you requested," his voice resonated, "everything is ready for your presentation." He whispered loud enough for all to hear, "Hope you don't mind, but I took the liberty of previewing it."

Bea saw her mother wince and force a smile. She touched the keyboard, and the screen came to life.

"What we propose to bring to Ashboro," she began, "is a park that will—pending your approval of the required permits, of course—bring an unprecedented economic boon to your lowly, excuse me, lovely community. Lights, please, Mr. Mayor."

Bruce Goodfellow turned off the lights and pulled down the shades. Slide after slide showed architectural renderings of Medieval-style amusement rides and intriguing structures. "In conclusion, Dragon's Lair theme park is designed to play up the legend of Burnt Swamp with its mysterious dragon lurking beneath the surface. It will attract visitors from all over the world."

A skinny woman with sagging skin squirmed and fidgeted at the far end of the table. Bea stifled a chuckle, amused by the woman's plight. *Either she's got to go to the water closet or she has something to say.*

"Any questions?" Mayor Goodfellow's back was turned toward the councilwoman who gave a series of loud "ahems" until he recognized her. "She's our environmental expert," he explained, giving her a nod. "Go ahead, Mabel. You've got the floor."

The wiry old gal tapped her pen on a three-ring binder. "Mrs. Daark, I have—"

"Excuse me. I prefer to be called Madam Daark."

"My apologies, *Madam* Daark." The woman cleared her throat, her discomfort delighting Bea. "I have the results of the soil survey we did on the land where you propose to build this elaborate amusement park of yours." She paused, flipping quickly through indexed tabs.

Had her pegged, all right. Bea studied the woman's narrow lips as they all but disappeared into a thin line. *Can't wait to hear what kind of spanner this "expert" is going to throw in the works.*

Mabel opened her binder. "First, let me say I was skeptical that the percentages of sand, silt, and clay—determining the textural class, we call it—would be able to withstand the weight of such a massive facility, not counting the problems that may be encountered while excavating. We have a high water table, you know."

Mayor Goodfellow tapped his pen on the table. "Mabel, can we speed this up? What problems did you run into with the soil survey? Is it something we can work around?"

"The majority of the materials in this region are Pocomoke and Muck soils—"

"Mabel." Again, the mayor interrupted her. "Cut to the chase, and tell us if it passed or not? Yes or no?"

"Yes."

"Yes?" Bea heard a corporate gasp from all corners of the room.

The councilwoman's face brightened. "Much to my amazement, the samples that were tested within the immediate vicinity of the Lodge are clearly Evesboro, suitable for the proposed construction."

The frowning minister spoke up. "This is a huge complex they're proposing, Mabel. How far out can they go before they run into trouble?"

"Rest easy, Fred," Mabel said. "There is ample room for Dragon's Lair. I vote in favor."

Madam Daark clasped her hands together. Bea hopped out of her chair, spun daintily, and sat down again. Excited cheers went up from the others.

Apparently Pastor Fred wasn't finished. "We're not voting yet, Mabel." He raised his voice and waited while everyone quieted down. "My other concern is the occult nature of the park. Am I the only one here who has reservations about the sinister theme Madam Daark is proposing?"

Mayor Goodfellow sucked in his gut and pulled himself to full height. "Look here, Fred, every time somebody comes up with a plan to improve this smoke-filled town, you pipe up with some cockamamie reason to shoot it down. Your fuddy-duddy ways and superstitions have held us back long enough." He raised his right hand. "All in favor of approving permits so Madam Daark can get on with construction of Dragon's Lair, raise your hand."

All hands shot into the air but one. Bea was pleased to find such little opposition, but she shouldn't have been—after all, whatever Mum wanted, Mum got.

"Fun for all and all for fun!" another board member shouted.

Rev. Bailey crossed his arms over his chest.

With the deed to the Lodge and a permit for Dragon's Lair safely tucked in Madam's briefcase, Bea and her mother took a quick limo tour of their property prior to boarding the Cessna once again. After two weeks on holiday in New England, conducting research for their family tree, they would return to London for a month of shopping and packing. During their absence, crews of carpenters, decorators, and landscapers were scheduled to prepare the Lodge for occupancy.

Oh, the plans we have for the netherworld portion of our new home. Bea's pulse beat faster as she thought about how the underground dugouts she had just seen would be expanded into a maze of tunnels and secret meeting quarters.

"Those slides were all new to me, Mum. When the Order first showed us the blueprints, bunkers and root cellars weren't part of the plan. When did the architects come up with that? Why didn't you tell me it's going to have a three-story lift and subterranean chamber?"

"I'll keep you informed on an 'as-needed' basis, Daaaahling." Madam Daark drawled out her sarcasm with a raised eyebrow that made Bea want to wither inside. "For now, it's sufficient that you know the sand hill behind the Lodge will serve as your training camp."

"What are you saying, Mum? You don't trust me?"

Madam Daark gave a slow, dreadful smile, which Bea hoped someday to emulate. It was the smile that sent a message without a word being spoken; the smile that made a person stop to wonder, yet know for sure, they'd never gain the upper hand.

"Candles," Bea suggested in response to her mother's silence. "I know we'll have state-of-the-art electronics, but we'll need lots of candles and kerosene lanterns, too."

"Yes, Love." Her mother continued smiling with her lips closed. "And why is that, pray tell?"

"Because it's up to us to bring light to this daaaark world. And we must use every means at our disposal."

CHAPTER SEVEN

GAVIN Caught!

The persistent, earsplitting roar of the indoor wind tunnel assaulted Gavin from every direction. Mousetraps flew and snapped and pivoted in the air, then lined up in perfect symmetry to form twin arrows pointing to the fireplace. Gavin fought with every ounce of strength to get away, but his feet kept slipping out from under him, and he couldn't get a grip on anything his hands reached for. Tables turned topsy-turvy, candlesticks rolled by, and with every beat of his heart, Gavin felt his body being vacuumed between the two rows of mousetrap arrows, ever closer to the hearth.

"Gaaaaa-vin!" Molly's muffled voice came to him from the other side of the windowpane. Twisting nearly upside down from the wind that held him in its grip, he saw his own panic reflected in her eyes.

He opened his mouth to shout for help, but the phantom wind tunnel screamed louder, exhaling charcoal and soot down the chimney that billowed out from the opening, choking back his cries.

Molly and Eric got out, so why can't I?

A cutting blast of frigid air gave him a brain freeze between the eyes, driving out all thoughts of his cousins. Suddenly, all chaos ceased and an otherworldly voice as illusive as smoke and as chilling as ice pierced Gavin's mind.

Who be you, intruder?

Gavin didn't know whether to try to answer or to keep his mouth shut. Had he really heard the words, or was it his imagination? If this was another vision, he sure wished Uncle Warney would show up. Wait! Was the phantom losing strength?

Twisting loose from the ghost-like grip, Gavin lunged for the door. Three steps forward, two steps back. The wind tugged at his body. *Only ten yards to go.* He tried crab-walking, but that only made it worse. In a last-ditch maneuver, Gavin took a sprinter's stance and tried to lunge forward. But he couldn't budge.

Then he heard a great *whoosh* gathering behind him as the voice spoke again, unmistakably this time. *Get out, and stay out.*

Gavin bolted and kept accelerating until he made it through the door. The screen slammed behind him as loud as a shotgun blast. Long-jumping from the back porch, he sailed over a grassy mound and landed on the driveway where gravel crunched under his feet as his knees gave way.

"Boy, am I glad to see you guys," he huffed to Molly and Eric as he regained his balance.

"What took you so long?" Eric smirked. "Get tangled up with a few mousetraps?"

"Mousetraps?" Gavin couldn't believe his ears. "More like monsters and living nightmares. I just about got sucked up the fireplace in there by some—"

"Let's not talk about it." Molly wrapped her arms around herself. "It'll be dark soon. Let's get out of here."

"Yeah, I'm outta here." Eric jogged on ahead and veered off the path toward the woods.

"Gavin." Molly spoke so softly he had to strain to hear her. "Don't let him out of your sight. We have to stick together."

By the time Gavin and Molly caught up to Eric, he was standing knee-deep in foliage, scratching his ankles with a vengeance.

"Quiet." Gavin grabbed Eric's arm. "Did you hear that?"

"Hear what?" Eric answered in a loud voice.

"Shhh." Gavin pointed ahead. "Over there—by the railroad tracks. What if somebody knows we're here?"

"I didn't hear anything," Molly said.

Eric laughed and went back to scratching his ankles. "Nah, me neither; must be your imagination." He sniffed the air and screwed up his face. "But, pshew, I sure do smell something. What *is* that?"

Gavin breathed in the most gosh-awful smell. "Skunk stink and swamp stench."

"Good tongue twister." Molly applauded and lifted her nose, too. "Smells faint to me, Eric, like it's almost gone."

"Nuh uh." Eric inhaled again. Shifting all his weight to his right leg, he leaned toward the trees and a ditch. "Nope, smells to me like it's getting stronger."

With that, he lost his balance and fell into the ditch where he landed on top of a black and white pelt—a dead skunk.

"Pee-uuu! Get this stink off-a me!" Eric yelled. He jumped up, hopped around, and shook his hands like they were on fire.

Gavin's eyes began to burn. He pinched his nose and backed away from Eric. The skunk pelt was stuck to the back of Eric's shirt, right in the middle and just out of reach. Eric groped and bucked like a wild bronco, then threw himself back on the ground and rolled over three times before the icky thing came off.

Gavin tried hard not to snicker, but it was impossible to hold it in. He snorted and burst out laughing. But when he sucked in a great gulp of air, the stench gagged him and threw him into a coughing fit.

Tears streamed down Gavin's face. He saw Molly take off in a run, quickly distancing herself from them. Through watery eyes, he saw Eric, still flopping around in the ditch. *Some athlete. If your teammates could only see you now.* Gavin grabbed a sturdy tree branch and held it out. "Can't give you a hand, good buddy—you'd get stink all over me—but here's a limb. Grab hold and I'll pull you up."

Back on solid ground, the boys caught up with Molly.

Eric yanked off his shirt and tossed it into the ditch, going bare-chested.

"Tomato juice." Molly closed and opened her eyes rapidly as they watered from the fumes. "Take a bath in tomato juice when you get home. And burn those jeans."

"Nice muscles," Gavin observed, not meaning to say it aloud.

Molly turned her back on them and marched ahead with her hands on her hips.

Again, Gavin heard rustling in the woods and held up a hand in a signal to stop. "Could be hunters," he said, chewing his bottom lip.

"Or a two-hundred-pound, ten-point buck!" Eric pointed to a deer with a huge rack of antlers less than fifty feet away.

Gavin had heard local hunters talk enough to realize that the intent to charge in this papa deer's eyes "Quick, run! Let's get out of h-e-r-e!"

The boys caught up to Molly, passed her, and were running at top speed when Gavin heard an ear-shattering whistle and realized the railroad tracks were dead ahead. He stopped, with Eric on his heels, barely in time to avoid stumbling over the rails.

Within seconds, tons of steel blocked their path. His heart pounded so hard, he thought the big buck must surely be able to hear it. Glancing back, a wave of relief washed over him when he realized the deer must have been as scared as they were and had run the other way.

Gavin paced back and forth. "Three engines. This is a long one," he said, trying to catch his breath as he looked down the tracks. "Let's count 'em. One, two, three . . ."

Eric jabbed Gavinin the ribs. "Might be more than fifty. Think you can count that high?"

Gavin rolled his eyes. "Seven, eight, nine . . ."

"You stand over there to count." Molly pointed, holding her hand over her nose and mouth. "Keep your distance. You stink!"

The three cousins counted the freight cars to the tune of the squealing rumble of iron wheels. As they counted, Gavin squatted on his heels and watched Molly shift her weight from one foot to the other while Eric wiped his hands on his jeans and paced around. Ten minutes later, they announced in unison, "One hundred and four."

Just as the caboose passed, the squeal of an airplane engine caused all three to look up.

Gavin gawked into the sky. "Wonder if it's that same jet."

"If it is, they've been circling a long time. Privately chartered, I'll bet—definitely not public." Molly craned her neck to follow the tiny silver streak across the sky. "Could be taking aerial photos—but, they're moving pretty fast. Wonder if they'll land at Ashboro Airpark."

"Nobody uses that any more," Gavin said.

"Yes, they do," Molly said. "Don't you remember? The big editorial in *The Encounter* about the runway expansion?"

"Yeah, well, I don't read the papers, remember? But you've gotta have a ton of money to charter one of those things." Gavin rubbed the tips of his fingers together. "What would rich folks want to come around here for?"

"Maybe it's the people who bought the Lodge." Eric wiggled his fingers in the air and made a spooky face. "Ooooohhhh, maybe they'll be witches."

Molly's hands found her hips again. "Well, if it is the new owners, we got out of there in the nick of time. You guys are never going to talk me into trespassing again."

"Come on, Molly," Eric said. "You have to admit the place was pretty cool."

Molly snorted. "Fascinating? Yes. Cool? No. That place is mega creepy. I'll bet an evil spirit lives there."

Eric gave Gavin one of his goofball looks, but their smiles faded when a siren pierced the air.

Through the trees, Gavin spied red and blue flashing lights speeding toward them, bobbing up and down on the dirt road.

"Yo! It's the cops!" Eric yelled.

"Oh no!" Molly gasped as the siren grew louder. "I can't find my backpack!"

"Your backpack? Forget it! The cops are coming!" Gavin said.

"But my article—and all my research—"

They scrambled into the woods and hunched behind a patch of prickly bushes.

"Ouch!" Eric glared at Molly. "How could you be so stupid? If the cops don't find us, they'll find your backpack and *then* they'll know it's us. If I can't play football this year, it'll be all your fault!"

Molly's face blanched paler than her cream-colored shirt. "I left it at the Lodge. I can't go back—I just can't."

"We can't just *leave* it there." Gavin's heart pounded.

Molly's shoulders dropped. "There goes my chance of meritorious honors."

"And I'll be grounded from sports forever." Eric moaned. "First the skunk, then the buck, then the train—now this."

"Hold on," Gavin said with a calmness that surprised him. "We don't all have to be caught. You two, go on and get out of here! They haven't spotted us yet. I'll find your backpack. Maybe I can get it before—"

"But Gavin . . ." Molly pointed in the direction of the flashing lights. The police car was almost on them.

"Can't you let me be a hero even once? *Go!*" Gavin trembled.

"This way, Molly." Eric sprinted off.

A sob escaped Molly's throat. She turned to follow Eric and glanced over her shoulder at Gavin. "Thanks. You're saving my reputation. Be careful."

Gavin nodded with a not-too-sure-about-that expression and shooed them away. He waited long enough to be sure Molly had left and then ran back into the woods. The muscles in Gavin's calves and thighs burned from pushing his legs past their limit. Racing deeper into the underbrush, he dodged trees and vines while trying to keep his bearings. *Whatever you do, don't get lost.* The siren grew fainter.

With hammering heart and clammy hands, he staggered into the clearing by the railroad tracks and flopped on the ground. *Phew, made it this far.* His breaths were coming so fast and short he thought he might hyperventilate.

In his whole life, Gavin had never felt so alone. What was he thinking? Why didn't he insist Molly stick around and find her own dumb backpack? A wave of frustration and fear swept over him as he coached himself. *Inhale, exhale. Inhale, exhale.*

The second he stood up to run back to the Lodge, the flashing vehicle rounded a corner and bounced straight toward him in a cloud of dust. No wonder he didn't hear the siren. It was turned off.

The dark blue Ford with "Ashboro Police" in gold letters fish-tailed and came to a screeching halt, spewing dirt and sand on Gavin, blocking his path.

Gavin's heart sank. Caught!

And then he saw a friendly ebony face looking back at him through the windshield. Panic and relief collided in Gavin's brain. *Officer Charlie, whew!* Gavin knew him from church and thought for sure he could talk his way out of this.

"That you, Gavin? Gavin Goodfellow?" The officer shook his head and eased his beefy frame out of the police car.

"Yes sir, Officer Charlie," Gavin said as he dusted himself off.

"Don't 'yes, sir, Officer Charlie' me, young man. This neck of the woods is off-limits."

Gavin's hope collapsed around his shaky knees. So much for church connections. "Um, yes sir—off-limits."

"You out here all alone in these parts, son?"

Gavin offered a sheepish half-smile. "Yes, sir. Sure looks that way, sir. All alone." Gavin was used to fibbing, but this was the first time he had ever lied to a cop. His conscience twinged. *Okay, so it's a lie, but it's basically true—I'm alone* now, *that's for sure.*

"The Lodge security system went wild. You wouldn't know anything about that, now, would you?"

"Well, sir," Gavin swallowed, "maybe so. You see, I was just scouting around—looking for something to do—and I wound up here in the woods. Next thing I knew, there I was at the Lodge, so I said to myself, 'Self, why don't you take a closer look?' I was real careful not to hurt anything. Just kinda nosed around, then left."

"Just the same, you know you've done wrong. Right?" Officer Charlie squinted at Gavin, the creases in his face deepening with concern.

Gavin felt somehow smaller.

"You had to see the No Trespassing signs, and you know what that means, right, son?"

"Yeah, it means stay out, but I figured it didn't mean me."

"Well now . . ." Officer Charlie clenched his jaw. "Looks like you figured wrong, doesn't it? Posted signs are there for a reason, and seeing as how I'm the law, it's up to me to enforce it. Not only were you trespassing, but if you went into the Lodge, then that means you were breaking and entering. That's serious." He looked Gavin hard in the eye. "What say you and me drive on down to make sure everything's in order?"

Gavin's mind was a whirlwind of torment. What if he didn't find Molly's backpack? What if he *did*? How would he explain that?

Officer Charlie guided Gavin toward the vehicle by the elbow.

Reality slapped Gavin's notion of heroics from all sides. *It's getting dark. What was I—nuts?* Till now, he hadn't thought about what it would be like to go back to the Lodge at dusk. What if the fireplace started up on its own again? Not even Officer Charlie could stop *that*.

"Shouldn't you take me to the station and turn me in?" Gavin stood back as the policeman lumbered toward the patrol car.

"We'll do that, all right, but first we're going to take a look so I can write up my report. What do you say you show me around?"

"Uh, okay, but . . . do we have to? It's getting dark, and there's not much to see."

"Sorry, son, but, yes, we really have to do this."

A sleek white jet flew low overhead as Officer Charlie opened the back door of the police car. He scowled when he saw it.

"Go on, son. Get in."

"Excuse me, sir," Gavin said a few moments later as Officer Charlie wedged his frame behind the steering wheel. "I know I'm in big trouble and all, but would it be okay if I asked you a question?"

"What's on your mind?"

"That plane." Gavin twisted his body around to look up through the window. "Seems like a lot of activity at the airpark today. You think it might have something to do with the people that bought the Lodge?"

Gavin sat down and fastened his seat belt.

Officer Charlie turned the key in the ignition but didn't put the car in gear. Instead, he placed both hands on the steering wheel and just sat there.

"You're pretty perceptive, young man," he said at last. "We got word from airport security that the new owners were flying in today for some sort of town meeting."

"They're rich, right?"

Charlie leaned his head back. "Yup, I'd wager they've got more money than all the people of Ashboro put together. They're from London, I think—a mother and daughter. I hear the girl's your age, maybe a year older."

Gavin chewed his bottom lip and inched forward, stretching the seat belt to capacity.

"Just be careful who you pick for friends."

"Uh, um, thanks—I guess." Gavin couldn't read the expression on Officer Charlie's face, but it made him wish he hadn't brought up the subject of airplanes or the people who bought the Lodge.

Officer Charlie put the car in gear and began driving. When the tires crunched to a stop in front of the Lodge, he reached for a flashlight. "How'd you get in, Gavin?"

"Around back. Come on, I'll show you." As they walked around the corner of the building, now dark in the shadows, Gavin silently vowed never to trespass again. He pointed to the window. "It was unlatched. That's how I got in. But I . . . um . . . locked it up good when I left."

Why'd I say that? I didn't lock anything up. I was too busy running for my life!

Officer Charlie tried to push the window up. It wouldn't budge. "Looks secure to me."

Whew! Lucky break. Still, Gavin recoiled at the memory of the window slamming shut from the mysterious whirlwind.

"No need to go in," the officer said. "The company reset the alarm and I don't have the code, so we'll just walk the perimeter, and I'll double-check the doors."

Another lucky break. Gavin's heart raced as they approached the front of the Lodge. There, through the twilight, he spotted a small denim heap on one of the porch benches. "Officer Charlie, I—um—left my backpack somewhere around here." He forced his voice to sound surprised. "Oh, yeah, there it is!"

"Good thing we came back after all, then. Hustle on over there and grab your bag, son."

Gavin scooped up the bag and rolled it into a ball so the turquoise strap and embroidered "M" wouldn't show.

Thunk.

Something was on the porch! He was sure of it.

His heartbeat skyrocketed. Gathering all his nerve, Gavin forced his chin to the left so he could look over his shoulder.

Relief surged through his veins. "Scared me to death, Ugly Cat." With the cat mocking him with one eye, he felt exposed.

"Beat it, Ugly."

The bag felt like it contained one of his dad's bowling balls as Gavin trudged back to the police car.

"Looks heavy," the big man said. "Want me to carry it for you?"

"No! I got it." The weight of the bag shifted under Gavin's arm, and Officer Charlie bent down for a closer look.

"What's that? A turquoise 'M'?"

"Uh, yeah. I . . . well, I wanted one with a 'G' on it but they didn't have any 'G's, so I got this one."

"Why'd you pick an 'M'?"

"Huh?" It was Gavin's standard response when he needed time to make something up.

"The 'M.' Does it stand for something?"

"Uh, yeah. It stands for—" His mind clicked through all the 'M' words he knew. "It stands for 'Mine.'"

"Figures." Officer Charlie threw back his head and let out a great peal of laughter.

Gavin laughed, too. But the cat's knife-like gaze stayed on his mind.

By the time Gavin and Officer Charlie made it back to the police car, the sun had set. Burnt Swamp, with the silhouette of the Lodge in the foreground, was dark except for the glow of red embers.

On the short ride back to town, images of mounted animals, pentagrams, and candle wax loomed in Gavin's thoughts. He licked his lips but didn't have enough spit. Stuffing his hand in his pocket, he found the Chapstick he'd borrowed from his mom's dresser, popped off the lid, and smeared the balm on his lips in an ever-widening circle. The strawberry scent made him hungry, but he was too worried to pay his appetite any mind.

Should he tell Officer Charlie what he saw in that place? No. What good would that do? Besides, he was in enough trouble already. *But he needs to know.*

"Officer Charlie?"

"Yes, Gavin?"

"Never mind."

"What's wrong?" The officer glanced at Gavin in a grandfatherly way and then turned his attention back to driving. "Concerned about facing your parents?"

"Nah." Well, that was about as big a lie as Gavin ever told. "It's just that I saw something at the Lodge."

Officer Charlie let up on the accelerator. "What was it?"

"Nothing, really. Sorry I said anything."

As they reached the outskirts of town, Officer Charlie pulled the car to the side of the road.

Gavin's stomach rumbled like the idling engine.

Beams from a streetlight illuminated Officer Charlie's face. It registered such genuine concern that Gavin felt a safety net had dropped around him.

"Tell me." Officer Charlie's tone reminded Gavin of the way Uncle Warney spoke when he spent a weekend at his shack and had a nightmare—all love, no reprimand. "What did you see? It might be important."

Every fear about the Lodge gushed out. During Gavin's spiel about stuffed creatures, wax puddles, and the chandelier with the hangman's noose shadow, Officer Charlie kept nodding his head and saying, "Yep, I see . . . go on."

"Oh, and I forgot about the mousetraps," Gavin said. "They were set all over the place but not baited, like they were meant to catch people instead of mice."

Officer Charlie smiled. "Now, now, son. Let's not get carried away. You were building a good case there, but mousetraps to catch people? Well, that causes me to take a fresh look at the whole picture. Except for somebody's odd choice of mounted wildlife, there could be a logical explanation for everything." Officer Charlie put his hand on Gavin's shoulder. "The wax drippings and chalk marks might be left over from a birthday party. But I'll be keeping a close eye on things."

A heaviness centered in Gavin's chest. He'd said more than he meant to say and seen more than he'd wanted to see.

Officer Charlie wheeled the car back onto the road. In less than a minute, they arrived at the Ashboro Police Department where the Magistrate's Court sign dangled from rusty chain links.

Gavin hugged Molly's denim bag close to his stomach so tightly it turned his knuckles white. *Secrets*, he thought as he got out of the car and started toward the brick building. *Everybody's got secrets.* But the one weighing on Gavin's conscience was heavier than Molly's bag.

CHAPTER EIGHT

WARNEY

Warnard Elijah Stokes

Warnard Elijah Stokes awoke with a jerk from his midday nap in the front porch rocker. Jumping to his feet, he steadied himself with his cane as he stared at the charred tree trunks on the fringe of Burnt Swamp.

"Something's wrong, Lord. What is it yer tryin' ta tell me?"

Though he didn't used to think so, the shell fragments that lodged in his spine during WW II were a gift from God. Just as some people can tell from their arthritis when a storm is coming, Warney's back was his "spiritual barometer."

Whenever the Lord drew near, it heated up like the inside of a toaster oven set on "high." But when evil stirred, the metal in his spine turned icy. His back was cold all the time now, even in the heat of the day in mid-July. Ignoring his physical discomfort, Warney shifted his weight to his left leg and listened.

Crack. Snap.

Was that a growl?

Distracted by a distant movement, Warney stretched a trembling hand to the back of his neck where the small hairs began to stir.

What in tarnation is that? He stepped off his porch and stared intently through the smoke screen beyond his shack to where the swamp fires continued to burn these many years. Something was moving in the trees at the far end of his property, something that made his blood run cold.

Too small and high up ta be one o' them bears that used to roam 'round, scarin' the daylights outta people. Too big fer one o' them pesky buzzards.

He clenched his teeth. *But nothin' lives in Burnt Swamp no more. Nothin' good that is.* Of course, that didn't count himself and Ugly Cat who lived as close to the swamp as a body could get without being in it.

Warney tried his best not to move anything but his eyes. He squinted and blinked to get the sleep out of them, but it didn't work. So, instead of rubbing them with the back of his hand like a normal person, he rolled his eyeballs around in their sockets and blinked again. The wrinkles of his long jowls twitched in grim satisfaction when his vision cleared.

Dread pimpled his aged frame with gooseflesh from head to toe. "So, I'm livin' to see the fulfillment."

Warney lowered his head in acceptance of what he knew could not be changed. For ten years the swamp had become a living, breathing, cauldron of evil, and now it was being stirred. That meant only one thing. His voice was low and gravelly, barely a whisper. "The infiltration's begun; the prophecy's comin' to pass—jest as the diary foretold."

A pool of stagnant water gurgled its confirmation and bubbled up into a sour burp. Or was it a strangled laugh? Nothing surprised him anymore. He knew the swamp was alive.

Ugly Cat inched closer and rubbed against Warney's leg.

"Are you protectin' me, or am I protectin' you?" Warney bent down to pet him, smoothing the row of coarse hairs that stood up on the cat's back. "Somethin' got ya riled up, old boy?" Warney tapped a finger against the right side of his nose. "There's gonna be trouble, you betcha. I'd stake muh nose on it."

His spirit on full alert, he cocked his shaved head to the right and listened with his left ear, his good one.

"Gimme a word, Lord. I been faithful, keepin' watch like Ya told me. A touch of warmth in muh back, maybe? Some sort o' sign to let me know Yer in this with me?"

Warney would have settled for any clue about the increase of the vile force that had crept into his beloved swamp. But he heard nothing—no sound or gurgling from the marsh, no voice from heaven above or from humans in the distance. Nor could he see any evidence of the evil that he knew lurked beyond his home at the edge of the swamp. Yet, an eerie sensation churned in his gut and caused him to wipe sweaty palms on the front of his jeans.

His attention drawn heavenward again, he spied a beady-eyed buzzard flying in lazy circles above him. Something fell from the sky. Warney tried to dodge it, but—splat!—a diarrhea-green bomb exploded on his forehead.

"Ack! Ya dirty buzzard!" Warney wiped the mess off with his bandana and smeared it on the steamy, moss-covered ground. "Good aim, Picky. Ya always seem to know right where ta find me. The Good Book says that a righteous man makes even his enemies ta be at peace with him, but I'm gettin' a mite sick of bein' yer target, ya old buzzard! Go find someone else to torment!"

Makin' peace is one thing, but ya cain't make friends with the devil.

He grabbed his gnarled walking stick and thrust it high into the air. Power exploded from the core of his being and coursed its way through his chest, surging down his arm and into his outstretched hand.

This must be how Moses felt when he stretched his rod over the Red Sea. Not that he looked anything like Moses. A picture of Charlton Heston flashed in his mind, and Warney chuckled. *No long beard.* He rubbed his palm against the stubble on his chin, then let it slide up and across his bald head, partly the courtesy of nature, the rest shorn off by choice. *And no long robe.* Unless a person counted the full-length gray riding jacket with maroon trim he kept on a peg for church-going. But he wasn't even wearing that now—just his usual faded jeans and gray sweatshirt with the sleeves ripped out.

Nope, he was more like the "crazy old coot" he was used to hearing most folks in Ashboro call him. Standing there, he caught a glimpse of his shadow and thought for a fleeting moment that he looked like a pot-bellied mosquito. He shook his head to rid himself of the silly image. *This is spiritual warfare.* He held the trusty walking stick high above his head as if to part Burnt Swamp. His lean, wiry arm locked into position, as sturdy and still as a shepherd with his staff poised to attack a stalking wolf. From its perch on the limb of a charred and leafless cypress, the buzzard cocked its black head and watched.

A rich baritone voice—Warney's prophetic voice—thundered from his parched throat like a radio announcer reading from the Authorized King James Version of The Holy Bible.

"As the Lord God of Israel liveth, before whom I stand, *there . . . will . . . be . . . peace* in the midst of this here place, a haven that none but the righteous may enter."

To Warney's surprise, the treetops rustled where he had sensed the earlier movement. The tree spat out six feet of gangly teen from the topmost branches. He dropped to the ground, his arms and legs flailing; then, before the old man could blink, the boy belly-crawled into a thicket and out of sight.

Ugly Cat, who had been resting on Warney's moccasins, shrieked like he did when his tail got caught in the rocker and raced off in the other direction as fast as his bent paw would let him.

"What in tarnation?" Tongues of the ever-present mist wound around Warney's body like a lasso, holding him hostage as he watched the heels of the teen disappear into the underbrush. Only then did recognition finally dawn on Warney's befuddled mind.

My soul. It's that rabble-rouser, Hee-Haw Downes. What's that snake of a lad up to, hidin' out here in a tree anyhow? No tellin', but it cain't be good.

Warney recalled his proclamation, and a realization washed over him like a waterfall. He'd called on God to allow none but the righteous in this haven, and the trees spit out Hee-Haw Downes like sour gum. A loud pop drew the old man's eyes to the orange embers that kindled at the foot of the brush near where the boy had disappeared. Most likely, he was halfway home by now, but the cloud of his reputation as a student of the occult lingered in Warney's already troubled thoughts.

Yellow flames skittered up a spicebush—from the roots to the branch tips, fanned by a powerful breath that bent the trees and tossed leaves into the air. Cool, fresh air that smelled of sea salt and spring rain swirled around Warney's body, replacing the swamp smoke and enfolding him like the very arms of God. As suddenly as the phenomenon began, it ended. The bush, with its red berries still intact, stood there looking as green and healthy as the bushes surrounding it, yet untouched by fire.

Fear and awe filled Warney's voice as he lifted his gaze to the heavens, blue and pristine above the umbrella of the swamp. "This is muh own burnin' bush experience, ain't it, Lord?" Even as Warney spoke, the shell fragments in his spine warmed like Burnt Swamp coals. The walking stick he had wielded in a demonstration of power and conviction only moments before was now heavier than his arm could hold. A willing but weary soul, Warney let go, and the knobby cypress staff dropped from his hand with a thud. Emotion wavered in his voice.

"Ten years, I been waitin' for Ya to speak to me 'bout them flames. Ten years, I heard exactly nothin'. No dreams, no visions, no stirrin' in muh soul. I finally seen Yer breath today, but now I'm crippled so's I can hardly walk." Warney chuckled halfheartedly at the irony. "Guess I'll never figure Yer ways. I *know* Yer here with me, Father God. Tell it to me straight. Is this holy ground? Or am I standin' in a livin' hell?"

Silence.

Picky fluttered down and perched on the remains of what was once a thriving, massive hundred-year-old oak. The huge bird bowed his head like he was going to sleep—or pray—and then he stretched out his wings like a black shirt with its arms spread on a clothesline.

Warney continued his prayer. "I'm tellin' Ya, I don't think that boy's ready for this. Then again, I don't reckon I am now either . . . at least not in body." Warney bent over to retrieve his walking stick.

"But maybe between the two of us, Gavin an' me . . . and *You*, o' course, Lord . . . we'll see the prophecy fulfilled." Warney tapped the stick on the ground. "No, I *know* we'll see the prophecy fulfilled." He shook his head, and his eyes burned with shame at his doubt. "I'm plum tuckered out. Fergive me. Sometimes this place feels more like Hades than hallowed ground."

Warney was about to turn away when he heard the rustling of wings. Two other buzzards, smaller than Picky, circled the charred oak tree and settled on either side of the huge bird who never flinched. They, too, put their beaks on their breasts, then fully extended their battered wings to the sides. The tips of their feathers drooped like dangling fingers.

The silhouette sent a prickling heat up Warney's spine. Three birds, their wings spread against a pale sky, reminded him of three crosses—symbols of forgiveness and love, pain and suffering.

Warney's bony knees hit the dirt. In the midst of his awe that God would choose such worrisome creatures to bring encouragement, he knew that things would get worse before they got better. But God would be with him . . . and with Gavin.

Warney closed his eyes and prayed. "Lord God A'mighty, if that boy's gonna to be fit fer the days ahead—"

The plate in his spine turned cold. *Gavin's in trouble. I know it, sure as I'm kneelin' here.*

CHAPTER NINE

GAVIN

Police Station

At exactly 9:15, just fifteen minutes after Gavin's arrival at the Ashboro Police Department, the heavy doors burst open with a bang as Bruce Goodfellow stormed into the station. Gavin jumped at the sound but didn't have to look up to know who it was. Dragging his gaze from the clipboard in his lap, Gavin watched his dad march straight to the front desk without as much as a glance his way. His mother, who followed in his dad's shadow, saw Gavin and hesitated a moment before breaking away to come to him.

Gavin tucked his head down to concentrate on the paper on the clipboard, double-checking to be sure his b's and d's weren't backwards. He heard his mom's footsteps coming closer but couldn't bring himself to look up at her.

"We were worried sick about you." Louise Goodfellow's voice sounded higher than normal. She slid onto the wooden bench beside Gavin and put her arm around his shoulder. Although her squeeze made him feel a little better, he continued to write until she placed her hand on top of his. Gavin stopped. But he still couldn't bring himself to make eye contact.

"Whatever it is, honey, it'll be okay," she said.

Gavin could hardly hear her for his dad's voice bouncing off the station walls.

"What's he done, Charlie? What kind of charges are we talking about?"

"Trespassing at the Lodge. First offense. Gavin and I had a nice little chat with the Chief. There'll be no charge for B and E."

"Breaking and entering?"

"That's right. Everything was locked up tight, and I saw no evidence of vandalism or theft, so there's no need for arbitration. The Chief agreed to handle it internally, so Family Court's not involved. We're putting Gavin on unsupervised probation with community service."

Officer Charlie glanced at Gavin. "He's a good boy."

"That's a matter of opinion under the circumstances, don't you think?"

Gavin didn't need to see his dad's glare to be stung to the core—which only added to the stew he was in about what the owners would find when they went inside. The stuff flying around the fireplace wasn't *his* fault.

"We figured a few hours of community service and a letter of apology to the new owners would be enough," Officer Charlie said. "He's drafting the letter now."

"Make it stiff—a hundred hours—five hours a day for a month. I can't have it looking like the mayor's son is getting special treatment."

Gavin stiffened in his seat. *Special treatment? How about* normal *treatment?* Even if Officer Charlie went light on his hours, his dad would make up the difference.

"Look at me, Gavin." His mother touched the bottom of his chin with two fingers and lifted his face toward hers.

The minute he gazed into his mom's I'll-love-you-no-matter-what eyes, they flashed open so wide he could see the whites almost the whole way around. She blinked twice and clapped her hand over her mouth, gasping like she was going nuts-o. Gavin figured she'd be upset, but he'd never seen his mom act weird like this.

"God have mercy—what have they done to you?" she said through her fingers.

"What do you mean, 'What have they done to me?' *I'm* the one who did something wrong, Mom."

Mrs. Goodfellow stared at him like he'd grown horns. "No, Gavin, your face! What's that stuff on your face?"

"What stuff?"

"That pink stuff!" On closer inspection, her horror gave way to laughter. "Oh, my stars," she said, reaching into her suitcase-sized purse. She pulled out a compact, opened the mirror, and handed it to him. "I think I know what it is. Take a look at yourself and tell me how that happened. You look like a clown."

"A clown?" Gavin snatched the mirror and held it up to his face. There, all around his mouth, from nose to chin, was a bright pink circle. He didn't know whether to laugh or cry.

"I *do* look like a clown! The Chapstick. It's . . . pink? But how—" And then he remembered. When he was sitting in the police car in the dark, he had managed to draw it over the whole bottom half of his face. Now, holding the mirror in one hand and wiping his mouth with the other, he managed to spread the mess around even more.

"I know I have a pack of Kleenex in here somewhere." Mrs. Goodfellow rummaged in her pocketbook and pulled out her wallet, a pack of gum, and a can opener—everything but tissues. "Guess you didn't know I use *tinted* Chapstick."

"But Mom, nobody told me. Nobody—not even Officer Charlie."

"Maybe they were trying to be nice, dear." She added a toothbrush and scissors to the collection in her lap.

"Or having a good laugh behind my back." *No wonder they looked so amused when they booked me.* "They took my picture. Bet that's a great-looking mug shot." A chuckle bubbled up in Gavin's throat. "So *that's* what they meant by 'the circus coming to town early this year.'"

Gavin and his mom burst out laughing.

"What's so funny?" Gavin's father walked over, shaking his head from side to side like an elephant about to charge. Gavin never told him to his face, but he did have big ears.

From the corner of Gavin's eye, he could see his mother's shoulders shaking and hear the muffled giggles behind her cupped hand.

His dad glared.

Trying to hide his humor and Chapstick-covered face, Gavin stared at his shoes. He knew that Mayor Bruce Goodfellow had no tolerance for nonsense, especially when Gavin was at the heart of it.

"Gavin, trespassing is serious. Do you know how poorly this will reflect on our family? Do you know what people will think? Can you imagine the ridicule I'll have to take? Shenanigans like this could cost me re-election—but no, you never think about anybody but yourself."

Yeah, wonder where I learned that.

"My own son arrested in the middle of the night. Inexcusable! How do you expect me to face the commissioners at the next town council meeting? How can I take a hard stance on crime when my own son is a juvenile delinquent?"

Yeah, yeah, yeah. You call nine o'clock the middle of the night? Tuning out the words he'd heard a thousand times before, Gavin kept his head down. He stole a look and wondered how a man's eyes could bulge so much and not pop out of his head. When his dad flung his arms out wide, Gavin imagined a policeman slapping handcuffs on his wrists for disturbing the peace.

At least his mom looked sympathetic, even if she didn't dare speak in Gavin's defense.

She opened her purse again and shoved both hands down deep. "I know I have wet wipes in here." Car keys and an overstuffed photo album tumbled out. "Do you know what kind of community service you'll be doing?"

Gavin rested his elbows on his knees and mumbled, "It's not bad, Mom. Stuff like sweeping ashes off people's steps, cutting grass, emptying trash cans—that sort of thing."

"Community service might be a good fit for your newfound *independence.*" Gavin's dad spit out the word like profanity. "You tell us you want more independence now that you're twelve, but we take our eyes off you for one afternoon, and what happens? How about that haircut you were supposed to get today, huh? What happened to that?"

Gavin opened his mouth but thought better of answering.

"We'll talk about your punishment on the way home. The first thing to go is *Infiltrators.*"

That figures. Why don't you just cut my heart out while you're at it?

"Look at me when I'm talking to you." Mr. Goodfellow raised his voice louder than usual, considering it was a public place.

Gavin's mom pulled out the packet of wipes. "I knew I had them." She peeled a moist towelette from the package and handed it to Gavin.

"You'd never find Molly or Eric in a predicament like this," his father added.

Gavin's head jerked up.

For the first time that night, his dad saw his face. "Gavin! What have you done?"

Gavin mopped wildly at the layers of greasy pink stuff. "It's my clown face, Dad. You know, comic relief." Gavin produced the Chapstick from his pocket and handed it over to his mom.

"Your mother's Chapstick?" His dad's face glowed brighter as Gavin's mom dropped the tube into her handbag. "Your mother was searching all over the house today for her Chapstick, and now we find that our son had it all along? You stole your mother's Chapstick?"

"He didn't steal it, Bruce. He borrowed it."

"But you didn't ask, did you? You took it."

"But I thought it was . . . you know," Gavin stammered, "family property." Even as the words came out, Gavin knew he had only made things worse.

"What on earth would you want with your mother's pink Chapstick, anyway? And what's it doing all over your face?"

"I didn't know it was *pink*, Dad." Gavin's voice sounded as small and weak as he felt. "I was nervous and . . . well, you know how I bite my lip sometimes and . . . well, I put it on in the dark when Officer Charlie was bringing me here."

His father turned balloon-red when he got mad. This time, Gavin just knew his face was going to explode. "You trespass, you steal, you write backwards. What else do you do that will make us the laughingstock of the town?"

Gavin continued to dab his face with the towelette.

"And another thing. What took you tromping around the Lodge anyway? You know you're not supposed to go near the swamp." This time, Gavin's dad paused and actually waited for an answer.

"I was, um, gathering leaves for a science project for summer school."

"No, you weren't! You're taking reading in summer school, not science. You're not even smart enough to be a good liar. When will you ever learn? So, what were you doing there? Were you going to see that worthless Warney?"

"Bruce, please don't call him that," Gavin's mom squeaked.

"You stay out of this, Louise. I'll call your cockamamie uncle whatever I please. He's a crazy old Gospel-spouting lunatic, always talking about demons and judgment."

Officer Charlie burst out of his office. "Emergency call—I need to leave." His face was a mask of alarm. "Gavin, you're free to go—just be sure you sign in first thing tomorrow. And, oh, bring that letter of apology with you."

"Anything I can do?" Bruce Goodfellow asked.

"No, it's personal. My daughter's been—" Officer Charlie choked up. "My grandson needs me." And he was out the door.

When Gavin stood up, Molly's backpack thudded to the floor with the embroidered "M" in plain view.

"And what are you doing with this?" Mr. Goodfellow seethed as he picked up the bag and held the turquoise strap at arm's length.

"Uh, it's Molly's backpack," he blurted out when his father raised his eyebrow.

"What? You stole Molly's backpack?"

"No, Dad. I, um . . . "

"Molly lost it, Dad." He tried to keep his story straight. "And I found it and—"

"You think I'm going to believe that?" The whole way down the steps and around the corner, Mr. Goodfellow shoved his son. "Well, young man," he snarled when they reached the Range Rover, "you're grounded for one month. No *Infiltrators*, no phone calls, no friends over—not even your cousins—and no TV. Just community service and time to catch up on those chores you've been avoiding."

"What chores? I did my chores."

Stepping closer to her son, Mrs. Goodfellow clutched her purse to her breast. "The shed, Gavin. Remember the shed? You promised to clean it out with me this summer."

"Oh, yeah, the shed."

Gavin's mom smiled. "Yes, dear, for the yard sale. Why, this month of restriction could turn out to be fun."

"Get real, Mom. Cleaning out the shed ain't my idea of fun."

Gavin's dad grabbed him by the shoulders. "Two things, son. Number one, respect. You speak to your mother with respect. Number two, there's no such word as ain't."

"Yes, there is, Dad." Gavin squirmed loose from his grip. "Molly says it's in the dictionary."

Mr. Goodfellow shook his head. "You'd never find Molly smart-mouthing her parents. Why can't you be more like her? I keep trying to believe you're going to amount to something, and look at you. A loser. Imagine that. Bruce Goodfellow raising a loser." He gave a loud "harrumph" and stomped the last few steps toward the car.

"Now, Bruce, speaking of Molly, why don't you give me that backpack, and I'll return it to her tomorrow."

Good old mom, always trying to kiss a bad situation and make it better. Gavin slid into the back seat and slouched in the corner. *A loser. Yeah, guess so.* Every time his dad called him that, Gavin believed it more.

The hum of the tires lulled Gavin to twilight sleep where flashes of the eat-the-book vision rushed back. Forcing himself awake to avoid sinking deeper into the dream, he rubbed the gooseflesh that popped up on his arms and felt a flicker of hope when the image of Uncle Warney's face refused to fade. *If only I could see him, he would know what to make of that vision. Yeah, like that's gonna happen. Dad'll keep me under house arrest till the swamp dries up.*

CHAPTER TEN

MOLLY

Rationalizing

olly glared at Eric. "If I'd known you'd be this crabby, I'd have mustered up the courage to visit Uncle Warney alone. I waited *two weeks* for you to agree to come along, and now you act like *this?*"

Eric jumped up, twisted at the waist, and slapped at a low-hanging branch. "Why'd you need me, anyway? I've got things to do that are more important than your stupid interview."

"If you hadn't talked us into going into that *stupid* Lodge, Gavin would be here, and you could have stayed with your *stupid* friends. But no! You had to be super snoop, and now Gavin's grounded, in case you forgot."

"Cut the guilt trip, Molly. If it weren't for *your* dumb backpack, we'd have all gotten off scot-free." He glanced at his watch. "I've got football practice at four o'clock, so in one hour and ten minutes I'm outta here."

"Don't worry." Slowing to a stop, she felt her brow knit in concern. "Eric, why are you so miserable around me? You used to bug me every other day to do something together."

Eric shrugged his shoulders and jumped up to slap down another low-lying branch.

No answer, as usual, so Molly kept walking. A patch of sun broke through the chronic smoke. She knew. But she wanted it to come from him. "You're not going to talk about it, are you?"

"Nope." Eric jumped up again, received an imaginary football, hunched over, and started zig-zagging along the path, providing his own commentary. "He's at the twenty yard line, the ten, the five, touchdown! The crowd is cheering wildly. Everett scores the winning point . . . and Sunken Bridge wins the game! Yeahhhhh!"

"You're getting to be just like Dad." Molly choked back tears.

Eric stopped and faced her, serious for the first time that afternoon. "And that would be so bad?"

"It's bad when it splits a family apart. He had no right to leave and take you with him."

"And you had no right to change your last name when Mom remarried. Molly *Pace*, a big disgrace." Eric did a chin strut in time with his mini-rap. "There's two sides to every story."

Molly stopped short. "The *disgrace* is what Dad did to the Everett name. And his *new wife* . . ." she grimaced. "Why did have to marry her anyway?"

"She's nice to me."

"I don't know you anymore, Eric."

"I don't care. You're my sister, not my mother or my girlfriend!"

"Girlfriend? Do you have a girlfriend?"

"Maybe I do, and maybe I don't. I don't have to answer to you or anybody else."

"But—"

Eric swiped the hair out of his eyes. "Do you want to stand here and argue, or do you want to see old Uncle Warney?"

Molly stood still, pondering her options. "I wish I could hate you, but I can't!"

"Because you're my sister?"

"No! Because I'm a Christian. Come on. We're late."

The two continued their trek in silence. Molly was only vaguely aware of the glowing embers ahead which seemed to beckon them into Burnt Swamp.

Warney coughed and wheezed like a train sputtering its last bit of steam. He yanked a bandana from his pocket. "Danged fire," he muttered, wiping his nose. "It'll be the death of me yet." Warney returned the rumpled cloth to his pocket as he watched Eric scoot around the corner in search of Ugly Cat.

"So, Molly, how come ya brung Eric with ya 'stead o' Gavin? Haven't seen hide nor hair of him in a couple weeks. What's goin' on with him? Izzy sick or somethin'?"

"It's a long story, but I need to do this interview. Did you say you have the *original* newspaper article?"

Warney gave her a searching look. "Why don't ya tell me that long Gavin story now?"

"Pleeeease, can we just do the interview first?"

"All right, but ya better tell me when we're done." Warney hobbled to the kitchen and rummaged in a drawer. "Got it right here. *The Daily*

Encounter, November 1, 1997, the mornin' after the lightnin' struck." With shaking hands, he opened the clipping, worn from years of folding and unfolding. "At my age, ya'd think I could handle this paper without gettin' all choked up. Here ya go."

When he handed the clipping over to Molly, it occurred to him that she was the spitting image of his sister—Molly's Grandma Jibbers— when she was a girl. Same long braid and freckled nose, two generations removed. His throat tightened with emotion when he saw how reverently she handled the article. And the confounded look that clouded her face when she read the words made him love her all the more.

"Can I borrow this?" Molly asked.

"Well, no, darlin'—that's one of them things I cain't bring muhself to part with. But yer welcome to copy it down."

Molly pulled out her pen and trusty notepad.

"I saw them lightnin' bolts with muh own eyes." He waited for Molly to finish writing. "And they was demons, I tell ya. Don't s'prise me none that they'd attack in the darkest part of the night on October 31st."

"Can I quote you on that?"

"Sure, honey, I got no secrets. Well, maybe I got *some* secrets, but there ain't nothin' secret 'bout muh feelin's where Burnt Swamp's concerned."

"Go on, then," Molly said.

Warney's mind saw it all over again—the horror he'd witnessed with his own two eyes that Halloween night. With an unholy passion, spears of non-stop lightning stabbed at his beloved treetops, again and again, like rapid-fire machine guns in the hands of a legion of madmen. Their blasts penetrated from every angle, splitting tree trunks down the middle—opening access to air pockets and root systems beneath the mossy soil.

Warney took in a deep breath that rattled his whole bony frame, then commenced. "Them trees had been growin' there, mind ya, since the end of the Civil War in 1865 . . ." After answering Molly's every question about the "relentless," "sizzling," "crackling," "mocking" flames that had devastated his swamp, he laid his walking stick across his knees. "So, did ya get whatcha needed fer that story of yers?"

"Sure did. Thanks!" Molly beamed, tucking her notebook away.

"Good fer you. Now, tell me. What's goin' on with Gavin?" He leaned toward her.

The smile faded from her face. "You haven't heard?"

"Ain't heard nothin'. Yer Aunt Louise has been 'round to see me o' course, but when I ask about Gavin, she jest says he's real busy."

"He's busy, all right." Molly snorted and clapped her hand over her mouth. "I hate it when I do that." She rolled her eyes and blurted out, "Gavin got arrested and has to do community service."

"Gavin? Arrested?" Warney felt like he'd been struck across the face with a fly swatter. "What'd he do?"

Molly took a deep breath. "He trespassed at the Lodge. Uncle Bruce put him on restriction, and he's not allowed to see you—or even me." Her eyes brimmed with tears. "I can't," she cried, putting her head in her hands.

"Whoa, whoa, baby girl! Calm down. Cain't what?"

"Can't tell you about it." She hugged herself and rocked back and forth. "It's all too weird. Besides, Eric will kill me if I tell."

"Eric's out there chasin' cats or raccoons, Molly. It's jest the two of us, and ya gotta get that weight off yer shoulders." He handed her a clean hankie. "Why in tarnation would yer brother wanna kill ya fer tellin' ol' Uncle Warney 'bout Gavin trespassin'?"

Molly sniffled and sobbed and divulged the whole account of the mishap—from shifting paths, to the terrifying Lodge experience, to Gavin's attempt at heroism and subsequent arrest while she and Eric got away. "So Gavin's being punished, and it's all my fault."

Warney couldn't decide which was worse—the possibility that his great-niece and nephews had danced with the devil unawares or the trouble Gavin had gone and got himself into. But with Molly turning into a bundle of nerves, he figured he'd best cater to her first.

"Okay, Molly, let's calm down a mite, and we'll try to sort this out. Ya say all three of ya saw the No Trespassin' sign and went on anyway?"

"Well, I was against it, but what was I supposed to do? Go back through the woods by myself?"

"No need to get feisty with me, baby girl. I'm jest tryin' to get a feel fer the choices ya made."

"Sorry, Uncle Warney. Yes, we all ignored the sign." Molly dabbed her eyes with the handkerchief. "But the Lodge looked so interesting nestled there in the woods. We'd all heard stories about it. I couldn't help it. Guess I rationalized it would be okay."

Yessirree, that's rationalizin' all right. Now, Lord, what do Ya want me to say to this young un?

"Funny how temptation has a way of playin' tricks so ya focus on somethin' that looks appealin' and miss the big picture."

Molly pulled on her braid and twisted the curls at the end like she always did when she was nervous. "Yeah, and even though I'm not in official trouble, it sure feels like it on the inside."

"Well, ya cain't undo what's done, that's fer sure." Warney sighed. "Ya willin' ta try a little experiment?" At her nod, he continued. "Close yer eyes and picture yerself back there when ya come up to that sign. Good. Now try to see yerself doin' the right thing."

"I can't." Her eyelids opened wide.

"Sure ya can, Molly gal. Play along with me on this. I'm tryin' to help ya find a way to keep from fallin' into the devil's traps. Ya got a good 'magination, I know ya do, and there's times when ya can trick yer brain into doin' right when yer flesh wants to do wrong."

"Trick *my* brain? I don't *think* so." She smiled and sat up straighter.

Warney noticed the sparkle returning to her eyes. "Let's say ya was here lookin' fer me, but I weren't home. Then here I come, barrelin' around the corner dressed up in a bear pelt—smellin' like a bear, lookin' like a bear, growlin' like a bear. What would ya do?"

Molly giggled. "I'd run as fast as my legs would carry me."

"See what I mean?" Warney laughed and wheezed. "Even though it weren't real, if yer brain thought it was real, it would act like it was real. So that's how ya can trick yer brain into doin' what's right when yer faced with the notion to do wrong."

"I think I see." She gave him a bland half-smile. "If I had it to do over again, when we came to the sign, I could have imagined red flashing lights. I could have considered the consequences and insisted that the three of us get out of there—fast."

"Yup, yer gettin' the hang of it. Now, ya say Gavin stayed behind so you two could get away?"

Molly nodded.

"So that means he's not only guilty of trespassin' but coverin' up fer ya?"

"Yeah," Molly said, a fresh wave of despair gathering in her eyes. "He lied for us, and now *I'm* stuck lying. Feels awful, but what good would it do for us all to get in trouble?"

Warney stood up to stretch his aching back and chuckled.

"What's so funny?" Molly asked.

"Well, I half expected ya to put yer hand over yer nose like ya did every time ya stretched the truth when ya was a little tyke in preschool, convinced that lyin' made yer nose grow."

"Yeah, *Pinocchio* was one of my favorites."

"Well, this ain't no story yer actin' out now. It's real life." Warney rested on his walking stick and drew a raspy breath. "Molly gal, I'm not one to tell ya what to do, but I'll tell ya this much. Two falsehoods never made a right."

"Thanks for the advice . . . and the interview." Molly stood up, gave Uncle Warney a peck on the cheek, and jammed her pad into her backpack. "We need to get going." She cupped her hand and yelled, "Errrric."

"Don't fergit now, I wanna see a copy of that story of yers when the paper comes—" Warney stopped mid-sentence.

Eric raced up, out of breath, drenched in sweat. "Was that ever hypernoxious."

"Hyper-*what*?" Warney asked.

"Hypernoxious." Molly gave an impatient shrug. "That's his new word of the day—his misguided attempt to increase his vocabulary."

"So tell us," Warney smiled. "What'd ya find out there that warrants such a high-falootin' word?"

Eric's eyes fairly danced, flitting from Warney to Molly and back again. "I chased a big—no, *huge*—frog into the swamp. And it dove right into the hot coals. Then, that crazy thing just sat there, staring back at me, calm as if it was sitting on a lily pad."

Uncle Warney's eyebrows knit together, forming a hedge of white over his eyes as Eric launched into all sorts of weird things going on in the swamp. In his version of how he and Molly had gotten lost on the way to his shack when the paths shifted, Warney noted there was no mention of the Lodge or them trespassing with Gavin.

"Well," Warney said when Eric finally ran out of steam, "thar's a heap a trouble stirrin' in Burnt Swamp, that's fer sure. Don't need to warn ya, but I'm gonna say it anyways. The swamp's dangerous, and it's gettin' worse. Ya gotta keep yer guard up every minute. I'll be steppin' up muh prayers fer ya."

Eric jumped off the porch and landed on stones that skittered every which way. Careening sideways, he recovered his balance. "Don't worry, Uncle Warney. It's all over town that the new people who bought the Lodge are gonna build an amusement park on the swamp. Pour enough concrete, and that'll put the fire out, for sure. Everything's gonna be fine."

The news nearly took out Warney's wobbly knees. Grabbing onto the porch rails, he lifted his walking stick and pointed it at Eric. "Watch yerself, young man. Everything's *not* gonna be fine—not till the evil that's tryin' to get a grip on Burnt Swamp's been dealt with. Let me tell ya, there's nothin' amusin' about settin' a fun house on top of a boilin' cauldron."

"Oh, Uncle Warney," Eric scoffed. "Don't be such a stick-in-the-mud. It's gonna be colossal!"

Molly flipped her braid over her shoulder. "Correction. It's not going *on* the swamp, Eric. According to Uncle Bruce, Dragon's Lair is going to be built near the Lodge." She rubbed her arms like she was cold. "Personally, the whole thing gives me the creeps."

Warney's stomach knotted up like a bucket of worms. "And when is this s'pposed to happen?"

Eric beamed. "Don't know exactly, but Dad says, 'In record time, Ashboro will be swarming with tourists, and the big bucks'll be flowing.'" He gave her braid a yank. "C'mon, Molly, we gotta go."

"Remember what I said, Molly gal." Warney waved, but Molly and Eric were almost out of sight.

A wretched gloom settled over Warney. The spiritual clock had been set in motion.

It's started, Gavin, muh boy. But are ya ready fer it? He shook his head, turned, and retreated to his cabin. It was time for him to bring that old diary out of hiding.

CHAPTER ELEVEN

WARNEY

Fire in the Soul

Coming home from his early morning walk around the outer edges of Burnt Swamp, Warney looked long and hard at the coals that fringed the wetlands near his shack. Ever since Molly and Eric's visit the day before, he sensed an urgency to fetch the diary. *Yep, today's the day.*

Glubrr-blub-puh-glubrrp. The muck stirred and seethed worse than usual, as if a monstrous giant beneath the murky waters could awaken at any minute. Tentacles of sooty clouds circled his head and sent him into a coughing fit.

By the time he settled down, the whole area was strangely silent. The birds had stopped chattering. Trouble was brewing. The only thing that dared to move now was a lone black vulture circling overhead. Warney looked closer. Picky, the bothersome buzzard.

Stiff legged and sore, Warney hobbled his way to the porch to sit down in the rocker. Ugly Cat plopped at his feet. "Yer a mess, but yer good company." Warney didn't get much company. He knew people in

Ashboro made it a point to avoid him, especially if they were in hearing range when he felt a notion to preach.

Ugly flopped sideways on the porch and rolled over to expose his belly.

"Tell ya who I miss, though—Gavin. Not bein' able ta see him really sticks in muh craw." Warney's back twinged when he leaned forward to pet the cat, and a frosty chill ran up his spine, riveting his thoughts back to the cauldron-like activity in the swamp.

"So tell me, Ugly, wadda ya think's goin' on? Yer a survivor. Things is heatin' up, ol' feller. And I 'spect you'n me's gonna have our work cut out fer us purdy soon."

Stretching his body out as long as it would go, Ugly Cat's only interest appeared to be getting a belly rub. In mid-stretch, his claws sprang out and he flipped right side up. Landing on all fours, his scraggly rod of a tail poked straight in the air like an exclamation point. His good ear twitched. He jerked his anvil-shaped head to the side and stared up with his bleach-blue eye—the good one.

Warney followed Ugly's gaze to a tree that overlooked the shack. He watched as the buzzard lazily swooped down and settled on a branch with the ready-to-eat expression of somebody sitting down to a picnic table full of fried chicken. "I know it might look like we're on our last leg, ya varmint, but Ugly an' me got lots of life left in us. So don't go thinkin' yer gonna git any dinner off of *this* porch, Picky." He tried shooing the bird away with his cane, but the scavenger just lifted a wing and nibbled at a bug.

Ugly Cat brushed up against Warney's leg.

"Ya can bet yer sweet fur that Hee-Haw boy's deep into hocus pocus and demon worship or some such."

124

Feeling a prayer building up, Warney steeled himself, inside and out. Planting both feet steady on the uneven boards of the porch, he shouted to the patch of blue sky peeking through the smoke. "Lord God A'mighty, we're in a heap of trouble."

He felt, more than heard, the rumble of the cat's purr against his leg.

"On top of everything else, Gavin's gone and got hisself arrested, Molly's pride's forcin' her to live a lie, Eric's got his eye on the glitter of fame and fortune, and that ain't the half of it."

A tickle burned in his throat, forcing Warney to cough and poke around for his bandana. All the while, the buzzard flapped its wings, never leaving its perch. "Flutter all ya want. Today ain't yer day, ya flappin' gut picker."

The acrid smoke had not only infused its deadly incense into the swamp but into Warney's lungs, as well—day after day, month after month, year after year. He wiped at the tears that flowed into his hollow cheeks and muttered under his breath. "Clogged tear ducts, shell fragments in muh back, and a wounded heart woulda been enough fer a feller to have wrong with him. Tarnfangled smoke." He pulled out his inhaler and greedily took in a long puff. "It's a wonder I can breathe at all with this asthma curse."

Soothing sounds came from Ugly's throat. Warney patted his head. "Fer every one of them ten years that danged fire's been burnin', it's been suckin' equal time from muh life." He inhaled another puff, held his breath, then exhaled slowly.

Ugly began to cough and retch.

"You, too, eh? C'mon, ya can do it. No stubborn hairball's got the best of ya yet."

A wall of smoke closed in around Warney. "Them doubters say the fire cain't be put out. What do they know? Swamp fires ain't nothin' to God. When He gives the word, them fires'll fizzle out fast as spit on a griddle." Warney wiped his face one more time as Ugly Cat gagged long and hard, finally producing the offensive mat of hair.

"Yessirree, Lord, with all I see goin' on 'round here—marsh muck bubblin' up and them new owners of the Lodge flauntin' plans fer some high-falootin' park, it won't be long before the prophecy comes to pass."

Jamming his bandana back into his pocket, a cockeyed smile stole across Warney's face. *Yep, it's high time to fetch that diary.*

Although his voice was barely a whisper aimed toward the smoke-rimmed swamp, it was filled with conviction. "Gearin' up to give Laddrach's dragon its freedom, are ya now? Well, get this straight, ya minions of evil—God is greater!"

Warney waved his walking stick at the buzzard. "Ya hear me, ya no good gizzard-plucker? God wins!" A handful of black feathers drifted down as the bird shot off the limb.

"See that, Ugly? Nothin' like a blast from the Good Book to scare off a pesky devil."

Bible promises were as much a part of Warney's life as his heartbeat. But that wasn't all that had become a part and parcel of what made him tick. There was the matter of the other book, the ancient Burnt Swamp diary, passed down from generation to generation and now entrusted into his care. In his mind's eye, he could see the last page he had read before the diary went and locked itself up. The faded blue ink was barely legible, but even now, recalling the mysterious writings made his spine heat up like a blazing furnace. His lips moved with reverence as he recited the words from memory.

"At the appointed time, when the swamp fires flare and Laddrach's beast strives to escape its prison, I will raise up young Gavin to sound the trumpet. He will be a good fellow—faithful and true."

Gavin. In Warney's view, his great-nephew was born looking like a plucked rubber chicken, long and scrawny and squawking like the dickens. But the moment Warney heard the baby's name, he knew Ashboro's deliverance was upon them all.

Yep. Time's right fer Gavin to get an inklin' 'bout the role God's got mapped out fer him.

"C'mon, Ugly, we got work to do." He entered the three-room shack with more spring in his step than he'd had in a long time. Before he could get the diary to Gavin, he had to get it out of hiding. "Yep, by cracky, that book's been in its safe place long enough."

Warney searched for a crowbar, first under the bed where he bumped his head on the frame of the box springs, then at the back of his one and only closet. He rummaged past the mostly empty wooden hangers, pushed his collection of old muzzle loaders and muskets aside, and got bombarded by a couple of hand-carved duck decoys that flew off the shelf. He came out empty-handed.

Not only did he have to find the crowbar, but Warney had to solve the problem of Gavin not being allowed to see him. He had to figure a way to get the diary to Gavin. *I'd send it by way of Molly or Eric, but . . . nah, that don't seem right.*

He headed out the back door toward the tool shed with Ugly at his heels. *Lord, it's a shame Gavin don't have a good friend besides Molly. A boy his own age, seated in faith, somebody he'd listen to and learn from. But he don't.*

On his way back from the tool shed with crowbar in hand, Picky and his black-winged buddies circled overhead. The menace in their beady eyes turned the metal in Warney's spine to ice. As he opened the door to his shack, Ugly *eeeyoooowed* and scooted inside while Warney lingered, turned to the buzzards, and hollered, "Git thee behind me, ya devils!" Stepping inside, he slammed the door, and the whole shack rattled from the force.

Warney's knees snapped and popped as he knelt down in the middle of the floor. Tossing the braided rug aside, he positioned the crowbar under one of the rough-hewn cypress planks and pried a floorboard loose. Then another, so he could reach it.

Ugly padded around, back and forth, his purr revving like a broken motor as he rubbed up against Warney. The closer Warney got to the secret compartment, the more animated Ugly became—tail twitching, paws batting, head butting against the floor gap. Repeatedly, Warney had to push him out of his way. By the time Warney could see the package, the cat looked animated enough to spring into back flips.

"Hey now, old feller, this ain't catnip. I know ya been a-waitin' like me all these years fer daylight to shine on this here treasure, but calm yerself down a mite."

Warney had an inkling why the cat was so eager. That infamous day the lightning struck, bleaching Ugly's right eye and sealing the other one shut, wasn't the only time his faithful pet had been touched by the supernatural.

The old man scratched behind Ugly's bent ear. "You recall it clear as I do, don't ya? Every time that ol' diary would see fit to open up, an energy force would pulsate from them pages, tinglin' anybody within arm's length, includin' you, huh, Ugly?"

The cat purred, and Warney thought for sure he was smiling.

"Leaves a body feelin' good on the inside, don't it now?"

As expected, the newsprint he'd wrapped the book in ten years before had yellowed. But had the book retained its power? Sure enough, the minute Warney's fingers made contact, he felt the same vibration he'd gotten when he discovered it in the trunk at Stokes Mansion. For a moment, he thought maybe the blinding light he'd first experienced at the old homestead would hit him again. It didn't. But the experience never completely left him.

There he was in a corner of the attic, fresh off the ship from his duty on the aircraft carrier and wearing his Navy uniform. He had been looking for a solid trunk to store his belongings. Emptying the beat-up footlocker of its contents—a satin wedding gown, framed tin-plated photos, a wool coat with a raccoon collar, and other personal items packed in evaporated mothballs—he stumbled into an appointment with destiny.

Nestled inside the folds of a frayed Army blanket, was a leather book, bound together with faded purple ribbon, stamped on the front in Copperplate lettering with the word "DIARY." Beneath the diary was a thin parchment envelope with his name on it. He knew what it was at first glance—the missing heirloom that had been handed down through the decades by a remnant of Christ-followers who, though born into a family of self-proclaimed witches, had retained and recorded their faith. Warney grew up hearing all about how his great-grandmother had bequeathed the diary to him even though he was only a child. The problem was, nobody knew the diary's location.

The envelope contained a copy of his great-grandmother's will, confirming his inheritance. Tucked carefully inside the will was another piece of parchment, about six inches square, with elegant handwriting.

There was no more God-fearing woman in Ashboro than Mum-Mum Phoebe, who was known for spending hours at a time on her knees in prayer. Once, he was told, she gave a prophecy over a woman. Folks said she spoke with authority like the words came straight from God. He thought about that every time he held the parchment in his hand. And every time he read the words, a blazing heat shot up his spine:

Warnard Elijah Stokes, son of the mist, you are chosen for favor and for hardship, for God has found you worthy of the role of Burnt Swamp Guardian. With your calling comes great responsibility. And with great responsibility comes resources beyond compare. Keep safe the book you now hold in your hand, for it will guide you in wisdom and understanding as you care for the swamp and for your loved ones in generations to come.

How that reporter from *The Daily Encounter* could have known about the diary made no sense to Warney. After all, he had never breathed a word about it to anybody—except Ugly Cat. Year after year, Warney simply and faithfully watched over the book and its secrets. At first, he didn't understand his role, but then, as the diary opened up to him and he was able to read selected entries, he began to comprehend its mysteries. The pages warned of a danger to come that would lurk beneath the swamp, locked there by heaven's fire. And it was up to him, Warnard

Elijah Stokes, guardian of Burnt Swamp, to keep watch and pray that the creature, so vile he couldn't even picture it in his mind, stayed put till the Lord had His way with it.

Warney pulled the diary from beneath the floorboards. By now, what he had written in heavy-handed pencil on the newsprint wrapper could barely be seen, but it was still legible if a body knew where to look.

Making his way across the room, Warney lowered himself into the rocker which creaked softly under his weight. His hands shook, both from anticipation and from the tingling sensation that came from the book. With Ugly Cat curled up at his feet, Warney's thoughts poured out in a whisper, more from his heart than from his lips.

"Now it's Gavin's turn—to read, to learn of the prophecy, to embrace his callin' by name as heir to the legacy of Burnt Swamp." A sense of urgency welled up within him.

He scratched Ugly's bent ear. "There's got to be a way to get this to Gavin."

From the corner of his eye, he saw the Ninja comic book on a side table—right where Gavin had left it. With that, a crazy notion came to Warney. Easing out of his chair, he headed for the closet. "Yep, Ugly." He smiled. "Extreme measures. That's what we need."

Ugly Cat stretched, long and lazy, making playful "happy claws" on the braided rag rug. He looked up at Warney, his good eye closing in a slow wink, then sprang to his feet and nosed the screen door open.

Warney watched Ugly skedaddle down the porch steps and take the path toward town. *Just what I had in mind, ol' boy. I'll git muh bike and be along after dark.*

Awaking at dawn, the whole episode seemed like a dream. But Warney knew he had set things in motion. Mission accomplished.

"For Gavin's eyes only." *Yep, that was a nice touch.*

CHAPTER TWELVE

Summer of a Summer

August poked along. Kicking up a cloud of dust, Gavin scuffed his way along the roadside to the police station as he had every weekday for the past three weeks. *First, summer school—now, dumping trash and pruning old ladies' bushes. Some hero I turned out to be.*

Day after day, before signing in at the police station, Gavin had to walk past the schoolyard and endure the jeers of Billy Bragg and the rest of the jocks who were there for football practice.

"Gavin the clown, the sheriff brought him down, so he's doin' the time, he's toein' the line . . ."

Hoping to find an ally, Gavin searched the faces for his cousin. The pain struck him even harder when he saw him. Instead of his champion and defender, Eric was grinning, hip-hopping to the infectious beat, and chanting the words along with all the others.

Gavin trudged along as fast as he could without breaking into a full run. If he had the nerve, he'd smart-mouth back; but that might lead to a fight, and he was in enough trouble already. Besides, they would crush him.

133

Climbing the cement steps to the police station, he ran his palm up the wrought-iron handrail and hit a rough spot in need of welding. *It's fallin' apart, like everything else around here.* A warped shutter dangled sideways from an iffy-looking hinge. *I'm surprised they haven't told me to fix that, too.*

He dragged his feet across the uneven floor, scribbled his name, picked up his assignment, and scuffed his sneakers again on the way out. Today's job was sweeping Young Saints Community Center on Main Street.

As if things weren't bad enough, who should be there to greet him but Ugly Cat. Ugly kept turning up here, there, and everywhere—more than usual. And every time, Gavin felt a deep twinge of regret about not being able to visit the one person who knew how to build him up. *It wouldn't surprise me if Uncle Warney didn't send him over to see what's become of me.*

Ugly rubbed against the doorsill, then sat to lick himself.

"Beat it, Ugly." Gavin waved his arms and stomped his feet, more out of frustration for his own stupidity than from annoyance with the cat. "I gotta get the broom."

The cat kept purring and licking.

Stomping past, Gavin yanked the screen door open and felt a pang of heartbreak, whether for the sad-looking animal or for himself, he didn't know. Pushing emotion aside, he greeted the heavyset man in coveralls who sat behind a desk with his nose buried in a newspaper.

"Over there, boy." The man pointed to the broom in the corner without glancing up.

Some supervisor, Gavin thought and then decided it was fine with him. At least the old guy wouldn't be breathing down his neck.

Gavin let the door slam behind him on the way out. He gave the broom a strong push that sent a cloud of ashes off the porch and—he noticed too late—straight onto Ugly Cat who disappeared into the shrubs with a raspy *meeeeowww.*

Beyond the haze of falling dust, Gavin spotted Molly across the street. "Hey, Molly."

Stepping away from Fennemore's Dollar Store, Molly approached him with drooped shoulders.

"Hi, Gavin," she mumbled.

Miss Wordsmith never mumbled.

"Oh, so you're talking to me now?" Gavin was glad to see her, but that didn't help him from being sarcastic.

"You're grounded, remember?" Molly said without looking him in the eye. "Your dad left strict instructions—no contact." She twisted her braid and mumbled again. "I didn't know if I was allowed."

"That's at home, not in public." Gavin decided not to make a big deal about it. "Hey, I get phone privileges again as soon as I'm done with community service."

"It must be awful." Molly's voice was barely audible. She gave a weak smile. "Three down, one week to go, right?"

So she'd been keeping track of him, after all. "Yeah, it's worse than I expected. They had me cleaning out sewer pipes one day and trash truck duty the next. I smelled riper than Eric's skunk pelt. But you know what's worse? Feeling like a criminal. You should see how people look at me—more like how they *don't* look at me."

Molly hung her head, lowering her gaze.

"Yeah, like that. You're not making fun of me, are you?"

She kept staring at her shoes.

"Hey, what's up, Mol? You're looking kinda pitiful yourself. Still bogged down with that newspaper story of yours?"

Molly shook her head and her eyes misted over. "Yes, well, I saw Uncle Warney and got a good interview, but he raised more questions than answers." She blinked back tears.

"Hey, what's this? Are you crying? You okay?" Gavin was sorry he asked. He hated it when girls cried.

"No, Gavin, I'm not okay." She choked back a sob. "Eric and I did a terrible thing leaving you alone to take the blame. And I can't believe you found my backpack and managed to get it back to me without getting me in trouble. Every day I think about turning myself in and telling the truth. And every day I chicken out. But my mind's made up. I'm going to confess to Mom."

"Don't, Molly. Pleeeeease. You know how I've always wanted to do something that mattered. For the first time in my life, I took a stand and did something, well . . ."

"Noble," Molly said. "And for the first time in my life I acted like a total, absolute blockhead."

Gavin considered hugging his cousin the way his mom hugged him when he was upset, but instead, he got up close to her face and lowered his voice. "No. Don't you see? You told us it was wrong and wanted to turn back. You didn't want to do it in the first place." He shoved his hands in his pockets and hung his head. "I've paid for what we did. If you go and tell the police now, it'll mess everything up. They'll know I lied about being alone, and I'll be in trouble all over again." He forced himself to look into her eyes again. "Please, Molly, please. Let it go."

Twiddling the end of her braid between her fingers, Molly blinked her tear-bright eyes. "Well, that's just great. I've finally gotten past my guilt by deciding to confess, and you tell me I can't without making more trouble for you? Some fix you've gotten me into. I'm guilty if I *don't* confess and guilty if I *do*."

Gavin whispered in rapid bursts. "Yes, I covered for you and Eric. I'm trying to do what's right. You're making me feel guilty about that. What good would it do for you to confess? Except to rob me of the good feeling I got by trying to protect you."

He could tell from the look on her face she wasn't getting it. What could he say to make Molly understand? "If you go and spill the beans now, you'll get yourself and Eric in deep trouble, not to mention catching me in a lie."

"Lower your voice," Molly ordered, "or everybody in town will find out anyway. But, hey," she tilted her head, "that might not be so bad."

Gavin paused to collect himself and propped the broom against the porch railing. "Look, Molly . . ." He clasped his fingers together and spoke in a low voice with all the feeling he could muster. "I'm begging you. Let this go."

"I have to do what's right, Gavin. Maybe there really is *no* right way out of this, but I'll pray about it and try my best to put it behind me."

Gavin gave her a hopeful look. "Your prayers seem to work a whole lot better than mine. I've been asking God for years to make Dad be proud of me, and now things are worse than ever. I get the silent treatment every night when he comes home from work, and when he does say anything, it's only to give me the third degree. A lot of good it did me to pray and do a noble deed."

Molly smiled and wiped her cheek. "Sometimes God doesn't answer our prayers like we want. Your dad loves you; he's just so busy trying to be a responsible parent and mayor that he has a hard time showing it."

"So you're on his side, is that it?"

"I'm not on anybody's side. The point is, we all mess up from time to time, including your dad. As for your noble deed, it's still a noble deed. You had good intentions. And you never would have gotten caught at all if the paths hadn't gone and shifted on us like that. The whole day was really bizarre."

"Yeah, no kidding. What does Eric have to say about it?"

"Eric?" Molly gave a disgusted snort. "What does Eric have to say? He says, 'Whatever,' his favorite word. As far as he's concerned, it never happened . . ." Her words trailed off as she nodded toward the donut shop. "Speak of the devil."

"Yeah, with his buddies." Gavin groaned.

There was Eric, laughing and poking another guy with his elbow. He looked up and caught Gavin's eye, then turned his back.

"Oh, forget him," Molly said. "Eric's changed ever since he made the football team. It's like his family is beneath him or something."

"He thinks he's hot stuff ever since they named him *quarterback*." Gavin scrunched up his face and stuck out his tongue like the word put a bad taste in his mouth.

"Come on, Gavin, change is inevitable. But there's no excuse for rudeness." Molly cupped her hand to her mouth. "Hey, Eric."

Eric gave his sister a recognition chin jerk but kept on talking while he wiped powdered sugar from his mouth with the back of his sleeve.

"See what I mean?" Gavin shook his head.

Molly called louder, "Oh, E-rrrrr-ic. I neeeed you over hee-ere."

Eric looked like he'd rather eat raw eggs, but at last he crossed the street with long, lazy strides. Gavin couldn't hear what he said to the boys before he left, but they laughed. Reaching the sidewalk just as two huge, black moving vans breezed by, Eric staggered from their gust, craned his neck, and bent over to gawk at the shiny vehicles.

"Whoa! Look at the size of those babies." Eric sounded like a kid seeing Tonkas for the first time. "And check out that wicked paint job."

"Wicked is right," Molly said. "Black on black."

"Yeah." Eric continued to stare as the vans rounded the corner. "Looks like they're headed toward the Lodge. Wanna go?"

"No, I don't want to go to the Lodge." Molly gave a spazzed out whimper, gripped her braid, and started twirling the curls at the end with her finger. "With its pentagrams, mousetraps, and fireplace tornadoes—are you, crazy?"

"Crazy is right," Gavin said. "Count me out."

Eric flicked the bangs out of his eyes. "I hear a new girl's moving in." He gave Gavin a man-to-man wiggle of his eyebrows.

Gavin ignored it. Instead, he picked up the broom and began sweeping. "Yeah, so I hear."

Molly leaned forward, fixated on the vans that idled at the town's only traffic light in front of the courthouse. "Don't you remember the occult symbols we saw at the Lodge, Eric?"

"Yeah, so what?"

A clear, unexpected voice chimed in from behind them. "Occult. You mean, as in . . . evil."

Gavin wheeled around to see who the voice belonged to. There stood a short, slender boy in a plaid shirt and pressed khakis. He looked like a miniature version of Officer Charlie.

"Hey," Gavin extended a hand.

Before the boy could respond, Eric stepped between them, arms at his side. "Excuse me," he said, balling his fists. "Do you always barge into conversations uninvited?"

Gavin saw a look pass between them, but the boy didn't answer. Instead, he flashed a white-toothed grin.

"Hello, I'm Molly." She nodded toward the boys. "This is Eric, my *rude* twin brother, and Gavin, my cousin."

The corner of Eric's lip lifted into a smirk. "So what makes you such an expert on eeeevil?"

Gavin felt sorry for the kid as Eric towered over him like that. How could he just stand there smiling?

"What's a-matter? Cat got your tongue?" Eric was getting ruder by the minute.

Tightening his fingers on the broom handle, Gavin considered swinging it at his cousin. Instead, to keep himself in line, he rested it against the railing. *What has gotten into Eric, bullying a new boy like that? Maybe I should say something—*

The newcomer took a couple of quick steps backward, but his smile never wavered.

"Back off, Eric," Molly said, beating Gavin to it. "Your scrimmage stench has robbed the guy of his breath."

What Gavin wouldn't give to sling barbs around like that.

"My name's Dexter," the boy replied, apparently unruffled by Eric. He held out a pack of candies. "Want a cinnamon mint?"

Eric spat on the ground and snatched the box of mints. "Whatever," he said, shaking the contents into his hand and returning an empty box to Dexter. "Nice to meet you." Dropping the mints into his mouth, Eric turned his back, shoved his hands into his pockets, and ambled away.

"Sorry about my lunkhead brother." Molly glanced at Eric who had rejoined his jock buddies. "There's no excuse for him, really."

Dexter smiled. "No problem; it's cool. I'm from the city. That's nothing compared to the gangs I've run across." He reached into his pocket and pulled out a roll of Hubba Bubba bubble gum tape. "I keep a good supply of candy and gum on hand. Want some?"

"No thanks." Molly smiled.

"Yeah, bubble tape's my favorite." Gavin took a strip and folded it, trying to figure this new kid out. He'd never seen anybody so cool under fire. "So, what brings you to Ashboro?"

"I'm Officer Charlie's grandson." Dexter's words were clear, in spite of the wad of gum in his mouth.

"I knew it." Gavin beamed. "I've seen you in church. And you look like him. Come for a visit?"

"No," Dexter said with the saddest eyes Gavin had ever seen. "I'll be living with him from now on."

"How come?" Molly asked. "Did your parents get divorced or something?"

"No, my parents are dead."

The brief glimpse of pain Gavin saw in Dexter's gaze told him that cool on the outside didn't mean okay on the inside. *He's really hurting and needs a friend, same as me.*

"I'm *so* sorry." The color drained from Molly's face. "It's just that so many . . . forgive me. How did they die? In a car accident or something?"

"No, my dad died of cancer two years ago and—" Dexter clenched his fists and his chin quivered ever so slightly, but then his eyes conveyed a flash of fury. "Mama was killed in a drive-by shooting."

"Oh, no." Gavin put two and two together from all the sympathy cards and flowers at the station. "So Officer Charlie's daughter is, *was* your mother?"

"Yeah. Her funeral was hard, even harder than Pap's."

"I'd heard about her dying unexpectedly," Molly gasped, "but nobody said *how*."

"It's no secret or anything, but Grandpap doesn't like to talk about it." Dexter's posture registered a deliberate shift. "Hey, can we talk about something else? Like those vans. I've got a bone to pick with those terrorists."

"Terrorists?" Gavin asked. "The van drivers are *terrorists*?"

DEXTER

Burnt Swamp Curse

"Terrorists?" Molly's freckles seemed to fade when her face flushed like that.

"Hold on a minute." Gavin moved away from the porch railing to take a quick peek inside the Young Saints Community Center. As he hoped, the man was sound asleep with the newspaper on his belly and his feet on the desk. "The coast is clear. Nobody's listening."

"So what are you saying?" Molly asked Dexter. "That Osama commissioned the vans?"

"Not likely. Wrong religion." Dexter's smile faded as quickly as it came. "I'm talking about the terrorist mentality behind the occult— people who do things, terrible things, and want to claim responsibility but not be caught and held accountable."

"What people? What terrible things?" Gavin asked.

"You're the ones who live here. Have you noticed anything strange going on?"

Gavin snickered and gave the broom a swipe, creating a cloud from the ashes and soot. "Duh, strange? How about a ten-year fire? Of course, there was that old tortoise your grandpap had to shoo out of the street."

"Wait a minute." Molly tossed an anxious expression Gavin's way. "I think Dexter might be onto something. What about the runes on the front door of the Lodge, and the shifting paths that took us there?"

Gavin bit his lip. *What's she doing?*

"Not to mention the mousetraps and that thing that tried to suck you into the firepla—"

"Back up. What do you mean, *shifting paths?*" Dexter stared up at her from where he sat on the top step.

"I talk too much." Molly clamped her hand over her mouth.

"Yeah. You do." Maybe she still felt a need to confess—but to a stranger? Gavin leaned on the broom handle and studied Dexter. "How do we know if we can trust you?"

"On my mother's grave." Dexter had the most sincere eyes. "So, what happened?"

Gavin lowered his voice and decided to take a chance. "We were on our way to Uncle Warney's when the ground went gushy under our feet. The next thing I knew, Molly and Eric and I were at the Lodge instead of on the path to his house."

"Whoa!" Dexter pushed the left side of his glasses up to balance them. "I've never encountered any shifting paths, but when you mention the occult and Burnt Swamp in the same breath, it hits at the heart of things, doesn't it?"

"The heart of what things?" Molly sat down beside Dexter.

Dexter glanced around cautiously and spoke even softer than before. "I wasn't always a city kid. I was born here, and I think the Burnt Swamp curse followed us when we moved."

"What Burnt Swamp curse?" Gavin watched Molly slip into her cynical reporter mode. "We've never heard of any curse," she said.

The sound of howling wind pricked Gavin's ears, but no air stirred around him. He glanced at the trees, expecting to see branches bending, but every leaf remained motionless. Nobody else seemed to notice.

"The curse ties in with the gushy soil and shifting paths . . ." Dexter turned toward Gavin. "And with what you told Grandpap. We were talking about all the strange things that have been happening around here, and he said I should look you up."

"Me? Officer Charlie said to look *me* up?" Gavin felt his voice squeak. Maybe he was too hasty in deciding to trust this kid.

Doubts gummed up Gavin's mind and put the world around him in slow motion. *What if Dexter's like his grandfather who seemed so nice at church but then went by the book and turned me in? What if Dexter learns the whole story about Molly and Eric being at the Lodge? Won't I be in bigger trouble? What if Dexter is Officer Charlie's spy? But those eyes. There's something safe about the look in Dexter's eyes. And he wouldn't have said 'on my mother's grave' unless he meant it. Besides, what choice do I have? Motor mouth Molly's already telling everything she knows . . . for that matter, so am I.*

"Yeah, that's why I came over," Dexter was saying. "Grandpap thought we might want to confabulate."

"Confab-you . . . what, who?" Gavin leaned back.

"Late," Dexter said.

"I'm not late." Gavin felt confused.

"No." Molly poked Gavin. "Con-fab-u-*late*. Brainstorm. Discuss."

"Thanks, Molly." Dexter grinned. "It's nice to meet another word person."

Gavin wracked his brain to remember their conversation. "What did I tell Officer Charlie?"

"You know—about the creepy stuff you found at the Lodge." Dexter shot a sideways glance at Molly. "You said there were runes on the door, right?"

Gavin began to sweep an already clean spot. "I don't know what you're talking about."

"Gavin, stop!" Molly grabbed the broom. "Listen to what he has to say." She turned her attention to Dexter. "So, what does any of this have to do with a curse that followed your parents?"

"Well, maybe it doesn't really. It just feels like it." Dexter took his glasses off, squinted at the specks of dirt on the lenses, and frowned.

Silence settled on the three youth like an open parachute.

"You can talk and clean your glasses at the same time, can't you?" Molly tapped her foot.

Slowly and methodically, Dexter finished his task. He looked like he'd just made a decision.

"From the time I was old enough to understand words, my folks talked about the evil behind the Burnt Swamp fire."

Molly gasped. "That's what Uncle Warney says—that the lightning that started the fire was *evil*, and that's why nobody can put it out!"

Gavin's stomach flip-flopped. "But nobody pays much attention to Uncle Warney."

"I'd listen to him if I were you," Dexter said. "Mama always told me I'd be better off armed with truth."

"So I hear." Gavin was surprised to hear it come out of his mouth like a wisecrack, but the root of sarcasm only gripped him stronger. "The truth will set you free, right Molly?"

Molly gave him a look of disgust. "Gavin. What's gotten into you?"

"Sorry." Gavin felt his face flush as remorse thumped his conscience. *What's wrong with me? The harder I try to do right these days, the more I mess up.*

Molly leaned toward Dexter. "Tell us what you know."

Dexter wrapped his wad of gum in the tissue, tossed it into a nearby trash container, and tore off another strip which he folded methodically and stuffed in his mouth.

"In the sixteen or seventeen hundreds, there was a witches' coven based in the swamp. Local Christians drove them out, but the last man to leave made a big, public stink about a dragon or dinosaur or something named Shimera. He said it would rise from the swamp in due time and kill, steal, or destroy anything or anybody connected with Burnt Swamp that reflects the glory of God."

"Is that all you've got?" Molly sighed. "Everybody knows that old story. I thought you were going to tell us something important."

"But it's not a myth, Molly. It's *true*. And it *is* important. The danger's real—now, more than ever."

"And you know this, how?" Molly blinked.

"Experience. Have you ever seen pure evil in somebody's eyes?" Dexter didn't wait for an answer. "I have, and it's more than scary. These are treacherous times." He turned to Gavin. "Treacherous, I tell you. We gotta keep watch."

A buzzard floated lazily down from the sky, perched on the roof of Young Saints Community Center, and began making hissing vocal sounds, then a series of snort-like chuffs and scratchy growls. The vile creature stretched out its wings, caused its neck to expand, put its head down on its chest, and swiveled its beak as though sharpening it.

"Don't move," Molly whispered.

"I'm not," Dexter whispered back. "But, if we don't move, he'll think we're carcasses."

Gavin sprang to life and took the broom from Molly with every intention of waving it at the buzzard. Instead, it slipped out of his hands, causing the handle to crash with a bang—which served the same purpose in getting the buzzard to leave.

Ugly Cat vaulted to his feet, back arched and tail in the air, and then jumped on Dexter's lap where he began to purr.

"Strange happenings. Yep, strange." Dexter exhaled. "Like the hollow look in that vulture's eyes."

That kid's a rock. Never even flinched. Gavin didn't understand what Dexter meant by all this talk about looking evil in the eye, and he didn't want to know. But he decided that nothing rattled Dexter. Nothing. Not even buzzards perching right next to him.

Molly edged away from the cat. "Let's talk about normal stuff."

"Sure. Like what?" Dexter blew a bubble the size of a melon.

"Like, how old are you?"

Dexter chuckled. "Twelve. Why?"

"It's just that . . ." Molly twisted her braid, "you sound a lot older than you look. But then, I guess experiences like you've had can mature people beyond their years."

"You know," Gavin said, "you remind me of Uncle Warney—the things you say, not the way you say them. Dad says he's crazy, that he's breathed too much swamp gas."

Dexter arched his back. "And you think I'm like your crazy uncle?"

"He's not really crazy. He's eccentric." Molly scrunched her nose like she always did when she defended family. "So Dexter—about this evil curse. If it's real and there's a dragon lurking under the swamp that's going to gobble us all up one fine day, what makes you think things are so 'treacherous' now? Any chance this curse can be reversed?"

Gavin held up the palm of his hand. "Slow down, Molly. It's not an interview for your dumb paper, you know."

"*Could* be," she countered. "In fact, it might be front-page news."

Dexter winked at Molly. "But even in interviews, isn't it better to ask one question at a time?"

Molly heaved one of her best disgusted sighs. "Okay. So here's my *one* question: How does the ancient curse tie in with what happened ten years ago?"

"Pastor Abe was the preacher here in Ashboro ten years ago. He lost everything in the fire that night and moved to the city to serve as youth pastor." Dexter inhaled a raggedy breath. "He used to come over and talk late into the night with Mama and Pap when they thought I was asleep. Pastor Abe said the fire was a curse. That he saw the whole thing up close and personal. That flames bounced off the treetops and shot right into the side of the parsonage like poison-tipped arrows. That things lit up brighter and louder than a fireworks factory explosion."

"Gavin!" Molly gave Gavin a wide-eyed look. "That's exactly what Uncle Warney said."

Gavin frowned. "Don't interrupt. Go on, Dexter."

Molly's cell phone rang. "Aaargh, not now. Hello? But Mom, can't it wait another half hour? Okay, sure. I'll be right home."

As she stood up, Dexter rose, too. "I take it you have to go?"

"Yeah." Molly shrugged. "Wish I could stay." Giving Gavin her you'd-better-tell-me-anything-I-miss look, she skipped down the steps with a snappy wave.

"So," Dexter stood and stretched. "Tell me more about your Uncle Warney. Is he a prophet? I think Pastor Abe mentioned him a few times."

"Yeah, that's Uncle Warney all right—the prophet and caretaker of Burnt Swamp." Gavin liked the way Dexter made him feel, so he opened up about the day he ended up in the police station. "The worst part is that Dad won't let me see Uncle Warney, and he probably doesn't even know I've been grounded." Gavin managed a melancholy smile. "The last time I saw him was in a dream." At the mention of the dream, the taste of dried apricots, juicy apples, and 7-Up filled Gavin's mouth, and he began to choke.

"Are you okay?" Dexter slapped Gavin hard on the back a few times, and the coughing fit passed as quickly as it came. "I'd like to meet your Uncle Warney," Dexter said. "I know! You could communicate with him in writing! If you want to send him a note, I'd be happy to deliver it."

"Huh?" Gavin's eyes still watered from coughing. Although glad that Dexter hadn't asked about the dream, the turn in the conversation was even worse. "Um, I'm not too good at writing."

"Come on—just a short note to introduce me."

"Well, yeah, but . . ."

"But what?"

"I have a little problem I don't like to talk about." Gavin crossed his arms and stared at the porch ceiling.

"What kind of problem?"

Gavin averted his eyes. "Dyslexia."

"Isn't that a learning disability?"

"Yeah, but . . ."

"So, what's the big deal?"

"It makes me feel dumb."

"That's stupid."

"See what I mean?"

"So you have to work harder to make the grade. You're not sick or dying are you?"

"No."

"Nobody's threatening your life or beating you up?"

"No."

"So, what's the big deal?"

"Yeah, things could be worse, couldn't they?" Still, Gavin felt ashamed.

"I'll bet you're good at lots of things. And I can help you write a note if you want me to." Dexter pulled a small tablet and pen from his back pocket.

"You would do that?" A fuzzy warmth lifted Gavin's spirit.

"Sure. Besides," Dexter said, "I'd like to meet your Uncle Warney."

The boys spent the next ten minutes composing three sentences which Dexter wrote down as Gavin thought aloud. When he was done, Dexter insisted that Gavin rewrite it in his own handwriting.

Dear Uncle Warney,

This is my new friend, Dexter, who is coming to see you because I can't. He'll tell you why. I miss you.

Love, Gavin

"Uncle Warney's shack is about two miles from town if you stick to the main road. You know where King's Ice Cream is?"

"Sure. Even city folks know King's." Dexter grinned.

"Well, right after King's you'll see a dirt path that goes into the woods, and it'll take you straight to Uncle Warney's. Provided the paths don't shift."

"Riiiiight." Dexter raised an eyebrow.

"I'm kidding—I hope," Gavin said.

Ugly Cat sprang off the porch with his bent paw twisted under him. He marched off with limping dignity in the direction Gavin described.

"Better yet," Gavin motioned toward Ugly, "you could follow him."

"Great!" Dexter said, giving Gavin a high five. "It's good to have a friend."

Friend. Gavin liked the sound of that word. "Oh, if you think of it, ask Uncle Warney if I left my Ninja comic book."

Dexter lifted his brow in surprise. "Are you into martial arts?"

"Nah, I just like the pictures. Hey, you'd better get a move-on." He resumed sweeping. "If Ugly gets too far ahead, you may never find your way there."

Dexter trotted after Ugly Cat.

A weird odor assaulted Gavin's nostrils. *Just the smoke*, he told himself. But it stunk worse than usual. "Hey, Dexter," Gavin called.

"Yeah?"

"Watch your back."

"No problem." Dexter skipped backwards a few steps and smiled. "God is my rear guard. He's got my back covered."

With that, he spun about and jogged after Ugly Cat.

Gavin watched until Dexter and Ugly Cat rounded the bend and were completely out of sight. *I sure hope so.*

Ugly led the way past King's and onto the dirt path. The last time Dexter tromped through these woods was three years ago when his dad took him deer hunting. Of course, they only pretended to hunt because they'd both watched *Bambi* too many times. But it was a good excuse to target practice. Funny how father/son talks came so much easier after a few rounds of tin cans.

Wonderful memories.

Good laughs.

Time alone—just the two of them.

All gone.

I miss you, Pap. I miss you something fierce. Mama kept me loved after you passed, but now . . .

"Big boys don't cry," he said aloud. Besides, he couldn't afford to let tears cloud his vision because he had to keep an eye on the cat or he'd lose his way.

Dexter tried to ignore the inner nudge that nagged at him to call his grandfather. *He's so overprotective. When will he admit I'm old enough and smart enough to take care of myself?* But, respectful of his elders as he was taught, Dexter dialed the number.

"I wish you'd asked before you left," Officer Charlie said. "I'll come get you."

"But I'm following Ugly Cat, and I think we've passed the halfway mark. Besides, it's shorter this way than the road you'll be taking."

"Okay. but call me every fifteen minutes. If you don't check in on schedule, I'll be after you with sirens blaring and lights a-flashing."

Dexter synchronized his watch with his grandpap's and flipped his phone shut so hard and fast it almost fell out of his hand. That's when the fear began.

A black buzzard circled in figure eights overhead—was it the same one with the evil eyes? He couldn't tell. Along with the smoke that spiraled around Dexter's head like a dancing lasso, he felt hot breath on his neck accompanied by a sickly sweet stench that made his head swim.

"Never let them see you sweat," he said aloud. "Courage is being the only one who knows you're afraid." But the platitudes his dad had taught him weren't working. *What was that other one? 'The greatness . . .'*

Ugly Cat stopped short, arched his back, and twitched his nose. After turning his head to the right, to the left, up toward the buzzard, and back, he relaxed his defensive posture and resumed his lead.

"'The greatness of our fear shows us the littleness of our faith'—that's it," Dexter said aloud. "God has not given us a spirit of fear . . ."

He looked at his watch and flipped his phone open. *Lord, help me out here.* His hands shook as he scrolled through the names in his phone list. *One ring, two . . .* "Hey, Grandpap." He checked his inflection to be sure it contained no hint of the panic he was experiencing. "No, no problems. I think we're almost there. I see a shack through the trees."

CHAPTER FOURTEEN

WARNEY

Confidant

Warney's mouth watered as he sat down to a plate of macaroni and cheese, fresh from the oven. He bowed his head at the rough-hewn table and thanked his Maker. But his fork stopped midway to his open mouth when he heard footsteps on the porch.

Gavin? His heart flip-flopping at the possibility, Warney dropped his fork and stood. In three giant steps he reached the door. Instead of his great-nephew, there, silhouetted by a halo of late afternoon smoke, stood a short, slender boy with black curly hair, brown eyes, and a grin that took up half his face.

"Excuse me, sir. But are you Gavin's Uncle Warney?"

Warney swallowed his disappointment. "Yessirree, young feller." He stepped onto a loose board on the porch he hadn't gotten around to fixing. "What can I do fer ya?"

The boy thrust out his hand. "I'm Dexter North, a friend of Gavin's." Ugly revved his motor and nosed the boy's spiffy leather boat shoes. "Your cat showed me the way."

155

Ugly didn't purr for just anybody. He took in the boy's clean-cut appearance; the boy's outfit, although not exactly fitting for swamp visits, spoke well of him. But something else impressed Warney—the warmth that flowed from Dexter's handshake, same as from his eyes. This boy knew his manners. Warney opened the screen door and ushered young Dexter inside.

"Now don't ya be callin' me sir," Warney said. "I'm Uncle Warney to Gavin. And that makes me Uncle Warney to any friend of his."

Excitement coursed through Warney's veins. Was this a kindred spirit? The shrapnel in his back seemed to vibrate, emanating warmth. "What brings ya all the way out here?"

"I have a message from Gavin, sir . . . er . . . Uncle Warney. He wanted to be sure you knew he'd be here if he could, but he's been doing community service and his dad has him on restriction."

"That much Molly told me." Warney caught a whiff of cinnamon from Dexter's gum. "Ya ain't nothin' but breath and britches, son. That gum ain't gonna put no meat on yer bones." He nodded to a chair. "How 'bout ya tell me what else's happenin' with Gavin over supper."

Dexter made a quick phone call, spoke softly, and then stood there looking hesitant. "It's okay as long as I don't make a pest of myself."

"Pshaw." Warney grabbed a plate along with some silverware and set another place. "Sit down and fill up, son." As Warney lowered himself into his chair, his stomach growled a long, low roll that sounded like it said *Elrrroy*. "'Scuse me," he laughed. "Muh tummy knows I'm not used to visitors, and it's tryin' to make conversation."

Dexter gave a hangdog smile as he stuck his wad of gum on the edge of the plate. "Would it be all right if I offered a blessing?"

"Praise be, yer a young man of God!" Warney nodded. "By all means."

"Dear Lord," Dexter's tender, young voice filled the room. "Thank You for seeing me here safely and for this meal we're about to eat. Give Mr. Warney a blessing for his kindness, and let our time together be pleasing in Your sight. Amen."

"Amen," Warney said, unable to contain his delight and excitement. "The Good Book says, 'Be not forgetful to entertain strangers: fer some have entertained angels unawares.' So, now, if'n ya don't mind, I'm gonna ask ya somethin' straight out."

Dexter nodded as he spread butter over a steaming biscuit.

Placing his elbows on the edge of the table, Warney asked in a hushed voice. "Ya wouldn't by chance be an angel sent from God, would ya?"

Dexter choked as he swallowed a bite of the biscuit. After washing it down with a gulp of milk, he said, "Well, sir, I mean *Uncle Warney*, I'm sorry to disappoint you, but I'm definitely no angel. I just came with a message from Gavin and, well, because I wanted to meet you."

Dexter handed Gavin's note to Warney, which he read quickly. Knowing how much Gavin hated to write made Warney's eyes mist over. But when Dexter relayed the conversation he'd had with Gavin and Molly about the occult, Warney dropped his fork. It was almost too much to take in.

"Another biscuit?" With all that talk about the black vans and curses, Warney had forgotten his manners. Besides, he needed time to ponder the news this boy had brought. "And land sakes, how about some collard greens? Picked 'em muhself, fresh from the field, and cooked 'em in fat meat."

"Mmm." The boy's face lit up as he reached for the bowl. "I haven't had a meal like this since . . ." His smile faded. "Since Mama passed and I moved in with Grandpap."

"Sorry ta hear about yer mama. How long has she been gone?"

"Three weeks. May I have some vinegar?"

Whether from the look in Dexter's eyes or from the quaver in his voice, Warney sensed a wall go up, so he decided not to push it. *Everybody has to handle grief in their own way.* "Didn't think I'd seen ya 'round these parts." Warney passed the vinegar.

"I used to live here," Dexter said, his smile returning. "You probably don't remember me because my parents moved us to the city ten years ago. I'm Officer Charlie's grandson."

"Well, I'll be tickled with a feather and hung out to dry." Warney's guffaw filled the room. "Don't matter whether yer a flesh-n-bone local or a heaven-sent angel, yer a godsend, far as I'm concerned. Ya see, twasn't that long ago I was a-prayin' fer Gavin to have a God-fearin' friend, and there ya go a-showin' up on muh doorstep, sayin' grace and all. Well, don't pay me no never mind. I don't usually chatter on like this. Must sound like a set of them plastic wind-up teeth."

Dexter grinned. "The Bible says believers are a peculiar people." He pulled a battered New Testament from the back pocket of his khakis and found the page he was looking for.

"Yep, right here. 'But ye are a chosen generation, a royal priesthood, a holy nation, a peculiar people.'"

A lump that wouldn't go away lodged in Warney's throat, no matter how many times his Adam's apple bobbed up and down in an attempt to dislodge it. "King James Version," he said when he could find his voice.

"Yer speakin' muh language." Now, if that didn't beat all. Here was a kid after his own heart and soul.

Little by little, Warney got Dexter to open up about his parents' deaths.

"So you see, that's one of the reasons I wanted to meet you, sir—I mean, Uncle Warney. I'm sort of on a mission. Maybe I'm wrong, but it seems to me my family's been on the receiving end of the Burnt Swamp curse, and I'm out to break it."

Warney marveled at the boy's understanding of God's power and grace to help him through the series of trials he'd experienced in his young life. And he admired his grit. But this kid was hurting. More than he knew. Breaking curses might be more than the boy could handle right now.

"I'll have ta cogitate a bit on that Burnt Swamp curse idea," Warney said. "Knew yer father real well, I did, and yer mother—she was one fine lady. String o' tragedies they had, that's fer sure. I was there the night Pastor Abe and yer family moved outta town. Cain't say I blamed 'em none, but them leavin' added to our heartache." He crossed his legs and stretched them out.

"Do you think you can help me break the curse?" A worry cloud passed over the boy's face.

"Let's slow down a mite and get ourselves better acquainted. We might need to tend to other battles first. How's about fillin' me in on yer schoolin' and such?"

It didn't come as any surprise that Dexter's IQ had taken him out of public school and put him on a fast-track for college. But for all his intelligence, he seemed happy enough to be enrolled in the seventh grade with Gavin at Sunken Bridge.

"Like I said, young Mr. North, yer the answer to an old man's prayer. Now, I'm just an old geezer who don't know much about young uns, but I know a thing or two 'bout pain and sufferin'. And it strikes me that yer the type that can work so hard at takin' care o' others that ya fergit about yer own needs."

Dexter's face showed no emotion, but he gave a slight nod.

"It's only been a few weeks since ya lost yer mama, and I 'spect ya been stuffin' emotional hurts way down deep inside fer a long time, thinkin' they'd go away if ya ignored 'em. But it don't work that way. Unsettled pain can weigh yer spirit down when ya least 'spect and grind yer life to a screechin' halt. Gavin needs a friend, and so do you."

Dexter's chin quivered ever so slightly. "I know friendship goes two ways, but I've never had much luck with friends before. How? How do I let Gavin be a friend to me?"

This was the breakthrough Warney was waiting for. "By lettin' him see yer flaws and yer weak spots."

"But—"

Now it was Warney's turn to nod. "The Lord'll show ya how. All I'm sayin' is it's not a weakness to let a friend see yer weak side when it decides ta show up. Yer bein' forged in the fires of affliction, and the good Lord's already bringin' somethin' good out of it."

"The problem with being 'forged in the fires' is that I don't fit in with normal kids." Dexter looked at the floor. "I guess I come across as a know-it-all or something, no matter how hard I try not to. Kids treat me like a grown-up—maybe because I act like one. I need a buddy like Gavin as much as he needs me."

"Yep, well, it's good ya don't fit in with *normal* kids, 'cause Gavin's far from normal." Warney rose and started to clear the table. "Fact is, though he don't know it yet, he's on the brink of becomin' a mighty man o' God."

"Let me, sir." Dexter beat Warney to the stack of dishes. "This was my job when Mama was alive. It blesses me to help."

It seemed the sadder the boy looked, the busier his hands got.

"Fair 'nough," Warney said as he watched Dexter gather the dishes and take them to the washstand. "How prayed up are ya?"

"Pretty prayed up," Dexter said.

Warney believed the boy, but did Dexter understand how prayed up he was gonna hafta be? "Ya cain't think it; ya gotta know it."

He saw the remark land on Dexter's face like a handprint. "Sorry, son. Didn't mean to come across so gruff. Here's the thing. Like ya say, we got ourselves a battle brewin' here in Burnt Swamp, and if ya want God to use ya on His side, ya gotta stay prayed up all the time. I don't wanna be settin' ya up fer failure."

Dexter squirted some liquid detergent in the steaming water and stirred up the suds. "With God's help, I figure if I'm still standing after gang wars, drug busts, and losing both parents, I can handle just about anything."

Warney raised an eyebrow. "Jest about?"

"Okay," Dexter said with a firm nod that shook his glasses halfway down his nose. "Anything. With God, I can handle anything." The words were right, but the passion was missing.

Except for the clank of dishes, silence spread through the shack. Dexter finished stacking the last of the dishes in the drainer and moved on to the pot with leftover greens.

Watching the boy work, Uncle Warney prayed. *Lord, that boy's hurtin', and only You can reach down that deep. I'm trustin' You to work it all out*. Warney also prayed about how much or how little to tell Gavin's new friend. By the time Dexter finished drying the last dish, Warney was ready.

With the humidity on the rise and the greasy aroma of charred cheese lingering in the air, Warney's lungs were starved for oxygen. A gust of wind caught the screen door and banged it on the outer wall. Despite the heat, he shivered.

"The Burnt Swamp curse is real—and dangerous."

"I know. It's already claimed Mama and Pap." Dexter's chin quivered again.

Warney pitied the boy but figured the best medicine was to keep on talking. "There's a lot more to it than ya know, and I aim to fill ya in as best I can."

"What can you tell me about shifting paths?" Dexter asked as he wiped his hands, composing himself quicker than Warney figured it was natural for a body to do.

"Don't know if ya've met Hee-Haw Downes yet, but I'd say he's in cahoots with the forces that are stirrin' up the swamp. Wouldn't surprise me none to find that he could answer yer question better'n me. But the best advice I can give ya is to steer clear of that troublemaker."

Dexter nodded. "Check. So, tell me more about Gavin."

"Gavin's a special boy with a powerful callin' on his life. Knew it from the day he was born. In fact, God spoke ta me soon as Gavin drawed his first breath—but I'm gettin' ahead of muhself." Warney meditated a bit. "Point is, 'til Gavin learns how ta cling to the Master, he cain't discern a pinecone from a pin oak. That's where *you* come in."

Dexter's brown eyes widened.

"The devil knows his time's short, and he's pullin' out all stops. Muh once-beautiful Burnt Swamp's a hot spot—a 'portal' to the underworld, if ya git muh drift—and things are happenin' mighty fast these days."

Warney stood up and leaned heavily on his walking stick, giving Dexter a chance for his words to sink in. When the boy didn't flinch, Warney went on.

"Seems clear to me ya got a big job ahead of ya, young feller. So does Gavin. A mighty big job. I done what I could to git him up to speed, but with him in the doghouse and things heatin' up so quick in the spirit realm, he needs a friend he can trust to help him catch the vision and latch onto his mission."

"I knew it! I saw in the Spirit that he was someone special. I hoped that we would be good friends." Dexter rested his back against the counter. "Tell me more."

"Let's sit a spell." Warney gestured Dexter toward a scroll-foot chair with the stuffing coming out at the seams, and then lowered himself into his caned rocker.

Ugly sauntered over and stood by the rungs of Warney's rocker, "rrrrmmming" his motor.

"That's funny," Dexter observed. "Your cat seems to be . . . what? Smiling? Grinning?"

"'Course he is." Warney dragged his fingers over Ugly's arched back and up his prickly tail. "Smarter 'n he looks. Ugly an' me, we go way back."

Dexter glanced at his watch and pulled a cell phone from his pocket. "Mind if I give Grandpap a ring? I told him I'd let him know when to come and get me."

Warney smiled. "See if he'll pick ya up at 7:30 so's we can have a bit longer to chaw the fat."

While Dexter talked with Officer Charlie, Warney tried to remind himself that Dexter was just a kid.

"So what's my role?" Dexter asked, flipping his phone shut.

"No beatin' around the bush with you, eh?" Warney laughed. "I see ya as Gavin's armor bearer."

"Ephesians 6, right? 'Put on the full armor of God.'"

"That's only part of it. Not many young uns yer age have a handle on the armor of God. As an armor bearer, you'll have ta carry Gavin until he's ready to fight the battle on his own. He don't know much about the armor yet. And judgin' from my talk with his cousin Molly, our Gavin's gonna have to strap on the belt of truth afore he goes much further."

"And the truth shall set you free."

"Yep, 'So that when the day of evil comes, ya may be able to stand yer ground.'" Warney continued to pet Ugly while he rocked. *Waddaya think, Lord? Is it okay to tell him?* Warney felt a release in his spirit nudging him to confide in the boy. "Ya see, Dexter, there's this diary that dates back ta 1640."

Dexter's hand flew to his throat. "The Burnt Swamp Diary? The one *The Daily Encounter* says holds the key to—how'd they put it— 'extinguishing the current blaze where modern technology has failed?'"

"One and the same." Shivers ran through Warney from head to toe. "It dates back to 1640 and was passed down in secret by 'white sheep believers' born into families that practiced witchcraft in the swamp."

"The paper said there's a rumor that you inherited the diary." Dexter sat unmoving, his eyes ablaze with interest. "Is there anything to that?"

Warney nodded. "You don't miss a beat, do ya, young fella? Yessir, bequeathed ta me by muh great-grandmother Phoebe." Warney leaned back in the rocker.

"So, how does this tie in with Gavin?"

"The last entry, that's what." For now, Warney decided to leave out the part about Laddrach's dragon. Instead, he quoted from the diary with deep emotion.

"Thus sayeth the Lord, 'At the appointed time, when the swamp fires flare, I will raise up a young boy to sound the trumpet. His name will be Gavin, and he will be a good fellow—faithful and true.'"

Dexter's whole body shivered. "Where's the diary now? Could I see it?"

Warney chuckled and shook his head. "If I'd a-knowed ya was comin', I coulda give it to ya to pass along to Gavin and spared muhself a heap a trouble." He reached into the magazine basket by his chair and, instead of the diary, pulled out a Ninja comic book.

"Oh, I almost forgot," Dexter said. "Is that Gavin's? I was supposed to ask if he left it here."

"Yep, it's Gavin's all right. Here." Warney tossed the comic book to Dexter.

"That fool comic book was what give me the cockamamie idea on how to get the diary to Gavin so's nobody'd see. I figured it wouldn't do fer me to give it to him straight out. Ya see, long before Gavin's dad put him on restriction, he made it clear he didn't want me goin' near the boy on muh own accord. So, I says to muhself, 'Self, if'n ya can sneak this to the school library where Widow Woebe'll come across it, curiosity'll get the best of her, and it'll only be a matter of time before she sees to it he gits it.'" Warney snickered, imagining the librarian's frustration when she tried to open the book and couldn't. "The diary's got a quirky habit of lockin' itself up. But that's a story fer another time. Night b'fore last, off I went on muh bicycle."

"Excuse me, but what's *this* have to do with it?" Dexter waved the comic book in the air.

A half-snort, half-chuckle rushed from Uncle Warney's throat. "Oh, yeah, I was about to tell ya what a fool I felt like, decked out like one of them Ninjas. If ya coulda seen me in that get-up, ya'da laughed yer head off. I had me a black hooded sweatshirt, black pants, even wore black gloves and pulled a pair of black socks over muh moccasins so's I'd blend in with the night. I wrote 'For Gavin's eyes only' on the package, wrapped it in muh bandana, and headed outdoors, prayin' to beat the band that the diary would find its way into the right hands. Then I mounted muh trusty old two-wheeler and pedaled from Burnt Swamp to the school, lookin' over muh shoulder all the way. Not a soul around."

"So you rode your bicycle in the dark to hide a diary 'for Gavin's eyes only' at school, hoping that the librarian would find it and give it to him in secret? Incredible!"

Uncle Warney rocked back and forth, back and forth. A smile worked its way across his face. "Seems silly now ta tell it, but it made right good sense to me the other night. By the time I rode into the parking lot and hopped off muh bike by the side door, I was breathin' so loud I thought the whole town would think the fire whistle'd gone off. And the noise muh bicycle tires made on the gravel sounded like a tank rollin' in. But nobody came, so I let muhself in through the back door."

"You let yourself in? How?"

"When muh daddy was a contractor, he had keys to every place he built in case of an emergency. Well, I knowed it was a stretch, but this seemed like a fair emergency to me. So into Sunken Bridge I went in muh Ninja outfit. Feelin' muh way down the hallway in the dark and seein' as how none of them new-fangled spy systems went off, I made it to the library without any notice. Felt around till muh nose told me I'd come to the old book section. Weren't no windows in that part, so I turned on muh flashlight and sure 'nuff, musty books stacked right on up to the ceilin'. I got into a coughin' fit and got to shakin' so hard, I thought the package would come bouncin' outta muh hand of its own accord, so I shoved it between two books."

"I'm surprised the janitor didn't catch you."

"It was after hours." Just thinking about how his asthma kicked up from the dust of those old volumes made Warney's wheezing worse. "My guess is that, unless the widow's gone blind, she's found it by now." He gasped for air.

Dexter stood up. "Can I get you a glass of water?"

"No, but reach down in that drawer there and hand me one of them puffers."

Dexter handed him the inhaler and Warney took a quick puff. "There's somethin' else that happened that night, if yer up to hearin' it. We still got another half hour before yer grandpap gets here."

"Sure. Are you kidding? I could listen to your stories till the bakery opens."

"More like till the frog croaks."

Tires crunched in the yard.

"Grandpap's early." Dexter sighed.

Warney nodded. "Hate ta see ya go." Pains shot up his back as he got to his feet. Leaning on his hand-carved stick, he hobbled toward the door with Dexter.

"Wait," Warney placed a heavy hand on the boy's shoulder and looked deep into his eyes. "I dumped a lot on ya today. Gavin needs ya. *I* need ya. Now, we didn't get into it, but I gotta tell ya one more thing seein' as how school's about to start."

"Yes sir?"

Warney stared deep into the boy's brilliant brown eyes. "The winds of change be upon us. The prophecy is comin' to fulfillment and battle lines are about to be drawn at Sunken Bridge Middle School. So, choose yer friends with care. Listen to the Holy Spirit. Be careful who you trust. Stay close to Gavin, even when he don't want ya to. Ya understand?"

"Yes sir, I do."

Dexter walked through the door to the waiting patrol car outside. As he and his grandfather drove away, Warney looked up into the tree at the edge of his property. Picky was perched near the top of the barren branches. Just as Warney's eyes fell on the buzzard, it lifted off, heading south toward the Lodge.

"Lord, help us," Warney mumbled as he shut the door and settled inside for his evening prayers.

CHAPTER FIFTEEN

Beware: Bea Daark

"Perfect." Bea admired her reflection. Checking her hair from every angle in the three-way-mirror at her dressing table, she was satisfied. Blonde locks cascaded down her back, spiraling much like the giddiness she felt in her tummy. After two tedious weeks in New England researching their ancestry, flying back to London for a month of shopping and packing, and arriving in Ashboro just three days ago, Bea was relieved to be settling into her new residence at the Lodge.

She smiled ever so slightly, aware that she had never in all her thirteen years felt more keyed up. Her first day in an American school where she could wear anything she wanted. No more everyone-must-dress-alike uniforms.

It was Tuesday, September fourth, and the moving vans had come and gone. Although other schools had taken the leap to open their doors in August, it suited Bea fine that Sunken Bridge Middle School waited until the day after Labor Day to kick off the academic year. *How opportune that their opening accommodated my calendar*, she mused.

Dabbing generous amounts of Black Amber perfume on her wrists and neck, Bea relaxed in the heady scent of vanilla and amber that blended into each other, and creating an air of mystery about her. She had chosen the exotic oil because of its hint of patchouli that was known for its pungent, musty aroma. She couldn't have been more pleased with her signature scent. It was delightfully overpowering.

Bea inhaled the lingering fragrance and swiveled away from her dressing table to face a small altar in the corner of the bedroom. Her morning ritual began with meditations—after bathing, dressing, and doing her hair and make-up, of course—that equipped her for whatever the day might bring. She rose slowly, like a princess in a trance, and moved toward the altar where she assumed the lotus position on the floor. One by one, she lifted the lids off five porcelain chalices representing the elements—spirit, water, fire, earth and air—and chanted her mantra.

"All day, in every way, I am moving higher, higher, higher. I have full and complete dominion over my senses and faculties. Always and forever, I am in control."

Centering herself, she became calm. Years of mind control lessons enabled her to tap into deep levels of her mind at will. She had learned to heighten her creativity and efficiency. Although not yet achieving full proficiency, the practice had increased her potential and her powers. In addition to helping her overcome the habit of picking at loose cuticles, mind control had improved her memory and given her an ever-expanding ability to control people remotely—for their own good, of course.

Concluding her morning rituals, Bea felt the urge to utter one more prayer for good measure. "Hail fair Sun, ruler of the day, heed my plea and light my way."

Running her right index finger inside one of the chalices, she reveled in its content of rose petals, semi-precious stones, melted candle wax, and dried leaves. A faint stream of smoke from the incense burner drifted upward to penetrate her perfume cloud. Her chamber in the Lodge's east wing almost smelled like the home she'd left in London.

Gliding back to the dressing table, she picked up the 1904 Art Nouveau hand mirror she discovered in one of the partially unpacked boxes. The mirror, ten inches long and six inches across, had a handsome design engraved on the back.

The last time she held the mirror was the day her mother told her they would relocate to Ashboro. The conditions catapulted mother and daughter into the grandfather of all arguments. Bea remembered her first reaction clearly.

"What do you mean I'll have to keep my power under wraps? What's the use of having power if you can't flaunt it?"

Only after her mother explained the scope of their mission and the increased responsibility entrusted to her did Bea understand. Although difficult, she had consented to try to cultivate the fine art of subtlety that would endear the commoners to her. One of her first tests of mortification was having to toss out all those sprung mousetraps some fool had set all over the lodge before she and her mother moved in—a few with dead mice in them. Bea fought a shudder at the repugnant memory. *Unlike those horrid creatures, my subjects will come to me willingly and unmarred, eager to receive the gifts I so generously bestow upon them in exchange for their loyalty.*

Now, for the final touch. Bea scanned the palette of twenty-four lipsticks with a critical eye. "You're the one," she said, picking up the deep violet tube and adeptly twirling her lip brush across its contents. "The perfect shade for my cashmere sweater. First impressions are so important."

After stroking the gloss-laden bristles over her full lips, she puckered a kiss at herself in the mirror.

"You're so stunning." She surveyed her image, turning first to the left, then to the right, striking dramatic poses to view her appearance from every angle. Behind her, mountains of unopened cardboard boxes awaited attention. But that task was relegated to another time. The blonde porcelain doll image, whose emerald eyes gleamed back at her, came first—now and always.

"Ashboro, look out. Beatrice Farrar—" She broke off, recalling her new identity. "Bea Daark is here. And you will never be the same." She looked closer to eliminate any flaws but found none.

This ought to catch the attention of those "saddos." She wished she could think of a stronger word to express her true feelings about the students who lived in this pathetic place. She doubted that any other girl in the eighth grade at Sunken Bridge—or the ninth grade, for that matter—knew how to work with make-up brushes like she did. After all, how many of *them* had had the chance to turn down dozens of European modeling agents? Bea's lips twisted into a polished smirk. Soon they would be falling all over themselves to learn her beauty secrets.

"And so, it begins." Startled by the whoosh of the door, Bea turned to see her mother coming toward her.

Donalda Daark's turquoise silk dressing gown billowed around her tall, trim figure as she floated toward Bea. Her salt-and-pepper hair tightly braided and wound around into a knot at the base of her neck, was pinned neatly in place with a silver hairpiece. Ornate bangle earrings sparkled in the sunlight as she came up behind Bea and placed her hands on her shoulders, meeting her daughter's gaze with a rare look of approval.

Bea basked in it. "You're up early, Mum," she said.

"I wanted to remind you who you are. This is no fanciful game— we're committed."

The corner of Bea's lips turned upward as she recalled the day they made their decision. "Tell me again what you said the day we chose our new name."

"Let's see." Bea's mother raised an eyebrow, her smile growing haughty. "What was it? Oh, yes. 'From now on, I shall be known as—" She paused for emphasis and lowered her voice to a sinister level. "'Madam Daark.'"

Bea giggled. "What an oxymoron. The Daarks have come to enlighten the commoners." Even her mother chuckled, which delighted Bea to no end, and they erupted into side-splitting laughter.

"Oh, Mum, you're so clever. I'll have so much fun enlightening my new friends."

"And influencing the community," Madam Daark added. "Off you go, now. Do you have everything?"

"All I need." Bea threw a lightweight royal purple cape over her shoulders, turned, and stepped into the hallway. "Ready or not, chums, your jolly Sunken Bridge Middle School is about to be revolutionized."

Madam Daark remained still, her head erect and nose tilted upward. "You're absolutely certain you want to take that horrid bus to school? Our driver is standing by."

"No, Mum. You know what the Order said. I must connect with the locals. That means I'll have to make some sacrifices, like riding that dreadful contraption."

"Yes, of course." Her mother's words said one thing, but the disdain in her voice said much more. They both knew what had to be done, no matter how repulsive it was. "I will have to get used to the idea of you cavorting with the peasants while you gather the chosen ones."

Walking together toward the great room, Bea's steps slowed while she pondered the timetable of her mission. "Do we have a date yet for Laddrach's release?"

A look of disgust flashed in Madam Daark's eyes. "How many times do I have to tell you? *Laddrach's* not being released. Laddrach is free now. He has the ultimate freedom to roam the earth at whim. The one to be released is—"

"His pet, Shimera." Bea lifted her chin. "Just teasing," she said with a smirk.

"Don't be flip with me, young lady." Madam Daark pulled herself up to full height. "You'll lament the day I lose my temper."

"Forgive me, Mum." Bea tried to sound genuinely sorry. "I just need to know if I have a deadline for getting our youth coven up and running."

"No one knows the day or the hour of Shimera's release but Laddrach. As for you, I suggest you concentrate on getting your hands on the Burnt Swamp diary. Its pages hold the clues we need to find the missing pieces."

Bea followed her mother's gaze to the bronze crest situated above the mantel of the stone fireplace.

"Have you selected a name for your coven?" Madam Daark's eyes remained on the crest.

"Daark's Dozen seems the best." Bea studied the crest, too, imagining how it might look once all the pieces were assembled and affixed to the bronze surface.

The high priestess of Laddrach and her daughter shared a rare moment of togetherness staring at the empty shell. As quickly as it came, the mood was broken.

"Just be diligent and put your ESP skills to good use."

Bea toyed with the buckle of her carryall and made no comment.

"You *have* been practicing, haven't you?" Her mother nailed Bea with a look that made her feel like she was sitting on a tack and couldn't get out of the chair.

"I know, I know. For your information, I have been practicing my *Effective Sensory Projection.*" She winked and launched into a textbook definition: "Where we project our minds into different objects such as brass, lead, and iron to explore textures and qualities."

"Bea," Madam said, lifting Bea's chin. "The last time you attempted mental travel through cloth, you left Mrs. Parker's parakeet with its feet in the air."

The memory of her failed projection attempt and the dead bird forced the last of Bea's sass out of her. "Well," she said, "it was a loud, wretched bird."

Her mother's glare didn't soften.

"So I haven't been as diligent as I should have been," Bea said. "I've been preoccupied with this move. I'll get back into the swing of things, I promise!"

"Promise what?" Mum whipped back at her.

"I will practice my ESP and help you find the diary so we'll be able to locate the pieces that go into the crest."

But in truth, Bea was puzzled. Why couldn't her mother, with her exotic powers and many servants, find the book herself? Sometimes, Bea felt more like a slave than a daughter.

"When, young lady? When?"

Bea sighed. "After school, Mum, or at the first opportunity. It's not like I don't have anything else to do. We just moved in. And I have yet to identify even one member of Daark's Dozen. Don't you think that should be my first priority?"

"The spirit of Laddrach will guide you, my dear. And don't underestimate your magick. You do have Clyccan, right?"

"Yes, Mum." Bea patted the pocket of her purple cape. "Clyccan's right here, safe and sound." She peered inside. "Aren't you, daahling?"

An indiscernible glow came from within, lighting her cape like a lampshade. With that, the deafening rumble of a "go-o-o-n-n-n-g" vibrated the floor under their feet, followed by a series of tinkling, off-key notes.

"What was that?" Bea held her hands over her ears and scanned the room with wide eyes.

CHAPTER SIXTEEN

Hee-Haw
Nemesis or Partner?

Before the offending vibration of the doorbell completed its cycle, loud banging resounded throughout the Lodge. Madam Daark recoiled in distaste as she cupped her hand to call for the butler.

"No need to bother Jenkins, Mum. I'll see who it is on my way out and send them away." Bea placed a light kiss on her mother's cheek and sauntered down the dark-paneled hallway, through the kitchen, around the boxes in the living room, and into the foyer. By the time she reached the door, the pounding had become violent.

Bea yanked the door open. There, with his arms raised above his head and hands clenched in mid-air, she found a lanky, greasy-haired, pimply-faced, teenager who was at least six feet tall.

"Yes?" she demanded, imitating her mother's imperious tone.

The boy lowered his arms. "Didn't know if you could hear me," he said with a blink as he extended his hand. "Nem Downes. You can call me Hee-Haw." His accompanying bray did not amuse Bea.

"And you're here because?"

"Thought you'd be expecting me. With us being *teammates* and all." His goofy buck teeth formed an overbite that made his chin look like it belonged to someone much smaller. The pungent aroma of human sweat and old socks assaulted her nostrils, driving out the expensive scents she had reveled in moments before. Tendrils of swamp smoke curled around Hee-Haw's knees like a cat currying favor from its owner.

Ignoring Hee-Haw's outstretched hand, she turned and called out. "Mum, come quickly! You've simply got to see this 'diputs' on our doorstep."

Turning back to the disheveled boy, she determined to put him in his place. "You must be off your trolley. I wasn't expecting anyone, and you are sorely mistaken about being teammates. I don't play sports." Bea felt her face contort at the notion of any connection with the poor excuse for humanity standing in front of her. "Certainly not with the likes of you." But something more than body odor raised the hair on the back of Bea's neck.

Madam Daark glided to the open door. "You're right. He is undoubtedly a diputs," she said, joining the game she had taught Bea from the moment she started to read at age four.

"Nem Downes. You can call me Hee-Haw." He greeted Madam Daark with one of his loud, harsh laughs. "By the way, what's a 'diputs'?" Again, an abrasive sound squawked from his throat.

"Stupid," Bea said, pleased with how quickly he fell for it. "I'd have thought someone as *backwards* as you would have figured it out on your own."

"Oh, I get it," he said with a mock-pained expression. "If I were you, I'd be careful about insulting a teammate right off the bat like that."

"Look, Mr. Downes." Bea stifled the urge to scream. "Perhaps you're hard of hearing. I'm *not* your teammate."

"Oh, yeah?" he drawled.

Madam Daark lifted her chin. "You may leave now, young man."

"I'm not talking about sports." Nem's lip curled into a sneer. "I guess my channels in the Order of Laddrach are swifter than yours."

Bea choked on a wisp of smoke that drifted around Hee-Haw and over the Lodge's threshold. "How," she coughed, "how *dare* you fling that name around!"

"How dare you *know* that name!" Her mother hissed, her breath expelling like steam from a leaky radiator.

Hee-Haw raised his brow in surprise. "You didn't get word from on high that we're gonna be partners?"

"As if *that's* going to happen," Bea said with a haughty sniff. *Isn't a narcissistic mother enough for one girl to have to deal with?*

Nem's expression darkened. "You think I like the idea of working with you snooty-patooty witches any better than you like the idea of working with me?"

Madam Daark fanned her face. Sidestepping to the intercom, she touched a button on the wall. "Ice. Bring ice. Immediately."

A distant voice crackled back. "Ice, Madam?"

"Yes, you fool," she shouted. "For my pulse points." She released the button and pressed two trembling fingers against her temples.

"Look," Hee-Haw said. "I may be no beauty, but the Order knows who it can trust. I've been laying groundwork in this place for a long time without any help from—how'd you put it?—the likes of you," he mocked, clipping his syllables to imitate their British accents. "My spirit guide, old Ooziss Naturus, cued me in, so you'd better get used to it."

Blah, blah, blah. Bea tuned him out but began obsessing over the name. *Ooziss Naturus.* For some reason, it made her dizzy to think of it. Suddenly, she knew why. *Ooziss is a powerful and dangerous spirit known for his hatred of humanity, unlikely to guide anyone anywhere except to destruction.*

"Just thought I'd be neighborly and get the jump on things by saying 'howdy.' Least you could do is show a fellow believer some courtesy." Nem turned to go.

As Hee-Haw walked off the porch, Bea reeled with thoughts that boomeranged inside her head. Surely, there was another, more logical explanation for this opportunist's knowledge of Laddrach and Ooziss Naturus. Maybe he was a wizard wannabe who gleaned his information from some pagan webzine. But what if the retreating figure was somehow right and he *was* connected with the Order?

"Mum, he said *Ooziss,*" Bea whispered, despising the way her lip insisted on curling downward as she uttered the name.

Jenkins, a short and stocky troll of a man with a thatch of black hair that always looked wet, appeared with cloth-wrapped ice chips.

"All right," Madam said to Bea as she pressed the compress against her pulse wrist. "I'll make a query to see if we can straighten out this misunderstanding." She whispered in Jenkins' ear, and he gave a nod.

"Young man. Right this way," the butler announced in a loud but flat voice.

Nem stopped, turned, and bounded up the steps two at a time. Jenkins led the threesome down the hall. Bea noticed that he took them the long way round instead of passing the great room with its double fireplaces—to keep their "guest" from noticing the bronze crest, no doubt. Passing through French doors, they entered the parlor.

"Sit, and don't touch anything. I'll be back in a few moments." Madam Daark checked her watch. "Seven o'clock here. Yes, well, I'll ring them up, but the Order is probably having luncheon, so don't expect much." With a sweep of turquoise silk, she glided ever so gracefully out of the room, powered by something more than her feet.

Nem meandered around the room, touching everything. "That rickety chair wouldn't hold a skeleton with osteoporosis."

"That's an ebonized American slipper chair, I'll have you know, and it's quite sturdy," Bea said. "You were told to not touch anything, so get your filthy mitts off the needlepoint upholstery."

"No need to get bent out of shape. I'm just admiring the merchandise. Like this gold castle clock here. Looks like it keeps pretty good time. Does that bell ring?"

"It strikes, yes, on the hour and half hour. It's French Gothic and dates back to 1827. Don't touch it." Bea looked at her watch. She had allowed plenty of time until this fool showed up. If her mum didn't return soon, she'd have to leave. She wasn't about to be late for her first day of school. But she also wasn't about to let Pimple Face work his way around the entire drawing room unsupervised. Even under her scrutiny, he managed to finger oval paintings, run his knuckles over the spines of countless volumes of leather-bound books, and almost topple a priceless marble bust. Bea had endured about all she could take of his harsh laugh and sick jokes of how many porcelain tea cups he could crack when Madam Daark swept into the room so quickly she disturbed even the heavy tapestries.

Her mother's face registered shock, confirming Bea's nightmare.

"It appears that the young man is correct." Madam Daark's voice was rigid as steel when she spoke. "The Order was going to give us another week to settle in before they introduced us." She shifted her gaze to Nem. "They were *quite* disturbed to learn of your initiative."

Her glare would have melted anyone else, but Nem just grinned broader.

"Nevertheless," Mum turned back to Bea, "it appears we have a partner called Nem."

"Hee-Haw Downes at your service." His shrill laugh assaulted Bea's ears. It was hard to tell which made her cringe more, his bray or the idea that she'd have to actually work with this grime-laden fool.

While she was trying to resign herself to the reality of the news she'd just heard, Nem grabbed Bea around the waist and twirled her in a clumsy victory dance.

Bea stomped on his insole, slapped him hard across the face with an open hand, and stared at him in disbelief. "Of all the nerve!" She wanted to scream *Get out, get out! Right this minute!* but her mother was approaching the boy with a stiffly extended hand.

Madam lifted her eyes toward the ceiling. "However inappropriate your behavior, I am . . . pleased—" the word sounded pained— "to make your acquaintance as our new associate."

Nem pumped Madam Daark's slender arm for all he was worth.

Aware she had no choice except to tolerate this miserable excuse for an ally, Bea subconsciously wiped her hands on her cape as she adjusted it and then hoped the grease from his face wouldn't leave a stain. "Yes, well, sorry to have to dash out," she said brightly. "It wouldn't do to miss the bus my first day."

Hee-Haw whirled around to face her. "Actually, I was planning on driving you to school."

"Do you always make plans without consulting anyone? Do you even have a license?"

"Sure. Got it a couple months back, but I've been driving for a few years now. Fixed up an old junker Cadillac from the salvage yard, and I go wherever I want. Are you ready?"

Bea shook her head. "No. Thank you."

"But—"

"No, I said. *No!*" Bea flipped her blonde tresses out from under the collar of her cape and headed for the doorway. "I wouldn't be seen dead in your company if I could help it, let alone set foot in an 'old junker.'"

"But—" Hee-Haw started to go after her.

As she glanced over her shoulder, she saw her mum place a hand on his shoulder and pinch his neck in an all-too-familiar way. That boy was about to learn his rightful place.

"Come. I want to talk with you a while longer, Nem." She motioned Bea on with her free hand. "Bea, daahling, have a lovely day at school. Don't forget what I told you."

"I won't, Mum." Bea winked and exhaled the breath she'd been holding.

Her heart thudded in her chest as she headed to the bus stop. What her mum had told her was to be subtle in recruiting her converts. *Sunken Bridge is my domain, and I'll take it captive any way I please, thank you very much. After all, it is my destiny to rule there . . . and beyond.*

CHAPTER SEVENTEEN

GAVIN

Speak Up!

"Quit *bugging* me." Gavin fumed as he and Molly walked to the bus stop on the first day of school. "Nag, nag, nag! I'm not a genius like you and can't spit out Bible verses on demand. Who do you think I am? Some preacher type that's got the Bible memorized?" He kicked a stone, and a puff of dust covered his red and black Nikes.

"No." Molly rolled her eyes. "It's just that when I get in a big debate, I expect you to *agree* with me and not sit there with a blank look on your face like you don't have a brain in your head. You *do* agree that my *father's wife* was wrong about the need to 'enhance our psychic ability,' don't you?"

Boy, can Molly stick to her guns. Gavin remembered that she had told him more than a year ago, when her dad remarried, that she would never *ever* refer to her stepmother by name. It had something to do with "justice." And now Molly was on *his* case. Gavin wished he still had his long bangs to hide behind, but with his hair cut off and standing up in a long flat-top, he had no choice but to look at her. Inhaling deeply, he regrouped. He was frustrated and ashamed at his habit of wimping out.

185

"Hellooooo, earth to Gavin. You do agree with me, don't you?"

Gavin didn't like Mrs. Everett any more than she did, but that didn't mean he wanted to get in the middle of the argument Molly had with her last Friday night. When she showed up as a chaperone at the Young Saints Community Center and tried to convince them that the Ouija board was just a game, Gavin knew there would be trouble. Molly's dislike of the woman flared into a confrontation every time they met. This was the worst ever. Molly started it when she got in her face and said, "Aren't we supposed to expose the works of darkness?"

And rightly so, in light of the fact that Gavin and his cousins had a devil of a time with a Ouija board in Fennemore's Dollar Store last June. He wanted to say, "Way to go, Mol! No wonder Eric's getting more messed up by the day," but he thought better of it. Besides, he figured Molly was doing a fine job without his two cents' worth. Now, spinelessness or not, Gavin felt something building up in him—a hair-trigger rage.

"Look, Molly. You're right. You should tell Pastor Fred. Does he even know Mrs. Everett was asked to chaperone? Where does she get off saying that evil will 'go away' if we ignore it? It wouldn't surprise me if she were to turn up wearing one of those Halloween masks with bloody eyeballs hanging out to prove that it's a 'harmless expression of creativity.'"

"Why couldn't you have said *that* Friday night? I was the only one who had guts enough to stand up to her. She's teaching false religion right in our own youth center, and does anybody see the danger? Noooo. When I looked to you for one little word to back me up, did you stand by me? Noooo. You left me, like, totally out there in the ionosphere."

"Eye-ahn-iss-fear? You and your big words."

"Don't change the subject, Gavin. You know what I mean. You could have at least nodded your head like you believed in what I was saying."

Gavin felt drained from his outburst. Where his big spiel came from he had no clue. It didn't sound like him. Oh, he liked it all right, the surge of passion, but whatever it was, the wave passed as quickly as it came. Why couldn't he be like Eric who routinely ignored Molly's arguments?

"But we're just kids." The fire in Gavin's belly had gone out, replaced by a dry whine. "Besides, you put me on the spot. Everybody turned to look at me and I, well, I went blank."

"That's a lousy excuse, Gavin."

Molly's words bored into Gavin's soul and felt like she'd punched him in the gut. His lip quivered, but he bit it and managed to keep from falling apart. "Pretend you're me for a minute, Molly."

"No way." She gazed down the road. "Is that bus ever going to get here?"

"C'mon. I just finished up my community service. I was almost feeling good about myself, and there you were, locking horns with your stepmother. You really wanted me to come out swinging?" Gavin hung his head. "You know I'm not good with words, and when people start to argue, well, it makes me want to run and keep on running. If Dexter'd been there, maybe he could've helped. He'd have had all the Scriptures you needed. But I'm not Dexter. I'm just me."

"Yeah, but Dexter wasn't there, Gavin." Molly's eyes looked softer. "And you were. At some point, you've got to learn to speak up for what you believe. Remember what Uncle Warney said?"

"Uncle Warney says a lot of stuff."

"You and I are lights in a dark place. God is counting on us."

"Big whoop. Now I get to let you, Uncle Warney, *and* God down."

Molly's voice softened. "You're wrong, Gavin."

"Oh, yeah? How do you know?"

"I just do. I know it in my knower."

"Well, your knower can't know what God can do in me."

"Can too."

"Can not."

"Oh, Gavin. If you can't trust God to shine through you, who can you trust?"

Gavin looked away. Avoiding the question might mean he could avoid the answer. Fear still gnawed and churned and knotted his stomach. "So, how was Sunday school? I overslept."

"That's what I mean." Molly sighed. "You've got to get with the program. You're either committed to Sunday school or you're not."

"Not," Gavin said.

"Oh, by the way . . ." Molly's eyes brightened. "Widow Woebe came up to me afterwards. She was acting kind of funny."

"So? She always acts funny."

"No she doesn't!"

"Whatever."

"She found a package in the archives that feels like a book—"

"Duh. She's a librarian. Of course, it's a book. So what?"

"So, this is secret stuff, and it has something to do with you."

"Me?"

"Yes, you. She seemed agitated and made me promise that I wouldn't tell anyone but you—it's highly 'hush-hush' or spiritually charged or something."

The mention of the book triggered an unexpected reaction in Gavin. Like a strobe smattering a wall with synchronized flashing lights, pulses of memory made him feel that he was moving in slow motion. He heard his heart hammering in his ears while he felt the color drain from his face. *No. Not again.* Forcing himself to stay in the present and get the blood back into his cheeks where it belonged, he bent down and rested his chin on his knee. It felt like forever for his pulse to recover and his head to clear.

"Why me?" Gavin fiddled with his laces. "What makes her think I'd want to see some dumb old book? Anything Woebe says is—"

"Because," Molly interrupted, "it has your name on it."

"What? My name?" Standing up, Gavin felt stronger than when the strobe lights hit, but he was still weak in the knees.

"Shhh. Here comes Eric. We'll talk about it later."

Gavin didn't want to hush up, but he didn't want to talk about it, either. It sounded too much like the vision book.

"Hey." Eric rounded the bend and loped over to them with a grin. "Look what I can do." He straightened his spine to an unnatural position with his rear end sticking out, cocked his elbows out wide as if holding invisible pruning shears, and crossed his eyes. As he rolled them around in their sockets, they looked like a couple of marbles banging together, again and again. "Who's this look like?" he asked, then answered his own question. "Strange old Uncle Warney." He relaxed his lanky body. "I heard him talking to himself when I saw him picking up trash along the road back there."

There he goes again, acting like a jerk. Gavin hated it when Eric mimicked Uncle Warney. "Come on, don't make fun of him. We all know he's strange, but he's family. And he doesn't look *that* bad."

"You sure?" Eric smiled, twisting his mouth into a cockeyed smirk.

"Hey. Enough about Uncle Warney." Gavin's mind raced. How could he get Eric to quit the bad-mouthing? Ah, yes. Get him to talk about himself. "I see you've spiked your hair with some of that slick gel. What's that? Your new look?"

"Yeah." Eric nodded. He leaned his weight on his left hip and wobbled his head like it was hooked to a Slinky. When the bobbing stopped, he grinned. "You got your windblown wheat field look, and I got my 'with it' spikes. Besides, it helps keep the hair out of my eyes. And if I'm gonna have to hear a bunch of garbage from Mr. Smoot anyway like, 'What in the world are today's youngsters coming to?', I might as well give him something to gawk at."

Gavin jabbed Eric in the ribs. "Planning to spend some time in the principal's office again this year?"

"Jerk."

Eric could dish it out, but he sure couldn't take it.

Molly twirled the curls at the end of her braid and stepped closer to Eric. "I think that gel in your hair makes you look taller—especially since it's standing on end. In fact, you look like somebody in the movies. Oh, I know. If you had it slicked back instead of straight up, you'd look like Snidely Whiplash, the villain that ties the girl to the railroad tracks."

Eric cocked an eyebrow and tried to match an evil laugh with her description. "Ya-ha-ha-ha."

A hot breeze swirled the dirt around Gavin's feet and swept over him. Whether real or imagined, he felt a sense of foreboding. The image of Eric playing the villain made Gavin feel like a victim himself, gagged and bound to a community that had embraced soot and gloom.

Shaking his head to get rid of the picture of Eric as one of the bad guys, Gavin felt a sense of defeat that held something more sinister than Eric's goofy antics. Yeah, it was something else, all right. But what?

CHAPTER EIGHTEEN

Optimistic anticipation flowed through Bea as she sauntered toward the bus stop and her first encounter with the students of Sunken Bridge Middle School. Slipping her right hand into her cape pocket, she fingered Clyccan, the fountain pen given to her by the high priest on her twelfth birthday. "A family heirloom," he had called it, "refashioned from an 1880-style wand into a cleverly practical pen." At her touch, the incantation-rich substance stored in the barrel responded. Bea's pocket glowed as though warmed by a pink lightbulb.

"There, there," Bea said. "We must be patient, now, mustn't we, Clyccan? Only a few more moments, dear."

By the time the bus stop came into view, she could barely control her excitement about their mission, especially in light of the Painter Landscape Company ad on the side of the shelter: "No Leaf Left Unturned." *An apt motto*, considering her quest to unearth every last object that belonged in the crest.

Positioning her feet on a small mound of grassy soil, Bea looked down her nose at three locals who waited for the bus. Startled by the sound of snapping twigs and clumsy footsteps, she whirled around.

"Hey, girly." The pimply-faced boy was back. "I had a short—but, let's say significant—talk with Mumsie."

Bea hoped she'd seen the last of the bloke, but there he was, standing on the knoll next to a rusty Cadillac convertible that left tire ruts in the dirt.

"What are you doing here?" she said.

Pimple Face ran his tongue over an eyetooth and sucked like he was trying to dislodge yesterday's bacon. "I go where I want. Took a short cut."

Bea's stomach churned; disgust filled her voice. "I meant what are you doing following me?"

"I wanted to get to know my partner, that's all."

"I'm not your partner."

"We've been all through that, remember? What the Order says goes."

"Keep your voice down." She pointed to the bus stop. "You want those kids to hear every word you're saying?"

Pimple Face rolled his eyes.

Bea lowered her voice and squinted at him. "How is it that someone with your—" she looked him up and down— "conspicuous lack of upbringing has connections with the Order of Laddrach?"

"Contacts, Baby. It's not what you know, but who you know that counts." He winked and actually sneered.

Bea crossed her arms. "This conversation is over."

The sneer vanished. Nem set his jaw and exhaled through his nose. "Sorry. My bad."

"Your bad what?"

"My bad. I never like to say I made a mistake, so—my bad."

"Oh, I get it," Bea said. "American slang."

"Suit yourself." He reached into the pocket of his holey shorts. "Here, I made somethin' for ya."

Bea studied the objects Nem held out to her—three stones that had been tumbled, polished, and etched with symbols.

"Marble runes?" The gems held her momentarily captivated.

"Go ahead, take 'em." He dumped the runes into her open palm. "Nope, they're shells from the beach. I collect 'em and Auntie Soshal tumbles and engraves them for her shop. I thought they'd make a nice welcome gift."

Bea looked closer at the runes. "Hmm. They seem to be emanating good energy." She recognized the "X" symbol of Gebo, working in cooperation, and the bow tie-shaped Dagaz "><" for attainment and wealth. She was all for that. And the "<" Kano emblem for keen insight and openings, something they would all need to accomplish their goal.

"Accepted," she said, carefully watching him from the corner of her eye. "Do you use these for divination?"

"Sometimes. My aunt likes 'em for spell-craft. The public believes the 'for entertainment purposes only' sign in the shop window, but we know better." Hee-Haw leaned into a giant yawn. "Me, I'm mostly into astral projection."

"So what are you? New Age? Occult? What?"

"Pagan, heathen—take your pick. I'm open to whatever path suits, wherever the power lies—witchcraft, psychic healing, voodoo—I'm not choosy."

Bea was beginning to think this kid might be useful, after all. "Mmm, I see. Agreed. Power is everything. You've lived here all you life?"

He nodded.

"You wouldn't by chance know anything about a Burnt Swamp diary, would you?" Sensing a vibration in her pocket, Bea gave Clyccan a gentle pat—her way of saying *calm down* without having to utter a word.

"Sure. You'd be surprised what I know. You're going to need me if you're planning to find the pieces for that oversized dinner plate above your fireplace."

Bea felt heat rush up her neck and into her face. "You know about the crest?" Her pulse beat wildly in her temple, and things she'd been longing to share with somebody other than her mother rushed out of her mouth. "Do you know where the diary is?"

"I'm working on it. So, let me ask *you* something. You believe in the devil?" Nem raised an eyebrow.

"A personal devil? No, of course not. Satan is just Christianity's scapegoat for irresponsibility and guilt." Bea wasn't sure where he was going with this, but she was glad he was moving away from the teammate focus. "Okay, you've asked your question, now here's mine: What's got you so bent out of shape?"

"None of your beeswax. But, see that boy down there—" he pointed— "the one with the red whisk-broom hair? He's trouble."

Bea studied the boy and laughed. "You're kidding! He looks harmless enough."

"That's Gavin Goodfellow, and he's got one heck of an aura. Ooziss says he's the one to watch out for."

"I don't see any aura."

"Well, it's not there now." Nem launched into the details of his out-of-body visit to the woods. "But his aura was so strong that day it caused a vortex that nearly sucked me to China."

The more Nem bragged about his sensational experiences and proficiency with astral travel, about his conscious mind leaving his physical body and moving into his astral body, the more Bea thought about how she liked the body she was in. He could keep his Silva method and his Montroe technique to himself, as far as she was concerned.

Not once had she desired to propel the essence out of her body, not even to hover over herself, let alone go somewhere else in the spirit. The mere thought made her nauseous. "My expertise is in mind control," she said.

"Sure, everybody knows you can't do OBE without mind control."

"OBE?"

"Out-of-Body Experience," Nem said with a look that made Bea feel like a worm.

"I knew that." It irked Bea that she always lost patience when she was embarrassed, but she let her annoyance show anyway. "Look," she raised her voice, "that's enough getting acquainted for one day. You're going to make me miss my bus. About those kids down there?" She waved a manicured hand. "I'll keep an eye on that Gavin chap all right, and there's something about that girl I don't like the looks of either. But that black-haired boy . . . Feeling a vibration, she thrust her hand into her cape pocket, and wrapped her fingers around Clyccan. "Yes, he's the one. Watch this. Let me show you what I can do with . . ."

Time stood still while Bea fixed her gaze on her target.

"With what?" Hee-Haw's grating voice broke through Bea's trance, making her jump.

"Don't be such a twit. You'll see." Clyccan wasn't ready yet. "By the way," she said, biding time. "How do you spell magick?"

"For illusion and baby games, I spell it m-a-g-i-c. But if you mean rituals and invoking power forces," Hee-Haw said, his pus-filled pimples turning a brighter shade of pink, "I spell it m-a-g-i-c-*k*, of course."

"Okay, then." If this crooked-toothed irritant wouldn't go away, Bea could at least show off her magick. A luminescent glow filled her pocket as she rolled the fountain pen between her thumb and index finger. In a matter of seconds, Clyccan's contents reached precisely 105°, the perfect temperature for a fever, and emitted a soft beep. Bea pulled it out.

"Time for a demonstration. Nem Downes, meet my favorite companion, Clyccan." She held out the pen for him to get a good look, then held it at arm's length in the direction of the bus stop. "Watch."

The barrel in her hand glowed fluorescent red and orange, the very shade Bea anticipated. Giving Nem sufficient time to ogle at the spectacle, she pointed Clyccan toward her target.

She tittered with glee as Gavin turned and stared up at her with his mouth open. The girl with the long braid and the black-haired boy turned and gawked, too.

The sound of voices set off an internal alarm Gavin didn't know he had. Instinctively, he turned toward the knoll. Out of the corner of his eye he saw Molly and Eric swivel around, too.

The first thing he noticed was Hee-Haw Downes, the biggest failure at Sunken Bridge—sixteen and still in the eighth grade. Every time he saw the gangly teen, he was afraid that he would share the same fate—failing multiple grades and staying at Sunken Bridge forever. And every time, Gavin had to remind himself that Hee-Haw wasn't dyslexic; he just didn't bother showing up for class.

What the devil? The girl with him had her right arm fully extended, pointing something in his direction. A magic wand? A laser light? In that moment, nothing stirred but the smoky fog that swirled around the perfectly poised manikin with her purple Merlin cape. Muffled sounds rode the fog to Gavin's ears, skirting around him and wafting across the road toward the swamp. Just when he thought it must be a mirage, the girl flicked her wrist.

"Watch that lanky lad with the black spiked hair," Bea said, taking aim. She looked down the barrel of the pen like a precision scope on a high-powered rifle. Pressing the clip, it was over in an instant.

A minuscule drop of the hypnotic matter shot from the chamber of the pen. Propelled on the ray of a laser beam, it found its mark.

The dark-haired boy jumped as if he'd been stuck with a hat pin. A cloud of reddish-orange encircled him.

"So, Nem. You like auras? What do you make of that?"

Hee-Haw grunted, reluctantly impressed.

"Enough. Leave me. I've more work to do. Alone."

He stood there like the simpleton she figured him to be.

For the second time that morning, Bea distanced herself from Nem Downes. Lowering Clyccan, she approached her prey and whispered words not intended for human ears, ending with, *"Clyccan, you know what to do, now do it."*

Bea glided down the hill. Within hearing distance, she lowered her voice to a whisper. "You, my pet, have been awakened from your slumber." Her smile belied the menace in her words.

Then, yes, there it was, "the look"—the awestruck look of admiration and subjugation. The first member of Daark's Dozen was properly identified. And marked. He just didn't know it yet.

CHAPTER NINETEEN

ERIC
Enchanted

*E*ric jumped. His already spiked hair sizzled like he'd been zapped by a thousand volts of electricity. He felt his ears turning red from bottom to top, like mercury rising in a thermometer.

Gavin's feeble voice said the very words he was thinking. "What . . . what kind of girl is *that?*"

A gust of wind caught her cape and lifted it off her shoulders, causing her long blonde hair to whip around like daggers in active combat. She stood tall and regal like a princess. Even from that distance, Eric could feel power seething from behind her eyes. She spoke, and the air around him prickled and gave him goosebumps. The wind abruptly died. Eric couldn't make out her words, but he could hear a velvet sound emanating from her vocal chords. He felt a distinct chill, but not from the September morning air. Awesome!

Hee-Haw said something to the girl and moved away.

The prettiest girl Eric had ever seen glided down the hill. The closer she came, the more nervous he felt. It was a good kind of nervous—the kind he felt when something good was about to happen—the kind that Super Bowl players must feel at game time.

And then, standing before him, she spoke. "So sorry to startle you," she said.

Never had Eric heard a voice so melodic, so dreamy, so magnetic.

Everything about Purple Girl, even her clipped accent, unnerved Gavin.

"Allow me to introduce myself. I'm Bea Daark, and I just moved here from London. This is where we pick up the transit for Sunken Bridge, right?"

"Huh?" Gavin glanced at Eric whose face now matched the color of his ears.

"If you mean the school bus, you're in the right place." From the look in Molly's eye, Gavin could tell she was gathering her reporter's steam.

"What's that?" Molly asked, indicating the object in Bea's hand. No beating around the bush for his nosy cousin.

The girl's face softened with innocent surprise as she turned from Eric. "Oh, this? Why, it's my pen."

"Oh." Molly appeared pensive, but Gavin knew she was far from done with this intruder. "From a distance, it looked like you were waving a wand—like you were casting a spell."

"Don't be silly." Bea flipped her fingers at an invisible fly. "If I could cast a spell, wouldn't you feel it?"

Ooooh . . . cat fight! Gavin couldn't believe how fast girls' claws could come out.

"So what's with the wizard cape, then?" Molly challenged.

"Its the latest rage in London." Bea chuckled.

"And the pen?" Molly was relentless.

Bea yawned. "I was showing Mr. Downes how I could gauge the distance between where I was standing and where I needed to be. Want to have a look-see?" She turned the pen upside down to reveal a glass portion on the end that contained a bobbing compass. Smiling sweetly, she tucked the pen into her right pocket and turned her attention back to Eric.

Gavin thought he saw her pocket twitch and poke outward three times but dismissed it as his overactive imagination.

"So, now that you know who I am," Bea said, "who might you be?"

"I'm Molly Pace. This is my twin, Eric Everett, and that's my cousin, Gavin Goodfellow."

"Nice to make your acquaintance." Bea wrapped her arm in Eric's and drew him close. "So tell me," she said, turning her back to Gavin and Molly. "Just why is it you and your twin have different last names?"

Molly appeared speechless as Eric and Purple Girl walked away, talking in low whispers.

Gavin searched for something clever to say, but words eluded him, as usual.

"Can you believe the nerve of that, that person?" Molly wrinkled her nose in disgust. "She actually ignored us and . . . where's she going with him?"

Gavin shook his head. "I'm used to it. People ignore me all the time. Hey, Eric!" he yelled. "Better get over here. Big Yellow's coming."

"Eric, you're too funny!" Bea wheeled around, leading Eric by the elbow. Her phoney laughter filled the air. "I'd love to meet your teammates. I suppose football to you is like rugby to us. Maybe I'll fly you to Europe if England makes it to the World Cup finals."

Gavin and Molly gave each other eye rolls. The minute Bea's back was turned, Gavin lowered his voice. "What do you call that?"

Molly gave a quick, head-to-toe glance at Bea and whispered back. "Smarmy self-importance."

"Well, yeah. But what's the deal with Eric? You think she did something to him?"

Molly's expression grew serious. "I don't know. But I don't like anything about that girl. I'm keeping my distance and suggest you do the same."

Just as the school bus lurched to a stop and the door squeaked open, a huge gray-brown bullfrog jumped from the marshy grass, landing at Eric's feet. Its bulging eyes shone in a way that could have been mistaken for delight if frogs were capable of affection.

"Ribbitt, ribbitt, ribbitt."

"Hey," Eric lit up. "I know this big guy from Uncle Warney's."

Bea gave a visible shudder. "Eeeww, if there's anything I despise, it's frogs." She gave Eric a piercing look as if to say, *Do something*.

"Get away, you slime bucket." Eric sneered and whacked the bullfrog with his sneaker. The blow sent the creature reeling into the tall grass where it landed on its back.

Gavin cringed when he saw the frog's white stomach exposed and his hind legs thrashing in the air. He couldn't believe his cousin's cruelty. He might act like a jerky jock, but he *never* mistreated animals, especially one he seemed so pleased to see a minute ago.

Eric shrugged, climbed the three steps into the bus behind Bea, and reached out to touch the hem of her royal purple cape.

"What's eating him?" Gavin asked Molly as they moved toward the bus. "He always *liked* frogs before."

"Yeah. I don't get it," she said. "He loves frogs—even insists one of them *talked* to him."

"Maybe Mr. Bullfrog said something Eric didn't like." Gavin shrugged.

Molly stepped into the bus. "Or maybe Bea put him up to it."

Gavin followed her up the steps. "She didn't tell him to kick it."

"She didn't have to." Molly turned and searched Gavin's face with her eyes. "Didn't you see that *look* she gave him right after she said she despised frogs?"

Leaving the question hanging in the air, she flopped down in the front seat by her girlfriend, Anita.

Standing in the aisle, Gavin glanced out the window and saw Uncle Warney limping toward the bus shelter. *He must have walked all the way here to see us off on our first day of school.* A powerful pang of sadness gripped Gavin. It had been so long since he'd seen his uncle; he felt as lonely as the old man looked. Uncle Warney's eyes searched the bus windows, and Gavin waved, but apparently he couldn't see inside. The bus jolted forward, putting even more distance between them.

"Take your seat," the driver snapped, no less impatient than he was last June.

Doing his best to keep his balance as he started down the aisle, Gavin scanned the seats for Eric.

But Eric wasn't waving at him or saving a seat like always. He wasn't even looking for Gavin. Instead, he was next to Bea who sat prim and proper, gazng out the window toward the swamp. Eric stared at her, googly-eyed, with his legs in the aisle.

Gavin stepped over Eric's boat-sized sneakers and took an empty seat directly behind him. A sick feeling churned in Gavin's gut as his cousin's fast-shifting loyalties began to register. It felt like something shriveled up inside him, something he treasured. Even Eric's finicky friendship was better than none at all. He tried his best to fight it, but the ache wouldn't go away.

How'd she do that to him? Well, it won't last, he consoled himself. And at least he was close enough to hear whatever they might say to each other.

Nonchalantly, Gavin stretched his arms above his head. Clasping his fingers, he pushed his palms outward until they reached the seat in front of him and then cracked his knuckles loud, right in Eric's ear. Yesterday, Eric would have laughed and cracked his knuckles back. But not today. Eric sat there limp, like Raggedy Andy staring at the live doll next to him.

Didn't he hear that? How could he miss it when the snap-crack-pop was right in his ear? Or is he ignoring me on purpose, ashamed to be seen with me?

While Anita chattered away in the front seat, Molly glanced back at Gavin and gave him a Don't-just-sit-there-Why-don't-you-do-something stare. Or was it a Didn't-I-tell-you-to-keep-your-distance stare?

Either way, all Gavin could do was shrug his shoulders and keep tabs on the slime show going on in the seat in front of him.

Bea turned her face away from the window and leaned toward Eric.

"Would you be so kind as to show me around school and introduce me? Maybe we could spend some time together at lunch."

"Sure!" Eric shouted. Every head on the bus swiveled in Eric's direction. He blushed, slumped down in the seat, and everybody lost interest—everybody but Gavin.

Eric whispered into Bea's hair. "I'll meet you between classes to make sure you find the right rooms—mmm, you smell good. What's your schedule look like?"

Gavin squirmed in his seat. *Eric's never thought about anybody but himself his whole life. Now he's Sir Lancelot? Gag. Barf. Just wait till she finds out how full of himself he is. She'll dump him like a load of Uncle Warney's horse manure.*

When Eric and Bea began talking in really low undertones, Gavin had to lean forward to hear better.

"Really, Eric," Bea said in a syrupy sweet voice. "I can't believe we're both in eighth grade, and we even have some of the same classes. I feel a connection with you already. In fact, I expect I'll be depending on you rather heavily for a time."

At that, Gavin stuck his finger in his mouth as if to gag himself. *Now, that really is enough to make a person sick.* He tried to turn his attention to the unimpressive scenery of Ashboro's weather-beaten houses as they blurred past the window. *Well, Miss Bea-whoever-you-are, I don't think you "depend on" anybody very much, but you sure know how to lay it on thick.*

After the longest twelve-minute ride of his life, the bus screeched to a halt in front of Sunken Bridge, but Gavin felt in no hurry to get off. It was just as well, because Eric stood up and let Bea go in front of him.

So when did you become Mr. Manners? Gavin grimaced.

"Oh, by the way," Gavin heard Eric say to Bea. "What did you say your last name was?"

She twisted gracefully at the waist and faced Eric as the other students scrambled off the bus. The light in Bea's emerald eyes glinted a shade brighter, and her face shone as she answered. "Daark. D, double A, R, K. And you might be interested to know that Beatrice means 'blessing' or 'brings joy.' You can call me Beatrice if you like, but Bea Daark has a nice ring to it, don't you think?"

Ooooohhhh, how appropriate, Gavin thought. *Just like our crummy old school. Dark and dreary, gloomy and boring.* Bea was far from boring, though. Gavin knew that much. What he didn't know was which emotion he felt strongest—disgust or distrust. *She's trouble, no D double doubt about it. She'll be stirring things up in no time.*

Gavin was just about ready to move from the window when a rust-eaten Cadillac convertible slid sideways and screeched to a halt, almost grazing the side of the bus. While everyone inhaled a collective gasp, Hee-Haw Downes stood up in the driver's seat and banged on Gavin's window. "Yo! Stupid!" he hollered through the glass. "Yeah, *you.* I got your number!"

Gavin's mouth dropped open; he backed away from the window. *This can't be happening.*

CHAPTER TWENTY

Widow Woebe's Summons

The last one off the bus, still shaking from Hee-Haw's unexpected, unwarranted, and totally confusing verbal assault, Gavin kept his head down and concentrated on the squeaking sounds his Nikes made as he scuffed them down the aisle of the metal floor. *I heard that guy could fly off the handle, but why me? He's got my number? What's that about? What'd I ever do to him?* Gavin decided then and there that he would keep his distance from Hee-Haw—the farther the better.

Pausing on the bottom step, he glanced up to see Eric and Bea head up the walk and melt into a cluster of kids who were probably talking about him. The whole group disappeared into the school like a swarm of locusts. Even Molly ignored him, chatting with her girlfriend as they waltzed through the double doors.

People either pick on me for no reason, or nobody gives me a second thought. Well, maybe Dexter, but I'll bet he's nice to everybody.

The *last* person Gavin wanted to pay any attention to him was Widow Woebe, or Woebegone, as the kids nicknamed her. But there she was in her second-story library window, waving her windmill arms at him. She looked like a mechanical scarecrow the way her flower-print dress hung on her bony frame. Even the tufts of gray hair that sprouted from the tight little knot on top of her head resembled wiry, dried-up straw.

Anyone but her. Gavin ducked behind a cement bench. What now? Hadn't he seen enough of her in summer school? Was it an overdue library book? Or the PTA's Read-A-Book program? Whatever the reason, the only thing Gavin hated worse than reading was how Mrs. Woebe acted like it was her God-given duty to help him develop a love of books.

Gavin crouched behind the hedgerow with his back to the library window and tried to avoid eye contact as he slunk his way toward the run-down building. Trying to ignore the taste of apricots, apples, and 7-Up—and memories of another strange book—he made it as far as the dumpster before her shrill voice caught up with him.

"Gavin Goodfellow, I see you there. Now get yourself out from behind that trash bin right this minute."

Busted. Gavin straightened up and stretched self-consciously, trying to get a kink out of his back. "Oh, good morning, Mrs. Woebe." He hoped his lopsided smile didn't look as fake as it felt.

Speaking through the screen, she chirped in her sweetest tone, "I need to see you in the library during study hall. And Molly, too. Be sure to tell her for me. I have something of . . ." she paused, "historic significance to discuss with the two of you."

Historic significance? That sounded as exciting as one of Pastor Fred's sermons. "Uh, sure. I'll let her know." *Like, NOT,* he thought.

"It's important!" Her gray bun tottered with an authoritative nod. "Don't be late." She withdrew her skinny frame from the opening and slammed the window.

Dragging his feet, Gavin headed toward the door and into the building. *What a great way to start the school year. Some hot-shot new girl gushes all over Eric, Hee-Haw threatens me, and now Woebegone wants me in the library.* "Historic significance," Gavin muttered under his breath, remembering the hush-hush package Molly had mentioned. "Yeah, right. Bet it's about that dumb, old book she found in the archives. Big deal."

No sooner were the words out of his mouth than an odd sensation sucked at his gut. He felt—what was it?—like he was being watched. Slowly, he looked up. There stood Bea, halfway down the hall, staring at him. Their eyes locked, and he cringed as Bea pulled away from her admirers and moved smoothly toward him. Try as he might, Gavin couldn't look away.

Bea's constrained tone wormed its way into his ears. "How *dare* you question the ancients?" she said. "Old books *are* a big deal, Master Goodfellow. Don't be too quick to reject the writings of old."

Gavin's pulse tripped. *How could she have heard me?* "Huh? You heard that?"

Instead of answering, she smiled as if to say she knew something he didn't.

"You must have awfully good ears," he said as Bea further invaded his personal space. The musty-sweet scent of her vanilla perfume made him feel light-headed and dizzy. Gavin felt his eyes bulge in their sockets and begin to water like an onion had been peeled under his nose.

He knew she hadn't been close enough to hear his mumbling. Could she read his mind? A cold shiver shook his whole body. This was one mega-creepy girl.

Bea placed a featherlight hand on his arm, freezing his legs to the spot. It was like something overrode his brain—something he could feel but that was undetectable to his eyes and ears. Internal warning bells rang louder than ever.

"I'm always intrigued by the mysteries revealed in the writings of old," Bea said. "Do let me know what you and Molly discover. Better yet, I'll join you and take a tour of the library."

"No!" Gavin's shout seemed to come from somewhere deep within, surprising him with its force. How could she know about Molly and the library?

The principal poked his head out of the office. "What's going on out here?"

"I beg your pardon," Bea answered. "I was asking Gavin for directions to my first class."

Did she just cover for me? Gavin stared at Bea, not sure what to make of her lie.

With his Marine-perfect posture, Mr. Smoot marched toward them, tall and stern.

Familiar heat crept up Gavin's neck, and he knew his face was turning radish-red. Was he in trouble? His mind spun in instant replay. Bea's smooth lie, how she read his thoughts, the way Eric fawned over her after she pointed that pen at him. *Bad news, all of it*, Gavin thought as the towering principal bore down on them with the promise of discipline in his eye.

With Mr. Smoot just out of earshot, Gavin found his voice, which came out sounding far more in control than he felt. "The library's a bad idea. Besides, there's really not much to see. Just books and stuff."

"This isn't over," Bea growled under her breath, a steely glint flashing in her eyes.

Gavin looked over his shoulder as Mr. Smoot approached and Bea relaxed her grip.

"Well, Beatrice," the principal smiled. "I see you make friends quickly."

Turning to Gavin, he scowled. "I thought you would have learned your lesson this summer, young man. You aren't becoming a troublemaker, are you?" Mr. Smoot continued before Gavin could answer. "Until recently, you were always such a good fellow." He chuckled over his pun. "*Goodfellow*, get it?"

"Yeah, uh, yes sir, I get it," Gavin mumbled. "I get it all the time."

Mr. Smoot gave Bea's cape a cheerful tug. "Well, you two had better be moving on. Classes are about to begin. We're glad to have someone of your social standing in our school, young lady. Hopefully your culture will rub off on some of our students."

"Thank you." Bea fluttered her eyelashes and waved her pen. "But this one," she said, nailing Gavin with a hard look, "is *such* a bore." With that, she walked off in a huff, leaving Gavin and Principal Smoot to stare at each other in puzzlement.

"Such a charming girl. I do hope she knows where she's going." Like magic, all trace of Mr. Smoot's irritation was gone. It was the first time Gavin ever remembered seeing Smoot smile.

"Maybe her pen guides the way," Gavin jibed, his humor falling flat with the principal. What *was* it with this girl? Gavin watched her purposeful retreat.

Eric loped around the corner—all elbows, knees, and grins as the bell sounded. "Hey, Beatrice, I lost you for a minute there. Let me walk you to your homeroom." He slipped his arm in hers.

Mr. Smoot straightened to his full height. "Well, she may not have warmed up to you much, Gavin, but she's quick on the uptake with your cousin."

"Yeah, uh, I mean, yes sir, I noticed that," Gavin said. And boy, was he glad for once that he *wasn't* Eric. "Gotta go. Don't wanna be late for class." He scooted past Eric and Bea without a word and, hanging a right, ran the last few steps down the hallway to his homeroom where Dexter stood in the doorway.

"*There* you are. I've been waiting for you." Dexter's grin turned to immediate concern. "What's wrong?" The boys dropped into their seats just as the second bell rang.

"Nothing," Gavin fibbed, struggling to catch his breath. "Just running late." His mind reeled—not just about the weird things that happened with Bea Daark and Hee-Haw, but about an uneasiness that had nothing to do with either of them. How much, if anything, should he tell Dexter? Knowing his luck, Woebe's old book would somehow tie in with the one Uncle Warney gave him to eat in the vision. That wasn't even real, yet more than a month later, he still had an aftertaste from it.

CHAPTER TWENTY-ONE

MOLLY
Clandestine Closet

After summer vacation, Molly was eager for the intellectual stimulus of school, more so than usual because of her new role as editor of *The Dragon's Voice*. Eighth grade was off to a jump-start as she headed for her next class. Already, with second period pre-algebra behind her, she had some fantastic notes.

"Pssst."

Startled by the errant sound, Molly stopped abruptly and stared at a closet door, slightly ajar. *What in heaven's name?*

"Pssst, Molly."

Edging closer, Molly spied a gaunt face peering at her.

Before the M of Mrs. Woebe formed on Molly's tongue, the woman put her finger to her lips, signaling silence. The school librarian hiding in a janitor's closet? Molly's heart pumped harder. There had to be a story here.

Looking both ways to make sure she'd drawn no attention, Molly took a reporter's pad from her purse and inclined against the wall by the

213

closet door. As editor of the school paper, her blank hall pass gave her a lot of latitude.

Once the bell rang and the hall cleared, Molly stepped inside the closet and flipped on the light. As she pulled the door closed behind her, she caught a glimpse of purple silk fluttering past her in the hallway.

Molly turned to find herself nose-to-nose with Mrs. Woebe. Was it only a year ago that she was ill-at-ease with the fidgeting librarian? *We don't call her "Woebegone" for nothing*, Molly thought as she waited for the woman to explain herself.

"The book, the book." Mrs. Woebe wrung her hands as though holding a wet dishcloth. "There's something wrong with the book." She waved two pieces of paper in Molly's face. "Two hall passes, one for you and one for Gavin. Meet me in the library during fifth period."

"But—"

"Be there." Before Molly could respond, Mrs. Woebe had nosed past her and scurried out the door and down the hall toward her inner sanctum.

Molly was used to Widow Woebegone's eccentric ways, but her frantic instructions—in the broom closet, no less—didn't make any sense. Something strange was going on, and Molly was just the one to get to the bottom of it.

When did it all start? That day in the woods . . . with the paths shifting and things flying around at the Lodge—the same day the Daarks flew in to meet with the Town Council. And then, for the month and a half or so that they were gone, things seemed to settle down. *But they're back, and things are getting weird again. Coincidence?* Molly thought not. Everything fit. The wax drippings and stuffed heads in the Lodge, the pointing pen—and what about that purple silk she'd seen just before she closed the door? That girl was bad news—but news was right up Molly's alley.

A chill ran through her at the notion that Bea Daark had been following her. What if she was standing outside the closet door when Mrs. Woebe was talking?

What if Bea was *still* lurking in the empty hall?

Opening the closet door a crack, she didn't see anyone.

"Now all I have to do is get Gavin to the library during study hall," Molly muttered to herself.

Gavin didn't even like to read. It was going to be no easy task convincing him to go to the library.

This is either going to be the best story ever written or Widow Woebe is truly gone, Molly thought as she stepped into the cooler air of the hallway and took a deep breath. The moment she did, an odd scent filled her nostrils—an overpowering aroma of musty-sweet vanilla. Cold, invisible fingers lifted the hair at the nape of Molly's neck. *Bea!*

CHAPTER TWENTY-TWO

Bea's Platform

Bea squirmed in her seat behind the cracked wooden desk. Annoyance drummed in her ears. Everything in her screamed *irritation*. Just when that chicken-faced librarian was squawking about the book, Principal Smoot came along and interrupted her eavesdropping. Of course, she'd claimed to be lost and laughed about mistaking a closet for a classroom, and he'd bent over backwards to see her to the right class. Not that the word *class* applied in any form to this dump of a school.

"What is this?" she muttered, running her finger around the perimeter of the hole in the upper right-hand corner of the desk.

"Beatrice, is there a problem?"

Bea sat up quickly and composed herself as best she could.

"No problem," she said. "I was trying to get a closer look at the, um, the . . . . For the life of me, I can't figure out why anyone would put a hole in what must have been a perfectly good desk."

A ribbon of soft laughter wound around the room.

Miss Jarvis shushed the students. "It's an inkwell, Beatrice," she replied, somewhat apologetically. "We don't use them anymore."

"I should think not." Bea smiled sweetly while she removed her Mont Blanc ballpoint pen from her handbag. *I wonder how long it will take Mum to get rid of this junk.* She tossed her hair away from her shoulders and leaned back. The chair tottered, and pain shot up her left thigh as her leg caught on splintered wood that threatened her designer skirt, not to mention her pride. She gritted her teeth and squirmed to avoid being pinched again, determined not to let anyone suspect the full level of her discomfort.

No wonder they wear those dreadful jeans. She looked around the stuffy room filled with thirty-two other students who had apparently learned to protect their legs. *Get ready, Sunken Bridge students, for you and your barmcake ways are about to change.* She smoothed her blue-violet silk skirt, now hopelessly snagged. Beads of perspiration dampened her forehead as she tugged at the neck of her cashmere sweater. In the UK, "back to school" meant cool weather and warm clothes, but here, the heat and humidity of early September made her clothing cling unmercifully. At least they provided a locker where her cape hung safely.

"This had better be worth the effort." Bea sat erect, trying to ignore the trickle of moisture that rolled down the center of her back. In order to avoid another encounter with the errant splinter, she didn't dare change position. *You'd think they'd have air conditioning.*

"Beatrice, do you have something to say?" The teacher turned away from the green chalkboard.

Yes, you old bat. You'll be the first to go, and soon. "I do hate to be a bother," Bea's British accent climbed up a notch, "but I must have a different chair. This one is ruining my skirt."

"Yes, of course. I'll mention it to the custodian," the teacher said, returning to the semester outline she was writing on the board.

"Excuse me," Bea continued. "I meant *now*. This is really quite bothersome."

The students laughed, and the teacher whirled around. "Excuse *me*?"

Good, Bea thought, controlling the smirk that teased her lips. "This chair is quite unacceptable. It is shredding my Jonnie Rayne. Mum will be absolutely livid when she sees that it's ruined . . ."

"Your what?"

"My Jonnie Rayne, you know, the haute couture designer in London."

"Be that as it may . . ."

"And since my garments are all one-of-a-kind and virtually irreplaceable—"

"Irreplaceable?"

"Oh! I am so sorry, Miss Jarvis. You buy off the rack, don't you?"

"What does that have to do with anything?"

"Jonnie Rayne is an internationally known designer who creates a line just for me, every year. This skirt, for instance, cost 450 pounds."

"You're wearing a $450 skirt to school?"

"Pounds, more like seven hundred and eighty-eight U.S. dollars," Bea replied, pleased that she'd moved the teacher so far off-track. Soft murmuring from her classmates assured her that she had made a strong impression. All was going as planned. "So you see, it really won't do to have my haute couture consumed by ill-kept furniture. So, if you could find me a desk without splinters, I would be most grateful."

"Yo, Miss Jarvis!" Eric practically tumbled out of his chair. "Beatrice can have my seat. It is absolutely splinter free!"

"Fine. Change seats, but be quick about it."

The teacher returned to the chalkboard, and Bea mouthed a "thank you" to Eric as she worked the room on her way to her new seat.

Situating herself comfortably, she put her ballpoint aside and eased Clyccan from her handbag. Gripping the barrel between her thumb and fingers, she rotated it several times. *This is going to be so easy. These provincials have no idea what they're in for.*

"Beatrice, does this new seating arrangement work for your wardrobe?" Miss Jarvis' sarcastic look matched her words.

"Quite," Bea replied in her most commanding tone. Her new vantage point from the back gave full access to everyone in the room. She gave Miss Jarvis her most attentive look while manipulating Clyccan in the palm of her hand. She didn't have to glance down to know that it was emitting a luminescent glow and had reached 105°.

"Good," Miss Jarvis said. "Now that the fashion crisis has been averted, please copy the semester outline. As for your math homework, turn to page . . ."

Bea placed Clyccan on the desk and flicked it gently so that it spun counterclockwise. "Now Clyccan," she whispered, and the pen began shooting droplets that turned instantly into a pixie dust-like substance that only she could see. Each smattering of particles found a target, and the students spewed out a wide variety of emotions, resulting in total chaos that delighted Bea to no end. Some laughed uncontrollably.

Others began to sob. A few hiccupped or jumped to their feet and started dancing. Some banged their fists on their desks and chanted, "Splunch, splunch. We want splunch."

The teacher appeared befuddled. She began erasing the chalkboard and muttering to herself. "No, I'm splorry." She blushed. "No, I mean, *sorry*. This isn't your semester outline, it's your splomework." She blinked. "No, I mean *homework*."

Bea basked in the commotion. *It appears that this class isn't so boring, after all.*

Just as she was about to charm the hands of the clock forward, the door opened and Hee-Haw entered. He winked at her and took a seat. The very sight of him drained the joy out of her, so she quenched the spell and returned Clyccan to her handbag.

"Quiet, class!" Miss Jarvis shouted. She must not have noticed, but order had already been restored.

Miss Jarvis' words faded to an indistinguishable drone. Bea offered Hee-Haw a plastic smile before glancing at her homework assignment. She learned this baby stuff two years ago.

Without any fanfare or comment from Miss Jarvis, Hee-Haw got up and left as quickly as he had entered. It was as though no one but Bea had seen him.

When will that blooming lunch bell ring? In answer to her impatient yearning, the buzzer whined like a dying fly. Before Miss Jarvis could dismiss the class, the students were on their feet and out the door.

Bea gathered her books, carefully slid out from behind the desk, and stepped through the doorway into the hall.

"Sir Eric, thank you for changing seats with me."

Eric took the books she thrust into his hands and started rambling on about football while they made their way to the cafeteria. She couldn't wait for this day to end so she could tell her mother about the book that Chicken Face had for Gavin. Could it be the same book her mother needed? Not likely. That would be much too convenient. But Laddrach and the gods *had* been smiling on her lately.

Any book requiring the librarian to meet Molly in a closet surely warranted looking into. Perhaps it *was* the diary that contained the clues they needed. Bea's pulse danced in her veins at the thought. If she could deliver the prize to her mum on the first day, maybe for once in her life she would receive the adulation she longed for. Of course, a hug from Madam Daark was out of the question since her mother wasn't the affectionate sort. Bea made up her mind to not only be in the library when the book was revealed but to have it in her possession by the end of the day.

In the meantime, she'd begin the task of choosing other members for her club. That meant getting acquainted with her dim-witted classmates.

Bea pulled the cashmere sweater over her head, deciding to finish the day in her orchid top. Flinging the sweater over her shoulder, the hallway became her runway where she tried to draw attention to her outfit. But the dolts seemed more focused on getting to the cafeteria than on meeting her. Judging from their lethargy, it was becoming increasingly clear that her fashions and style were wasted in Ashboro. She consoled herself with the idea that she was on a mission—a glorious mission that would change everything.

"Eric, be a dear and take these books to my locker," she said as she stopped to open her handbag. "Here's my combination." She jotted down the numbers on a scrap of paper. "I'll see you in the cafeteria."

While Eric walked away, she retrieved Clyccan once again, along with a 24-karat gold chain with a hollow crystal charm. Carefully, she inserted Clyccan into the crystal case, looped the chain over her head, and adjusted the pendant that dangled from her neck.

"If only you could speak real words, Clyccan," she whispered, stroking the crystal case that glowed red from its chemicals. "I see you're ready to go to work. Let's put you on display."

Within seconds, two girls from her class came over to her. "Oooh, what a beautiful necklace!" One of them reached out to touch it. "It looks like an upside-down cross."

"Watch out. I wouldn't do that if I were you." Bea stepped back from the girl's extended fingers. "This is more than a piece of jewelry. It's magical, endowed with high-tech chemicals. To the uneducated eye, it looks like a fountain pen, but it is really my compass and mood enhancer."

The two girls looked at each other in puzzlement, then laughed.

"What, like a mood ring that changes colors depending on your body temperature?" the dark-haired girl asked.

Bea chuckled at the brunette's naiveté. "Sort of." She wrapped her fingers around Clyccan, and it glowed blue, icy blue, signaling that these two would never be members of Daark's Dozen. They were unworthy.

"Wow," the girls spoke in unison, "it's *blue*."

"You must be, like, totally mellow," the brunette said.

"Like, that's totally awesome," the plump girl chimed in. "Really cool. I'd love to have something like that."

"It's an exclusive. You won't find it around here." Bea smiled as she moved away from the girls. Clyccan was working perfectly. Its beeps and colors would draw those with The Gift to her. Surely, there had to be someone here who possessed it, aside from Donkey Boy.

"Watch where you're going," she groused as she dodged an elbow in the overcrowded hallway. A curly-haired boy gawked at her and fixated on her necklace, which left her momentarily stunned, something she never allowed. *How utterly rude*, Bea thought as she turned her back to him.

She grabbed hold of the crystal case, which emitted a rainbow of colors. *Too many students too fast.* Clyccan must be confused by the cloud of bodies that assaulted its aura. Bea cringed and then willed her thoughts to consider the bright side.

At least Clyccan had managed to identify Eric as the perfect lackey. As pliable as putty, she could twist him into any shape that suited her. And he would be able to open doors to facilitate her plans.

Where is he, anyway? Bea stewed as she neared the cafeteria. *How long does it take to get to the lockers?*

Her eyes came to rest on Gavin who leaned against the opposite wall playing a handheld computer game. Not counting the riff in the hallway, and his eavesdropping from the seat behind her on the bus, there was something about that boy that irked her from the instant she saw him at the bus stop. She'd seen his name before. Ah, yes. She remembered. The letter their realtor had left on the kitchen counter upon their arrival last Saturday—some sort of lame apology for trespassing at the Lodge—was signed by none other than Gavin Goodfellow.

For one so humble on paper, how dare he have the nerve to rebuff her when she'd suggested oh-so-perfectly that she should be included in the library tryst during study hall. Was he so stupid that her charm had no effect on him? She'd had him off kilter, but somehow he pulled himself together.

He's trouble. Donkey Boy's warning played over in Bea's mind. What was it the oaf warned her about? Gavin's aura?

Well, aura or not, Bea sniffed in indignation, *I'm scheduled for study hall right after lunch, too, and I intend to be there at your meeting with Chicken Face.* Although not fond of the idea, she decided it might be expedient to befriend Gavin until she got what she was after.

Clyccan turned icy blue confirming Nem's warning about Gavin.

Fine. She'd be discreet and remain hidden, if necessary. But she'd go to the meeting in the library. Whatever it took, she intended to get her hands on that diary.

CHAPTER TWENTY-THREE

GAVIN

Infiltrators

After wolfing down the bologna and cheese sandwich he brought from home and spending a few minutes with Dexter, Gavin had found a quiet spot in the hallway and, ever so carefully, pulled *Infiltrators* from his backpack. It had been under lock and key while he was grounded, and school policy only allowed him to play it outside of class. *But I'm home free now*, he thought as both thumbs traveled over the buttons with lightning speed. Nagging thoughts of Woebe interfered with his concentration. *I'll look for Molly in a minute.*

Where Uncle Warney got the money for such an expensive birthday gift—or where he found it in the first place—was beyond Gavin, but who cared? *Infiltrators* was way cool. He'd even looked it up on www. gamefaqs.com. The fact that nobody had ever heard of it was truly strange, but that made it even more special. Gavin asked Uncle Warney about it once, and all he got out of him was a wink and something about it being a "spiritual experiment." Best of all, it had super graphics, great sound, and hardly required any reading.

By now, Gavin was adept at thumbing the buttons. Images of the magical crest floated beyond his grasp. There was something about the crest that reminded him of the Lodge, but he was too busy trying to land one of the six pieces in its place to think about it. If only he could get his warrior to grip the handle of that twirling knife.

Guess I'm out of practice, he groaned, pressing faster and harder. But the game met him with taunting beeps as if to say, "Ha, missed again!" The images appeared, but as he pounded the "A" button to capture them, they faded away beyond his grasp.

"Gavin," a voice sang out.

His head jerked up from the game in time to see Bea weaving her way through a dozen students. She seemed glad to see him.

"Were you waiting for me?"

"Like, not!" He shrugged off an involuntary shudder.

A high-pitched trill drew him back to his game. Pressing a series of buttons, he defeated one of the generals that threatened to overtake his army in a brilliant stroke of luck.

He felt her staring at him and turned the game away to block her view of the screen. Suspicion crept into his mind the same way it had when, running late as usual, he'd spotted Bea with her ear pinned to the janitor's closet before third period. It looked like she was eavesdropping, but what would there be to listen to on the other side of a broom closet door? Instead of stopping to see what she was up to, he'd scooted away from her as quickly as he could and continued on to his next class. Now, here she was again, creeping him out every time he turned around.

Without moving his eyes from the miniature screen, he said, "Bye. I'm sure you've got better things to do than hang out with a lowly seventh-grader."

"Actually, I was hoping you could tell me more about that old book we were discussing."

Beeep, rrrbing. "Nope. Haven't seen it. Don't intend to. Besides, I'm waiting for Molly." He glanced up, pretending to spot her. "Uh, there she goes now; must be headed to the cafeteria." Turning on his heel, he ducked around Bea without so much as a "See ya."

Gavin heard Bea mumble, "Well, of all the inconsiderate . . ."

Just as Gavin escaped one worrisome female, Molly (whom Gavin hadn't *really* seen headed for the cafeteria) stepped into the corridor from the opposite direction.

"Gavin!"

"Oh, I . . . I thought I saw you over there," he fibbed, pointing toward the cafeteria. Gavin glanced around to see if Bea had heard him, but she had left. At least, one pain was gone.

But Molly bore down on him like a woman on a mission, until she dropped one of her books. In the split second it took for her to bend down to retrieve it, Gavin slipped around the corner and into the boy's restroom.

Privacy, he thought, stepping into a stall.

He wished he could sit on the lid, but there was none. It was lucky that the rust-stained toilets were working at all. Deciding it would be better anyhow if his feet didn't show, he situated his bottom on the unsteady water tank and carefully placed his feet on the rim of the seat, as good a place as any to resume his electronic game.

Ignoring a pang of conscience, he refocused on the screen. It was on pause as he left it, but the moment he pressed "start," Gavin noticed a solidified image he had never seen before.

Ugly Cat? None other, with its one eye, broken ear, pole-straight tail, and singed fur.

"Cool." Uncle Warney must have a programmer friend who knows how to personalize games. The old man was full of surprises.

The cat opened its green eye, capturing Gavin's gaze. Try as he might, Gavin couldn't look away. It seemed to probe beyond Gavin's eyes, down deep to the place where he kept his secrets. Uncle Warney always said animals knew "what was what" about people. Could they see a person's soul? Guilt churned through Gavin over the lies he kept hidden there, including the two he'd just added to the pile.

It was wrong, a voice from within told him. Why had he been lying so much lately? The moment Gavin admitted his secret to himself, that it seemed easier to lie than to face the consequences, Ugly's face dissolved and the game went back to normal.

Relieved, Gavin resumed play. In a streak of particularly good luck, his warrior picked up several treasures in a row and landed them in their proper spots in the crest—a jeweled cross, a wooden flute, and a spinning stone used for sharpening knives. Much to his surprise, a new figure began to appear on the screen—a battered leather book. Slowly, the pages of the book opened, and the words "Be Ye Ready" appeared over the image on the screen, the first time ever.

Was this level two? *Oh, Uncle Warney, did you have to go and put that stupid book in here?* Excitement warred with the anxiety in his chest as he manipulated his warrior closer to the diary. The instant the warrior picked it up, another image began to materialize. He strained to make it out. A dog leash? No, it was . . . a belt, one of those big ones like wrestlers wear, but still a belt. What did that have to do with the crest and his warrior?

Tapping his long, arthritic fingers under his chin, Warney prayed for Gavin—again. He bent to the ground and grabbed his walking stick from the smoldering ashes that lay by his feet, planting it firmly on the gravel surface of the road.

"The Holy Spirit is all over me," Warney said to Ugly Cat who padded along beside him. Goosebumps raised the hair on Warney's arms. "Gavin's playin' the game." He knew it as sure as them buzzards were circling overhead.

Spirit of the livin' God, I'm a-countin' on You to use that contraption ta reveal truth ta Gavin in Yer own good time. If 'n it's too soon, fix it so's it won't mean no never mind to him.

A sizzle in Warney's spirit told him that Gavin was making poor choices again. "I know keepin' that young un on track is a mite like herdin' cats, Lord, but see to him fer me, would Ya?"

The bathroom door crashed open, nearly causing Gavin to fall off his perch, and Mr. Smoot's voice echoed off the tile walls. "Check the bathrooms every period. We don't want any smokers hiding out."

Oh, no! Bathroom patrol. How could I have missed the bell? Gavin hugged his knees to his chest, silenced the game, and held his breath.

"Yes, sir," one of the youth monitors said. "I don't smell any smoke, but I'll check the stalls."

None other than Billy Bragg's smelly sneakers approached. Gavin heard stall doors open and close with a series of bangs. Then a sneakered pair of feet stopped directly in front of his stall. The door rattled.

"Trouble?" Mr. Smoot boomed from the other side of the bathroom.

"Well, sir . . . it's stuck." It was Billy Bragg's voice, all right.

Gavin held his breath. The monitor dropped to his knees and the top of a curly-haired head appeared in the space beneath the door. Yep, Billy Bragg's hair.

"Doesn't seem to be anybody here," Billy said. "Maybe it's out of order and the janitor forgot to put up a sign. Want me to crawl under and check it out?"

"No. We can do that later. Let's finish our rounds."

Whew! That was close. Gavin's heart had never beat so fast.

"Probably some prankster locked the door and crawled out . . ." Billy's voice faded as he and the principal exited the boy's room.

The door had barely closed when a dying gasp drew Gavin's attention back to his game. In his carelessness, he had not turned off the sound, after all; even worse, he had dragged the knife straight into the heart of his warrior. Watching in morbid fascination, he saw the screen dissolve to blood-red.

"Noooo!" He couldn't lose Level Two now. He'd never get it back again. As he rose in disgust, shaking the game, his foot slipped off the edge of the toilet seat, plunging sneaker and leg into the bowl. The water splashed clear to his knees, thoroughly soaking his pant leg.

Gavin yanked his foot out of the toilet and sloshed over to the paper towel dispenser where he twisted the handle for all it was worth. Three measly towels and—empty. What next?

Why does everything have to happen to me? He groaned, grabbed his backpack from the hook on the door, and tucked the game into its pouch. Leaving a trail of wet footprints behind, he headed for study hall, water squirting out of the top of his right Nike with each step.

"There you are, Gavin," Mrs. Hoffman said when he walked into the room. "If it weren't for this hall pass Molly left for you, I'd have to mark you tardy." The study hall teacher handed over the slip of paper.

Gavin's shoulders fell when he saw it was for the library. "Thanks—I guess."

Surprise registered on Mrs. Hoffman's face. "Better hurry. She's waiting for you. You're excused."

Gavin's wet rubber sole screeched on the linoleum, fueling a wave of giggles as he turned to walk away. *Squish, thunk, squish, thunk, squish.* Gavin shuffled along, willing the floor to open up and swallow him.

"Wait," Mrs. Hoffman called after him.

Gavin pretended not to hear and sped up, squish-thunking in double-time out the door. How would he ever explain his wet foot?

"Excuse me, young man." Mr. Smoot's deep voice bellowed in his ear as he entered the hall.

Gavin's sneaker screeched as he turned around to face the inevitable.

"Sir?" he asked, looking up into the cavernous and hairy depths of Mr. Smoot's nostrils.

"Gavin, your pant leg is dripping."

Ya think? Gavin wanted to say, but all he could do was wince as Smoot's eyebrows knitted into a hedge over his eyes.

The principal assumed his military pose, crossing his arms over his chest. "Where are you going and how'd that happen?"

Gavin flashed his hall pass. His mind raced. "To the library . . . uh, outside at lunch . . . I stepped on a doggie log," he whispered. That would work. Dogs were always using the school grounds as a bathroom.

"Speak up. I didn't hear you."

"Stepped on a doggie log at lunch and tried to clean it up."

"A doggie log!" Smoot exclaimed, bewildered. "What are you talking about?"

"You know." Gavin winked. "A *stinky* doggie log."

Mr. Smoot's face grew dark with anger. "Gavin, what do you mean, 'a stinky doggie log?'"

For whatever kind of a degree principals had to have, Smoot could be dumber than dirt sometimes. "Poo." Gavin blurted out. "Poo, poo— doggie doo!"

Muffled laughter came from the classroom. Gavin glanced through the glass door and realized the only studying going on in there was of him. The only one who wasn't laughing was Dexter, and he looked worried.

Even Mr. Smoot stifled a chuckle. "I see. So you stepped in dog poop at lunch and then did what? Stuck your foot in the sink to clean it up?"

"Sir. Yes, sir." Making up a story about sticking his foot in a sink was certainly more acceptable than the truth. Gavin launched into a report on the boys' room being out of paper towels.

Talk about a day going to the dogs. The only thing worse would be if his father found out Gavin was late for class and got quizzed by Smoot twice in one day. Suddenly, the thought of Mrs. Woebe's library seemed better than spending another second under the principal's probing gaze.

CHAPTER TWENTY-FOUR

GAVIN

Mysterious Old Book

ecret books and stupid girls. Gavin frowned as he ducked around the doorjamb and into the library.

So, where is everybody? Gavin maneuvered around cubicles, tables, and stands. The sound of hushed female voices drew him to the back of the musty archives room.

He looked around the bookcase, finding Molly and Widow Woebe with their backs to the door and heads together, inspecting something under a Plexiglas case in the center of a round table.

"Oh, there you are," Gavin said in a voice way too loud for a library.

Molly wheeled around with a glare. "Shush!" In the blink of an eye, her ire melted into an up-to-something smile. "Come over here. You've got to see this."

"You never know who's lurking in the halls," Mrs. Woebe said, looking furtively around Gavin.

Oh brother, if she only knew, Gavin thought as he watched the librarian reach into a cardboard box. Or maybe she had seen Bea flitting around like a purple butterfly with radar ears.

"Put these on." Mrs. Woebe thrust something into Gavin's hands.

He scrunched up his face. "White balloons? What am I supposed to do with these?"

Slowly and deliberately, as though speaking to an imbecile, Widow Woebe said, "They're gloves, Gavin. Latex gloves."

"Gloves?" Gavin looked closely and saw that the balloons did indeed have five pouches extending from the end.

"Well, they look like balloons to me," he said with an embarrassed smile. "But my hands are clean." He turned his palms right side up and then over again to show her.

Molly drilled him with her I-couldn't-be-more-disgusted-with-you look.

"They'll keep the oils in your hands from damaging the book." Mrs. Woebe sniffled and dabbed a lacy handkerchief to her beak-like nose.

Gavin tried his best to figure out where to put his thumb. He stretched and pulled one of the gloves at odd angles, then held it over his head and looked up at it.

"Give me those." Molly snatched Gavin's gloves from him. Deftly grasping the wrist band, she held the glove open and waited for Gavin to shove his hand in it. "Sometimes you're dimmer than Eric." When his hand was secure, Molly let go. The latex snapped like a misfired cap gun, stinging his wrist.

"Ouch. That hurt!" Gavin's voice shattered the library's silence.

"Shhhh!"

"Shhhh!"

Gavin couldn't decide who had shushed him loudest, Molly or Mrs. Woebe. Before he could protest again, Molly snapped the other glove on his hand, and he found himself between them in front of the table with the mysteriously wrapped package.

Woebegone's hands were shaking so much that the hinges rattled when she lifted the case. "In addition to these large letters, 'For Gavin's eyes only,' obviously written recently—" She pointed to the aged newsprint wrapping, awe filling her voice. "Look closer. There's another message. The pencil impressions are barely legible, but . . . oh me, oh my . . ."

She handed Molly a magnifying glass. "Here, hold this for him." She began pacing and muttering in a higher pitch than normal. "The end is near; the end is nearly near."

"What's she talking about?" Gavin said as the fretful librarian collapsed into a nearby chair and leaned forward, resting her forehead on her hand. Through the magnifying glass that Molly held, Gavin could barely make out some letters. Gingerly, he removed the package to see it better. The edge of the flimsy, brown newspaper crumbled in his gloved fingers. A piece floated to the floor.

Widow Woebegone sat up, stunned. "How can that be so delicate? Moments ago, that paper was as tough as rubber." She shoved herself up from the chair, breathless.

"Gavin, be careful!" Molly gasped.

Startled, Gavin lost his grip and dropped the package like a hot potato. "You guys sure know how to make a person nervous," he growled as he knelt to make out the rest of the print. "It looks like it says, 'Sealed until' . . . something . . . 'shall come,' but I can't make out the rest."

Molly pushed him aside and squinted at it through the magnifying glass. "I can read it fine. 'Sealed until the Day shall come when—'" She paused, her voice growing softer. "'Gavin Goodfellow becomes of age.'" She looked at Gavin is if he'd grown a wart on the tip of his nose.

Gavin grabbed the magnifying glass from her hand. "What? Let me see that!" He picked up the package from the floor and held it close to his face, his eyes widening in disbelief. "That *is* my name. But maybe it's a different Gavin Goodfellow."

"Don't be silly," Molly said. "It's not like you have a real common name like Smith or Jones."

"Okay. Okay then, Miss Smarty Pants, why would *my* name be on this thing?"

Mrs. Woebe began to pace beside the table. "I've asked myself the same question a hundred times. Why would someone write *your* name on a book and place it in my library? Why, you hardly ever set foot in here."

Gavin started to counter her insult but couldn't get the words out.

"And even stranger," she continued without so much as a breath, "try as I might, I haven't been able to unwrap it. It's like the paper's glued to the book."

Gavin flicked a piece of the loose paper off. "It isn't now."

Mrs. Woebe's face took on a new level of panic. "Now look what you've done! That paper could have historic value." She shivered visibly as though struck by another thought and lowered her voice. "It could be cursed. Do you think someone has cursed it?" She crossed her thin arms over her chest as if the temperature had dropped. "Curses are real, you know, as real as blessings." She began chewing her practically nonexistent fingernails.

Gavin could even see her pulse beating in the blue vein in her temple.

"Its . . . its appearance is supernatural," she said in a shaky voice. "I know the rare book collection by heart, and I tell you—" She slid back into a chair, slumping her shoulders together like weak bookends. "Th-this package appeared on the shelf out of nowhere."

"Well, I'm sure there's a logical explanation." Molly picked at the corner of the newsprint wrapping. "Let's see what's inside."

"Hey," Gavin shouted to Molly. "It says for my eyes only!"

Mrs. Woebe shushed him. "You're in the library, young man."

"All right, then, why don't you try to open it?" Molly challenged, handing the parcel to Gavin.

"Okay. No problem. I love to open presents."

In one swift ripping motion, he tore the newsprint right off. From Widow Woebe's gravelly gasp, Gavin thought sure she would faint, but she didn't. She stared at the book in his hand.

The thick leather cover, embossed with the word "DIARY," was hand-bound with two holes drilled through the left side and laced with a faded bluish-purple ribbon. For all the fuss, the book didn't seem to have very many pages. But the way it made him feel compelled Gavin to put it ever so carefully on the table. Like his composed answer to Bea earlier, he felt surprisingly calm, as if someone else was directing him. His fingertips tingled. Glancing up at Mrs. Woebe and Molly, he wondered if they felt anything.

"You can look at it if you want." He offered the book to Mrs. Woebe. After all, she was the book nut, not him.

"I'm not touching it," the old woman answered in a mouse-like squeak, her face bunched up like a prune. "It's for your eyes only."

"I will," Molly said, picking it up without hesitation and attempting to open it. "That's weird. The cover won't budge. It's like this thing has an invisible lock."

"I told you it was cursed . . . or something." Widow Woebe's fingers fluttered at her neck.

Gavin barely heard her. Something wasn't right about Molly having the book. He knew it and felt it. The word NO hammered in his brain so loud that he could hardly hear the conversation between Molly and Mrs. Woebe.

Then, he couldn't see them. Instead, he saw a re-run of Uncle Warney holding out a musty-smelling diary and instructing him to "eat it." Gavin tasted the dried apricots, juicy apples, and 7-Up. Repulsed and thrilled at the same time by the bittersweet memory of the vision he'd had in the swamp, this time, he didn't faint. Gavin's senses were keener than ever—in fact, every nerve in his body was on alert. He could feel the hair raising on his arms.

"Excuse me," a prim British voice intruded.

The vision disappeared, and Gavin found himself back in the library.

"Could you kindly direct me to where I might find Mrs. Woebe?"

The overwhelming scent of vanilla invaded Gavin's senses. *Bea!* Instinctively, he knew he couldn't let her near the diary. Gavin leapt into action. "Let me have that." He grabbed the book out of Molly's hand and scanned the room for a way to escape Bea's detection. "It's not safe here." His words were low but spoken with such authority that the librarian stepped back and gaped as he tucked the book under his shirt.

"You're right," Mrs. Woebe agreed, shaking as violently as an off-balance washing machine. "By all means, remove this book from my library. It feels like it doesn't belong here."

Molly narrowed her gaze at the librarian. "Books don't feel."

"This one does," Gavin replied. *Maybe old Woebegone isn't so gone, after all.*

"Gavin Goodfellow, what's gotten into you?" Molly demanded with fists clenched as tight as her braid.

Gavin couldn't explain. He didn't understand it himself. "Later! We can't let Bea see this book!"

"I have no idea what you're talking about, but . . ." Molly was shocked into submission by Gavin's commanding tone. "At least get that book out from under your shirt before you go messing it up."

Gavin removed it and almost laughed from the unexpected tickle it gave him.

Molly turned to the librarian who was leaning against the wall, fanning herself with her hand. "Mrs. Woebe, would it be okay if we let Uncle Warney look this over?"

"P-p-perfect," Woebe answered, relief washing over her drawn face. "Warney knows about such things."

Mrs. Woebe, with her eyes darting, herded Gavin and Molly toward the back of the library to the "staff only" door. "If at all possible, get it to your uncle before the end of the week, and find out what this is all about." She hesitated and patted her hair with trembling fingers. "Let me know when. Maybe I should come, too."

Gavin and Molly looked at each other.

"No," Woebe said. "On second thought, just give him my regards."

"Hello, is anybody here?"

Mrs. Woebe glanced toward the approaching voice as Bea drew near.

"We will," Gavin assured her, handing the book over to his cousin. "Here, Molly, wrap this in your sweater."

Molly took the diary and did as he said. "But *this* is mine," she told him, rolling up the newspaper. "Old papers always have something good in them."

Keeping an eye out for Bea, Gavin peeled off his latex gloves and dumped them in the wastebasket. "Take those off and act normal," he said, glancing at Molly's gloved hands. "You can read that paper later."

He saw Mrs. Woebegone press her hand against her neck as if she'd had heatstroke. She heaved a sigh and then headed to the workstation at the center of the library.

"Gavin, you're up to your neck in something big here," Molly said, dropping her gloves into the trash can.

"May I help you, dear?" Mrs. Woebe distanced herself from them.

"Yes ma'am." Bea's voice followed Gavin and Molly to the staff exit. "Are you here alone? I was sure I heard voices."

Mrs. Woebe's response was cut off by the gently closing door.

Molly stopped Gavin on the opposite side of the door. "Look, I didn't want to drill you in front of Woebe. What's with you grabbing the book and looking so weird?"

"I think I had a sort of vision, maybe," he admitted.

"What kind of hare-brained nonsense are you talking about? Dreams and visions? And what's this got to do with Bea? We've got enough of a mystery with this crazy diary that materializes out of nowhere with your name on it and locks itself up."

Molly caught her breath, and her eyes misted over. "I'm scared, Gavin. None of this makes any sense. What do you know that I don't?"

"We need to see Uncle Warney, and we have to keep this book away from that new girl. She's creepy." Gavin leaned closer to Molly. "I think she can read minds or something." He chewed his lip.

"Really?" Molly shuddered.

Gavin nodded his head solemnly. "She's eerie to the umpteenth power."

Molly glanced over her shoulder and then frowned at Gavin. She had a way of making him feel it was somehow all his fault.

His gaze drifted to Molly's backpack. "All I know is that Bea is bad news. I can feel it in my bones."

Molly chuckled. "Now you sound like Uncle Warney."

Gavin couldn't disagree. Uncle Warney's bones told him all kinds of things. And Uncle Warney had visions. Now Gavin was having them. It was like inheriting some sort of bad gene. Why him?

"You've got the book, right?" Gavin felt paranoid.

"Yep." Molly patted her backpack and adjusted it over her shoulder. "Safe and sound right here. I'll get it back to you after school."

"That'll work." Gavin cracked his knuckles, a nervous habit.

"Now," Molly flashed a smile, "let's just finish out the day and try to lighten up."

"Easy for you to say. It wasn't your name on that thing." *It won't be any easier to lighten up than to ace history.* "And if you get any bright ideas of how I can convince Dad to let me go to Uncle Warney's, let me know, huh?" Gavin sighed.

Not likely. His dad had laid the law down a long time ago. The way Gavin figured it, Uncle Warney—his mom's uncle—must have either said or done something that ticked off Bruce Goodfellow, big time. Maybe it went back to the argument they say his dad got into with Uncle Warney at the Leavitt Thanksgiving dinner in 1996. Whatever the reason, his dad seemed to despise his mom's side of the family. Gavin hated how it felt to be in the middle of a family feud.

"Hey! Isn't Thursday Uncle Warney's birthday? That ought to work. We can go after school—"

A clap of thunder came so loud and fast that Gavin thought he'd been shot.

CHAPTER TWENTY-FIVE

GAVIN

Nailed

"Hey, Molly," Gavin pointed as he broke through the clearing about a quarter of a mile from Uncle Warney's shack. "There he is now. This is great—let's surprise him right here."

"Happy Birthday!" Gavin and Molly cheered in unison.

The old man stumbled backward two steps and grinned as he clasped his chest in feigned heart-failure. "My lands, you two sure know how to give a body a start. If you ain't a sight for sore eyes."

Molly held out a homemade pie wrapped in plastic. "Mom timed it to come out of the oven right after school. Sweet potato, your favorite."

"Yer thoughtfulness takes muh breath away." Warney wheezed.

"Maybe we shouldn't have jumped out at you like that." Gavin fretted as Uncle Warney pulled out his inhaler.

"Not to worry. I'd be in this fix with or without ya. The stables seem to be gettin' farther off every day." He pulled two long draws from his puffer and smiled. "Other than you, one of the few joys in muh life is carin' fer them gentle giants."

"They're real beauties, Uncle Warney."

Gavin knew he meant the magnificent pair of Clydesdales grazing in the pasture next to the run-down stable. They were Uncle Warney's only reason to visit what remained of the family estate. Anytime Gavin asked why he didn't live in the big house, Uncle Warney would say he'd rather live like a hermit in his shack of a home than to risk people barging in and robbing him of his peace of mind.

Uncle Warney shoved his hand deep into his pocket and fingered something. The faraway look on his face made Gavin cringe. He knew that look. Preaching always came with it.

"Found this on muh way back." He pulled out a two-and-a-half-inch steel-cut nail. "One o' the last things I got from Abbott Supply Company when they went and sold out. It's got a nice feel to it—not rough and jagged like you'd expect, but smooth and time-worn. Kinda like me and muh eighty-three years."

Yep, here comes the sermon.

"Something told me to hang onto it," Warney said.

Gavin glimpsed at the nail, probably from an old roof. It didn't look like anything special, but for some reason it made him gulp and feel jittery inside, reminding him of the diary which freaked him out.

"Are you going to start collecting nails now?" Molly asked as if everything were normal. "To go with your assortment of strings and bottles?"

"Maybe so." Uncle Warney shoved the nail back into his pocket and never said another word about it.

That's it? Gavin's heart began hammering the minute he saw the nail, and it was still going strong. The absence of a sermon hit him harder than if Uncle Warney had preached for an hour. At least he didn't have to worry about carrying on a conversation. Molly chattered enough for all three of them.

By the time they entered the shack, Gavin couldn't stand it another minute. "I brought you a present," he blurted out, producing the diary from his backpack and placing it on the table.

"Well, I'll be." Warney scratched the stubble on his chin with a gnarled finger and glanced from the book to Gavin. "'Bout time." His eyes fairly danced. "Here, Molly, let's have that pie. This is cause fer celebration!"

"Waddaya mean, *about time?*" Gavin threw up his hands in exasperation. "You knew about this all along?"

"Guilty as charged." Warney offered a sheepish grin as he placed the pie on the counter and gathered up several plates.

Molly pranced around in a circle, barely missing Ugly Cat's paws. "I *knew* it was your handwriting." She spread the old newspaper on the table and smoothed out the creases. "Only you could come up with—'Sealed until the Day shall come when Gavin Goodfellow becomes of age.'"

Warney's face crinkled into a smile.

It was impossible for Gavin to steady his erratic pulse. "Why all the secrecy? If you wanted me to have this moth-eaten thing, why didn't you just give it to me?"

"How was I s'pposed to give it to ya when yer dad won't let ya near me?"

For a fleeting moment, Uncle Warney sounded testy but his cheerful disposition returned so quickly, Gavin thought he must have imagined the frown.

"We got this here diary starin' up at us, and I reckon ya got plenty more questions. That right?"

"You bet I do." Gavin decided it was his turn to be testy. "One big one. What's this got to do with me?"

Uncle Warney pivoted with his walking stick and motioned the youngsters to sit down. "A week or so after the fire started—when you was nothin' but a little tyke, Gavin—the Lord give me a clear word to wrap the diary in that thar paper and put yer name on it 'til ya come of age. I learnt long ago not to try to figure everything out at once. So I done what I was told." Slicing the pie in slow, methodical swipes, Uncle Warney served up plates to each of them. "Then the Lord goes and tells me ta seal up the words of the book in a safe place. So I prayed protection over the diary and stuck it under muh floorboards, never attemptin' to open it again."

"All this time you've had this priceless treasure under your floorboards?" Molly stared with her mouth open.

Gavin squirmed in his seat. "Why bring it out now? And why me? You still haven't answered that."

"I'm gettin' ta that. One thing at a time. Go ahead, now, eat yer pie. Sure smells good."

Gavin took a bite and savored the spicy blend. "Mmm, still warm. Go on, Uncle Warney," he said with his mouth full. "Talk."

"Now, where was I? Oh, yeah. Week before last, the Lord tells me it's time, so Ugly and me, we dug it out and come up with a right smart way to git it into yer hands without dishonorin' yer daddy's limits."

"Couldn't you have just waited 'til now and handed it to me?"

"Didn't rightly know when I'd be seein' ya again, now, did I? Lookin' back, it might not a been the smartest thing I ever done." He chuckled. "But, keep in mind, it don't do to question the Lord's timin'."

Gavin waved his hand in a gesture of dismissal. "Okay, so I got it. But what good is a book that won't open up? See?" Gavin reached for the book. This time, though, when he lifted the cover, the pages opened as easily as any ordinary book.

Molly gasped and Gavin felt as though his eyes would pop right out of his head.

"It's been a long time since I laid eyes on them pages," Uncle Warney said softly.

Gavin inspected the faded ink and tiny, curly-Q penmanship. A hand-drawn border of ivy leaves decorated the pages.

"Let me see that!" Molly grabbed the book, only to have it slam shut the minute her fingers touched it. "But, but . . . I didn't . . ."

"You didn't what?" Gavin demanded. "Do anything? Yes, you did! I get it open and you go and mess it up!"

"Calm down," Warney chuckled. "That book can be a mite temperamental. It's fer yer eyes only, Gavin. Guess the diary's smart enough to know whose hands got a hold of it."

Gavin would just as soon never touch or look at the thing again, but he had to admit that the thought of it being "for his eyes only" made him feel special.

Ugly Cat gave a low, guttural growl, more like a dog than a cat, and rubbed against Warney's leg. The cat's pink lips pulled into a threatening curl and his ears, even the broken one, laid flat against his head. Squinting his one good eye, he stalked toward the window like a cougar slinking toward its prey.

"What's wrong with him?" Gavin asked.

"Shhh." Warney crept to the window and wrinkled his nose while he looked outside as if sensing something unpleasant. "Think I'll let Ugly go out for a spell."

As Warney moved, the cat's back shot into an arch, and he darted to the back door where he waited until Warney hobbled over to let him out.

Gavin heard Ugly's war screech, then a clear but faint *ribbitt*, the muffled sound of running feet, and the thud of an overturned trash can. "What's that?" He suspended his fork in mid-air.

"Pay no never mind to that ruckus," Uncle Warney said. "If we had any intruders, sounds like Ugly's taken care of 'em." He placed his hand on the diary and gave it a tender pat. "So ya want to know what this book's got to do with you, eh?" Warney said.

Gavin nodded, his mouth full of pie.

"There's a bittersweet callin' on yer life, Gavin. Bitter 'cause them forces of darkness are real and close. Sweet 'cause the Lord is yer strength and ever-present help. God chose ya 'cause—"

"But I'm the *last* person God should have picked." Gavin was freaked out enough before, but now a true shiver of panic shot through him. He could feel Uncle Warney's eyes boring into him. "There must be some mistake. How about Molly? She'd be great. Why can't it be *her*?"

Uncle Warney studied Gavin for a moment and then spoke gently. "God don't make no mistakes, Gavin. He knows who He picked and why."

"Besides." Molly smiled. "I just thought of a verse that makes sense. 'God chose the foolish things of the world to confound the wise and the weak things to shame the strong.'"

Gavin didn't know whether to yell at Molly or to thank her. He knew he felt "foolish and weak," but did she have to say so, especially in front of the only person in Ashboro who thought he could do something right?

"I'm a better reader than Gavin," Molly said with a sudden burst of enthusiasm. "I'll bet God wants me to help him solve this mystery." She reached for it again.

"Ouch!" Her hand flew to her mouth. "That thing nearly burned my fingers!"

"Whoa!" Gavin snickered. "Not very quick on the uptake, are you, Mol?"

"Settle down, now." Warney held up his hand like a stop signal. "Think ya mighta learnt yer lesson this time? Told ya that book can be a mite persnickety."

"More like scathing," Molly said.

"Whatever," Gavin said. "I don't want anything to do with that, that . . ." He pointed a shaking finger at the diary. "*That* . . ."

"Before ya throw a tizzy fit, hear me out." Uncle Warney leaned forward.

Gavin didn't want to hear another word. All he really wanted was to leave, but then that would prove Molly right. She already thought he was a coward and a quitter. *Maybe I am.*

"Can I ask a question?" Molly said.

"Sure, fire away," Warney said as he got up from the table to let Ugly in.

"Who wrote the diary?"

"Ah, good question." Warney smiled. "That warrants a fittin' answer that would take too long to go into today. Fer now, how 'bout if ya both jest promise me one thing?"

"What's that?" Gavin asked.

"Sure, anything," Molly said at the same time.

"Can I have yer pledge that ya won't breathe a word about this?"

"Not to anyone?" Molly looked puzzled. "What about Mrs. Woebe? What are we supposed to tell her?"

"Yeah," Gavin said. "She's gonna quiz us for sure."

"Jest leave the widow to me." Warney sighed in a respectful way. "You'd never know it from her skittish ways, but she's a mighty prayer warrior. She'll be on her knees about this—prob'ly already is. Now whadaya say? Can I have yer word?"

"You have my word," Molly said.

"Scout's honor," Gavin vowed, holding up three fingers and straightening his posture.

Molly frowned. "What kind of promise is that? You're not a Boy Scout."

"I know. Okay, then . . . cross my heart." Gavin fingered an X on his chest.

"A simple 'I promise' would be best." Molly looked at Uncle Warney. "And I do."

"Me, too. I promise," Gavin said reluctantly. After all, he didn't want to ruin Uncle Warney's birthday.

Somehow Gavin had thought he'd be able to give the diary to Uncle Warney and that would be the end of it. Instead, saying his goodbyes on the porch, he realized his entire uneventful life had been turned topsy-turvy. This was the kind of stuff that happened to kids on television and in the movies, not in real life. If there was any way to wiggle out of this, he was going to have to find it.

"Ya got that book tucked in thar safe 'n sound, right?" Uncle Warney patted Gavin's backpack and wrapped his strong, bony arms around him in a bear hug.

"I'll take gooohoood care of it." Gavin felt like Uncle Warney squeezed the words right out of him.

A piercing scream ripped through the air, sending Gavin's heart thudding against his rib cage.

"Somebody's in trouble!" Molly swung around in the direction of the scream.

"A girl, it sounds like," Gavin ventured, almost afraid to think or say another word.

"It's comin' from the swamp." One of Uncle Warney's gnarled hands clutched Gavin's shoulder; the other pointed toward the path that led deeper into the swamp. "That-a-way!"

"But I'm not allowed to go into Burnt Swamp." Gavin didn't like the sound of that girl's scream.

"Not in a matter o' life or death?"

"Come on, Gavin." Molly grabbed him by the arm. "No time for debate—that girl's in big trouble. We've got to save her!"

CHAPTER TWENTY-SIX

Quicksand and Brimstone

The more Bea thrashed in the quicksand, the harder it pulled her down. With her arms and legs flailing, she strained with all her might to wrench herself out of the soupy mixture of sand and water. But the gritty liquid held her feet firmly in its murky bed as the water level inched its way almost to her waist.

If only that mousy librarian had told her what she needed to know about the diary when she cornered her on Tuesday . . .

If only she hadn't trailed Gavin and Molly into these blasted woods . . .

If only she hadn't stepped on that *huge* frog. It was as if that ghastly thing knew of her phobia and chased her into this trap.

She screamed again, gripped by a fresh wave of reality. There was no one to help her. Or was there? It was hardly feasible, but— "Shimera!" Bea cried out. "Help me! Show yourself strong. The Order has sent me to do your bidding. How would you like a big fat frog for dinner?"

What if the dragon refused to reveal himself? No one had seen it yet. But no one had *needed* Shimera until now. Her need would surely compel Laddrach's beast to the surface. She relaxed at the thought of being the very first to see it. Wait? Were the murky chains loosening? Bea tried pulling her feet up once again only to find herself more bound than before.

"Stupid frog!" She couldn't see it, but it must be out there somewhere. "If you're not the one that Eric kicked, you should have been! You and that cursed cat!" Angry, Bea struggled all the more, only to be driven deeper into the quicksand.

"Help me, somebody! Anybody!" Exhausted from her struggle, she considered her surroundings. Having run too far, too fast, she had plunged headlong into this sinkhole and was fully in the grip of the festering swamp. The best she could figure, the slime pit she'd fallen into was three to four meters long and twice as wide. The small clearing she had stumbled upon was surrounded by dense clumps of blackened cypress trees that extended an umbrella of charred branches overhead, well beyond her reach. A scraggly mishmash of low-lying scrub bushes and thorny underbrush were surprisingly green, apparently untouched by the flames. Bea had been yearning to cross the line of no return and enter into the mysterious Burnt Swamp, but not this way!

"This can't be happening to me!" Still sinking, Bea fought to gather her wits as a fresh wave of acrid odor assaulted her nostrils. The smell was worse than Donkey Boy and the heat unbearable, except for the hint of a breeze that stirred the simmering coals.

Surely Shimera would come. But soon enough? What if he was too deep in his cave to hear her?

Stay calm.

Magick could not be rushed. Bea took deep breaths to try to calm herself. Instead, a wave of panic overcame her.

"Help! Somebody, anybody—*help* me!"

But how could anybody hear her this far from civilization? Maybe this was a test from the Order. Surely, they hadn't sent her to this dreadful place to be swallowed up in the same swamp that was to be Ashboro's gateway to enlightenment. She was sent there to lead—not to be swallowed!

Wait. Hadn't she been given authority over the creature who dwelt beneath? Yes. And it was high time to use it. The time for pleading was over.

Bea recited an incantation under her breath, then shouted with authority, "Show yourself, Shimera. In the Name of the Order of the Knights of Laddrach, I command you to reveal yourself!"

Nothing. Nothing aside from the usual sparks the swamp gave off at its whim, igniting around her like misspent firecrackers. Fear-fed panic swept through her. *"Now!"* she commanded. "Show yourself *now*, you worthless phantom!"

A haunting silence remained. She might as well have recited a nursery rhyme. No swamp dragon was going to deliver her.

Clyccan gave a jolt. Grabbing the pendant from around her neck, She held it above the rising sand. The magic pen vibrated in her hand, radiating every color of the rainbow.

Ducky. Just ducky. "Some help you are." Her voice was hoarse with frustration. "Danger, danger, is that what those colors mean? No kidding!"

Bea tried hard to kick the muck away, doing her best to keep her balance while she relocated the pen to a safer place behind her ear. She envisioned the gunk claiming her arms, her chin, her mouth. What would it be like when that awful stuff reached her nose?

Bea shuddered, looking about frantically until she spied a nearby tree branch. Of course! She'd seen this done in the movies a hundred times.

But the more she twisted her torso in an attempt to reach the overhang, the tighter the swamp glue gripped her foot. She lunged and flailed, almost committing the rest of her body to the soupy pond. Aside from the branch being too far away, it looked rotten and was scorched black.

A flicker of something stung Bea's arm. A hot cinder! The quagmire glowed orange. Everything around her festered. Sparks flicked and skittered among the dry leaves on the ground, igniting them and singeing her mint green Jonnie Rayne blouse.

Calm down. It could be worse. At least the liquid around her waist felt warm, not boiling. Or did it feel hotter now than when she first fell in? Was it her imagination? No, the temperature was definitely rising.

I can't die like this! I won't be boiled alive! Thrashing, she released another scream.

Suddenly, a piece of charred wood plopped next to her. Glancing above, Bea spied a pale shadow of Hee-Haw floating overhead. Her mind reeled in a crazy mixture of fear and hope as she tried to make sense of the wisps of matter that resembled the boy she despised. She had never seen an out-of-body person before.

"Over here!" She thrust a hand into the air.

Hee-Haw's transparent body circled the perimeter before drifting toward her, but her relief turned to instant horror. Every time his spirit body floated past a tree, another limb broke loose, crashing to the ground. Now hot coals surrounded her and seemed to be closing in like sharks circling their prey. Hee-Haw floated in front of her nose where he remained, his grating donkey laugh confirming Bea's suspicion that he was toying with her.

"Wipe that grin off your wretched mug and help me," Bea said.

"What? The pretty witch got herself in a brew she can't get out of?" Hee-Haw brayed again.

"How dare you mock me! The Order will be furious if you don't get me back on solid ground at once."

Hee-Haw floated closer, gazing into her eyes.

An icy bolt ran through her, so cold that it made her quiver in the warm quicksand. She felt a sinister presence probe her soul.

"Me?" he gloated. "It's not my job to get you out of your messes. Why don't you just call on that snazzy pen of yours to pull you out?"

Bea touched Clyccan. Still tucked behind her ear, she was both comforted by the tingle of its warmth and dismayed by its proven uselessness. "I've tried that."

"What about your spirit guide? Have you called on him?" Hee-Haw's toothy grin was as offensive as his taunts.

"I don't need a spirit guide. I'm under the direct supervision of the Order of Laddrach. Now, get me out of here!"

"What's the magic word?"

"Please," Bea replied in a small, frightened voice that felt like it belonged to someone else. It sickened her to beg, but what choice did she have? "We're partners, remember?"

"Sorrrrry." Sarcasm dripped from Hee-Haw's lips. "My spirit man can't lift anything." His voice was absolutely emotionless, and it chilled her.

"You impotent ghost!" Bea railed.

Hee-Haw's form flickered. "Hey, just be glad you can see me at all. Few people can, you know." His voice faded away. "So, why don't you wait here while I go get my body. If you're a good little witch, I just might help you out of your mess—or not."

Bea felt weak all over. Her legs began to shake, and she fought collapse. "No, don't leave me! I can't be alone—"

But he was gone, dissolved into a puff of smoke. A dozen branches tumbled in his wake, causing another shower of red hot cinders to explode near her face. Misery gave way to sheer panic.

"Help, help!" She tried to yell, but her vocal chords wouldn't work. A pathetic squeak no louder than a series of squirrel chirps leaked slowly from her lungs in a defeated sort of way.

And then she heard it.

A faint but clear, "Helloooooo."

Someone was coming!

The gods had heard her, after all, and help was on the way.

"Over here!" she cried, barely eking out the words as a floating log inched within reach. Gavin and Molly burst into the clearing.

"Oh, no!" Molly panted. "Look at you!"

Is there no end to my humiliation? This must surely be a test.

"There's a circle of fire all around you!" Gavin shouted and ran back the way he came. "Uncle Warney! Hurry, we need your cane!"

"Try to relax," Molly said, inching as close as she dared. "The more you struggle, the faster you'll sink."

"Right. Relax, you say?" Bea fought against every instinct and tried to let her arms go limp. "I can't."

"I know it's hard, but if you just lean back and relax, your body will float."

"I can't. The muck's got hold of my foot."

"Try anyway. Relax." Molly raised her voice.

"Easy for you to say. *Your* feet aren't stuck in this wretched filth!"

Attempting to regulate her breathing, Bea watched Gavin return, urging the old man who was wheezing his way toward them to walk faster. Irritation displaced panic as she waited for her rescuers to get her out of the slimy mess. A soft rustle drew Bea's attention to the backpack Gavin slung over a bush. Could it contain the prize she coveted? Was this why Shimera failed to rescue her? So she could retrieve the book?

"You are indeed wise," she whispered, tearing her gaze from the backpack and wobbling slightly in the mire. She studied the old man Gavin was tugging her way. His ruddy face looked stern.

"Here she is, Uncle Warney." Gavin gestured as though directing traffic. "Stuck, see?"

She didn't like this Uncle Warney person. Not one bit. She didn't like the shape of his shaved head or the look in his eye as he stood over her with his hands crossed on the head of his walking stick.

"Got yerself in a pickle, young lady?" His relaxed smile and deep voice sent a shiver through her.

Bea avoided his hazel eyes, fearful that they could see into her heart. That would never do. *Steady, girl.* Her mind reeled. "Well, are you going to get me out?"

"Yep," he said simply, continuing to stand like the fossil he was.

Molly put her hands on her hips. "I told her to relax, Uncle Warney."

"What are you waiting for?" Bea would have stomped her foot if she could. "Get me out of here!"

A stern look came over the old man's face, and he began to glow as if encased in a full-body halo. Was this one of the auras Hee-Haw had prattled about?

"The Lord is not slack concerning His promises as some men count slackness but is longsuffering . . ."

Although Bea saw the old bloke's lips move, his words echoed with the resonance of a distant place. Discomfort settled in her spirit as Clyccan started vibrating even harder than before. *Danger! Danger! Get away, danger!*

"The Lord is not willing that any should perish, but that all should come to repentance."

Every word penetrated like the blade of a knife. Bea bristled. "Shut up and get me out of here!"

Gavin leaned down to her. "Sometimes he gets like that."

"We have to hurry," Molly said. "Gavin, *do* something."

"Can I borrow this?" Not waiting for an answer, Gavin took the gnarled stick from his uncle's hand. "Grab onto this," he commanded, holding the cane out to Bea. Molly stepped back.

Bea gripped the walking stick with both hands. Instantly, a series of electric shocks passed through her body. Wave after wave of current washed over her. She gasped for air, but smoke from the fire burned her lungs. It was more like the cane had a hold of her than she did of it. Was the old man some kind of rival wizard?

Gavin tugged, straining against the pull of the quicksand that tightened even more against her foot while the old man stood at a distance with a blooming grin on his face.

Bea met Gavin's gaze over the length of the cane, and an inexplicable feeling crept up her neck. Terror yielded to arrogance. This klutz, with no sophistication or power other than his scrawny arms . . . whose only attraction was the diary in his possession . . . made her feel—what, vulnerable? Never.

Gavin gave one more tug, causing Bea to lose her grip. He sprawled on the ground, cane in hand.

The old man stepped forward. "That ain't how it's done," he said matter-of-factly. "Gentle like, real slow, young lady. I want ya to wiggle yer legs."

"I can't." Bea didn't relish taking orders from the old windbag. "My foot's stuck."

Molly leaned toward her with a disgusted look on her face. "Do you want to get out of there or not?" She didn't wait for an answer. "Uncle Warney knows what he's doing. You need to wiggle your legs to create small spaces in the packed sand for water to flow through. Got it?"

Bea fought to keep her angry tears under control. She'd never been so mortified in all her life. Wiggling her foot ever so slightly, she was surprised to feel the substance begin to release its grip. "It's coming loose!"

"Now lean yer head back. Try ta float on yer back." The old man's voice sounded soothing, but she couldn't bring herself to trust him.

"What? And put my hair in this mess?"

"Suit yerself," he said.

Molly scowled at her.

"All right, then," Bea said as she retrieved Clyccan from her ear, held it above the water, and leaned back. "Eeewww. I think it's working," she whispered, keeping Molly in her peripheral vision.

But it was the old man who answered. "Sure 'nough. Now make small, circular motions with your legs."

"My foot's free!"

"Great," Molly said. "Now, roll over and doggie paddle your way over here and I'll help you out."

"Aaaaargh," Bea positioned Clyccan between her teeth and rolled over. Doggie paddling to terra firma, she thanked the gods that none of her future followers could see her in such a humiliating condition.

"These flames are looking way too weird," Gavin said, moving to where the old man stood on a mossy patch.

Molly threw her cotton sweater over the burning embers. "I don't know if this will do much good, but if the yarn doesn't burn, it'll give you a spot to stand."

"It's about time!" Bea chirped as she stepped on Molly's sweater, pressing it into the glowing ashes before taking a few more delicate steps onto solid ground.

Gavin drew a deep breath and turned away. "Guess some folks don't know the words, *thank you*."

Bea knew the words, all right, but they stuck in her throat. By Shimera's toes, she was grateful not to be in dire straits any longer, but who was to say the powers of Laddrach hadn't orchestrated her rescue? Pretending not to hear, she took inventory of her appearance.

Her thick tresses were matted with sand and twigs. Sidestepping the flames that licked at her ankles, she discovered that her now ruined shoes somehow remained on her feet. Never had she looked such a mess.

"Molly, how's my make-up?"

"You don't look like a raccoon, if that's what you mean. Waterproof mascara, right?"

Bea wrung out her once-beautiful skirt. "Yes. My eyes are my best feature," she said, turning them toward the old man who repelled but fascinated her. "What are you? A wizard?"

The old man raised his walking stick, wet and dripping from the mire, and shook it in the air. "I am a prophet of the Lord Most High and guardian of Burnt Swamp." His voice thundered, amplified by an unseen source. "These flames are kindling compared to what the unrighteous will suffer."

Bea blinked, feeling light-headed.

"The Lord's return is near, young lady." He leaned closer and lowered his voice. "Seek the Lord while He may be found."

Warney walked past Bea to the place where she had emerged from the sand pit.

"Hear me, demons of the deep, the God of Abraham, Jacob, and Isaac reigns in this place. It is not yer time. In the Name of Jesus I declare this threshold *closed*."

Bea watched, flabbergasted, as the waterlogged soil, that only moments before had held her captive, began to bubble and boil like a cauldron. Steam began to rise, and all the soupy matter vanished. Within seconds, the whole area solidified. In less time than it took to gasp, the quicksand that had threatened to suffocate her was suddenly a patch of cracked, hardened clay.

Turning away from the mire, Warney placed his cane on firm ground and limped away in the direction he'd come from, as though finished with both the pit and Bea.

"Whoa! Uncle Warney!" Gavin turned to run after the old man. "How'd you do that?"

I don't care what he says, he must be a wizard. Bea trembled. "Barmy as a rabid bat," she mumbled after the retreating form of the man. Bea's gaze fell upon the almost deserted backpack.

"Oh, Molly." Bea hugged Molly's neck. Clyccan, sandwiched between them, remained cool with indifference. "I could never hope to find a better friend than you. Be a dear. I think I dropped my handbag over there somewhere. Would you see if you can find it?"

Molly pulled away, startled. "Well, I, uh . . . sure." She stepped out of the small clearing to look for Bea's bag.

Bea bent over, grabbed Molly's charred sweater and headed for Gavin's backpack. Quietly, she opened the main compartment and saw the leather book. *It says "DIARY!" This must be it! Old, small, secretive!* She took the diary, wrapped it in Molly's sweater, and returned the backpack to its original condition.

Taking two steps away, she spied her bag and dropped her prize inside.

Quickly returning to the spot where Molly had placed the sweater, Bea dropped it on the ground and called, "I found my bag."

Molly came running back with Gavin on her heels.

"I insist on replacing your sweater." Bea bent down to pick it up.

"That's not necessary," Molly said, returning to her side.

"Have you seen my—" Gavin looked worried. "Oh, there it is! "he said, grabbing the straps of his backpack. "Come on, Mol, we've got to get home." He hiked the bag over his shoulders. "My dad will kill me if he finds out I've been in the swamp."

"Uh, let's keep this little episode between the three of us. I would prefer it if no one knew that—"

"Who would believe it anyway?" Molly said as she turned to follow Gavin.

"Who, indeed?" Bea twirled in the direction of the Lodge, the diary tucked safely in her bag. She'd done it!

CHAPTER TWENTY-SEVEN

BEA

Ours at Last!

B ea catapulted up the front steps of the Lodge and gave the doorbell a playful push as she burst through the door. A deafening "go-o-o-n-n-n-g," followed by a distorted version of Westminster Chimes, announced her entrance.

"Whatever is *wrong* with you?" Madam Daark appeared in the shadows of the foyer, holding her hands over her ears. "The doorbell isn't repaired. Turns out that the local repairman is as inept as everyone else in this forsaken place. Jenkins has contracted an electrician from London, but he won't arrive until tomorrow."

Panting from her marathon, Bea waited for her mother's tirade to subside.

Jenkins appeared in the hall. "Shall I cover the button over, Madam?"

"See to it." Her mother waved him away.

"Mum!" Bea caught her breath and moved toward her, into the light. "You won't *believe* what I've got."

"I can't believe what I *see*." The ghastly expression on her mother's face was priceless.

In Bea's elation over the diary, she had actually forgotten how she must look. "How unlike me," she giggled. "Well, it's a small thing, really, considering . . ." She opened her bag and reached inside.

"Small thing? You're getting the hardwood floors wet. *Look* at you! What happened? Have you been attacked? Who did this to you? Where have you been? Some moonstruck boy named Eric drops off your books, and you show up an hour later looking and smelling like you've been taking a mud bath in a pigsty. How—"

"Actually, I have been in the swamp—literally. But first . . ." Bea paused for effect. "I have a surprise for you." Slowly, she revealed the book in her hand. "Could this be what you wanted?"

The remaining color drained from Madam Daark's face. "Is that what I think it is?"

Hardly able to contain herself as she saw the sheer yearning in her mother's demeanor, Bea handed the battered book over. Her chances of finding it so soon were far-fetched enough, but to actually capture it? Well, only the gods could have managed such a thing. This was a moment to savor.

Her mother examined the book with its frayed leather cover and water-stained edges. "It's old," she said, "but . . ."

Bea tried to ignore a creeping shadow of doubt. The book had to be the genuine article. It wouldn't do to disappoint Madam Daark.

When her mum failed to comment further, Bea reminded her of the secrecy surrounding the book and nervously launched into an account of how events had unfolded.

But Madam Daark seemed too mesmerized by the diary to give Bea her full attention. She turned the book over in her hand, front to back, and traced her long red fingernail over the cracks in the cover. Then she studied the ribbon binding.

Bea's heart sank in exasperation. "Mum?" She hadn't even gotten to the quicksand part.

A smile surfaced, claiming Madam Daark's face. "Yes!" Her voice turned to a whisper. "I believe this is it." A tear trickled down her cheek, cutting a path through layers of powder.

When was the last time Bea saw her mother cry? She couldn't remember. Of all the shocking things she had seen and done in the past six months, this surprised Bea most. So her mum had another emotion besides disgust. Envy tugged at Bea's heart as she watched her mother hug the book to her breast. At least she could share in Mum's joy, even if she couldn't be the source of it. But her mother's elation gave way to curiosity as Madam Daark fingered the deckle edges common to hand-made papers of the diary's era. Bea watched her mother closely, poised to discover its contents.

Bea could stand it no longer. "Go ahead, Mum. Open it!"

The moment of truth had come. Was it truly the book she coveted or not?

"Let's retire to the great room," Madam Daark said dreamily.

Bea followed her down the hall and through the doorway.

In the serenity of paneled walls, surrounded by antiquities, Bea stood in anticipation near the massive fireplace, trying not to worry about the drips her skirt was making on the hardwood floor.

Madam Daark rested the volume in her right palm, took a deep breath, and pried at the cover with her left thumb.

"It's stuck," she said.

"Let me try."

"No, I'll get it." Madam gripped the book with both hands. But no matter how hard or at what angle she pulled, the cover wouldn't budge. "It must be the moisture. Mildew has a way of gluing pages together."

Madam Daark glided across the room, carrying the book before her as though it were a rare artifact—hopefully so. "Follow me. I know how to take care of this."

Following her mother to the fireplace beneath the empty crest of the Knights of the Order of Laddrach, Bea noticed the book was too large to be one of the pieces intended to complete the crest. But in her world, appearances were often deceiving.

She kept her question to herself as Madam Daark raised the book up high, lifting it toward the bronze shell like an offering, and chanted.

"Laddrach, oh mighty one," she said, "the book is in our hands. But, alas, it is sealed. It is our desire to open the book that we might begin the business of deciphering its clues. What must I do? Send your wisest spirit guide to give us wisdom."

Bea followed her mum's example and closed her eyes to receive instruction. At least if she fell into a trance, there was a thick Oriental carpet on the floor to catch her body. Blocking out the trials of the day, she recited a quiet mantra to empty her mind and invoke the spirits. Tuneless sounds to the uninformed ear, it was the vehicle that transported her to a place of deep rest.

Gradually, her consciousness began to lower. Her ears registered her mother's fading voice until it droned like a distant bagpipe . . . then silence.

But the exercise took an unexpected turn. She began drifting to a place she had never been, going deeper. Instead of the light-filled atmosphere she expected, she entered darkness. Alarmed, Bea tried to will herself into a recognizable plane, but she could not.

The stench of burning swamp sulfur filled her nostrils and turned to a powdery, suffocating substance. Her lungs began to ache, starved for air. A sickening entity wormed its way into her stomach. Just as Bea thought she would vomit, words exploded on the canvas of her mind.

Do not proceed apart from Nem Downes.

"Who are you?" Bea cried out in silence.

I am Ooziss Naturus, and you will heed my words or face my wrath.

Bea's mind was awash with visions of the torture she would have to endure if she disobeyed the command—maybe hot needles under her fingernails or worse, having her head shaved. A small sampling of pain skittered up the back of her neck.

"Noooo!" Bea's scream was hoarse and loud, shattering the silence of the room. Her eyelids flew open.

"You insolent fool!" Madam Daark wheeled around and glared down at Bea. She grabbed a fistful of Bea's hair and yanked her to a standing position. "What do you think you're doing? Can't you see I'm communing with the great one?"

Instant tears stung Bea's eyes as she massaged her scalp and tried to process what was happening. Never before had her mother laid a hand on her. "But—"

"But *nothing*," Madam barked. "There is no excuse for this. How dare you interrupt when I'm meditating at such a crucial time."

Bea sought a word that might arrest her mother's ramblings so she could relay what had happened.

"Ooziss," she blurted out.

"Ooooozisssss?" Madam's initial rage fled her face. "What's *he* got to do with this?"

"Nem Downes, that's what," Bea said, still trembling. "Remember? Ooziss Naturus, his spirit guide?" Bea clung to her mother's arm. "Oh, Mum, I've just had a visitation from him, and it was *awful*. I felt like my mind was . . . invaded." Her skin still crawled. "He says we are not to proceed until Nem Downes is present."

"Nem Downes? What do you mean he must be present?" Her mother pried Bea's fingers from her arm.

"Ooziss says."

"But, but . . ." Madam paced in small circles, gnashing her teeth in distaste. "Very well," she said at last. "It will be as he commands."

"Jenkins," Madam called. "Locate Mr. Downes immediately. We require his presence."

"My knees are shaky." Bea started to sit on the chaise lounge.

"Not there!" Her mother held up her hand. "You're a filthy mess! Are you dry?"

Bea crumpled her skirt and felt her spirits doing likewise as she moved to a leather chair. "Dry enough, Mum," she sighed. "May I tell you about the rest of my day?"

As Bea unraveled her tale, she knew she still didn't have her mother's full attention. By the time she got to Gavin, Molly, and the old man showing up, Madam Daark seemed totally preoccupied.

"Didn't you hear me, Mum? He said he was a prophet of God and keeper of the swamp."

"A demented old man," Madam Daark said, gathering some old newspapers she had spread out on the table and carrying them to the hidden wall safe.

"But he had a powerful aura and his voice—"

"What do you know about auras?" her mother interrupted, as she sat the papers down so she could maneuver an oversized painting aside to get to the safe. Slowly she dialed the combination and opened the door.

Bea caught one of the headlines before her mother started stuffing the newspapers in the safe. It read, "Abernathy Toddler Lost in Fire."

"Auras? Not nearly enough according to Nem who claims to be some sort of expert. But that old man had one like an all-over halo. Speaking of Nem—" Bea's indignation flared as she recalled him gloating over her in the swamp. "That oaf saw me drowning in the quicksand and—"

At that moment, the doorbell gonged, rattling the framed oil paintings on the walls.

"Terribly sorry, Madam," Jenkins said, poking his head in the doorway. "I haven't gotten to the doorbell yet."

"That will be Mr. Downes," Madam said, as she closed the safe and returned the painting to its original position. "Fetch him at once," she said as she walked to the center of the room where she awaited the entrance of the intrusive Hee-Haw Downes.

"Mr. Downes, how kind of you to come on such short notice." Madam motioned him to an adjacent chair. "Please sit down. We have something extraordinary to show you."

"Wouldn't happen to be an old diary, would it?" His obnoxious laugh rebounded off the walls, more grating than the doorbell. "Not much goes on in Burnt Swamp that escapes my watchful eye. I see you got out of that quicksand."

No thanks to you, Bea thought as she recoiled from his knowing wink. She fought a shiver, recalling it all too well. "You actually enjoyed my despair, didn't you?"

"Ha! A little melodramatic, don't you think? The pit was shallow enough; if your foot hadn't been tangled, you could have stood up and walked out." Nem eyed the diary. "But then, you wouldn't have had a chance to work your sleight of hand to capture *that*, would you?"

Bea hadn't thought of it that way. "Yes. And it appears to be *the* diary that holds the clues we need to find the icons." Bea's gaze wandered from Hee-Haw's irritating visage to the naked crest above the fireplace.

Madam Daark eased her slender frame toward the edge of the chaise. "The pages appear to be mildewed together." She crossed her ankles to the left. "We were in the process of seeking advice on how to open it when Ooziss appeared to Bea and said your presence was required."

Nem hee-hawed. "I figured it'd only be a matter of time before you needed me."

Bea despised his smirk. "Now that you're here, I presume we'll have no more difficulty opening this."

Nem held out his hand. "Mind if I take a closer look?"

"Yes, I mind!" Madam Daark sprang to her feet and stood in front of Bea. "You'll not be putting your grimy hands on this if I have anything to say about it." Still glaring at Nem, she reached out to Bea. "Give it here."

A giddy anticipation ran through Bea as she released the book into her mother's hand.

A smile playing at the corner of Madam Daark's mouth, she once more tried to open the book. Again, it wouldn't budge. Her smile faded to shock and then gave way to fury as Madam tugged and pulled on the book from every angle.

"Careful, Mother. You'll tear it."

"Hush! You know nothing."

Curses in dark tongues spilled from Madam's lips, cutting Bea to the core and causing Nem to grin. Bea shuddered as much from his ugly teeth as from her mother's unexpected wrath.

"You *will* open for me, you shabby, wretched, worthless book." Madam's nostrils flared. "I know. I'll undo the binding." She pulled on the ribbon, and the bow cooperated by coming undone. "There! I think I've got it!" But her elation vanished as quickly as it came when she realized the pages still would not part.

Bea had never seen her mother so utterly out of control. She watched in dread as the book sailed across the room and slammed against the stone fireplace. When it landed on the floor, still unopened, Madam proceeded to stomp on it like a toddler having a tantrum.

Nem inched closer to Bea. "And she was worried about my grimy hands? Looks like the high priestess has lost it." His voice was tinny, carrying a hint of well-disguised fear.

"Mother! What *are* you *doing?*" Was this the same woman who had raised her? The one who taught her to maintain control of every situation? The one whose hair stayed in place, even while she slept? The empire-builder who specialized in causing others to lose their tempers but never lost her own? All her life, Bea had wondered what secrets her mother kept that made her so driven, but never more than now.

Madam Daark stopped jumping. If looks could burn, which they often did in Madam's case, the diary should have incinerated, but it was unaffected.

Madam Daark stopped, gazed wild-eyed around the room, then stared at the diary. She slowly inhaled a ragged breath and plucked the book from the floor. "Well, that was interesting, wasn't it?"

Bea watched the regal woman standing calmly by the fireplace. She resembled her mother, except this woman looked like she'd just emerged from battle. Her clothes were disheveled. Strands of black hair sprang loose from her top knot. The absurdity of the situation brought loosely hidden giggles to Bea's lips.

"Why, Mum," she allowed the laughter to surface. "I believe you've come undone."

With a brittle laugh, Madam reached up to pull her hairpins the rest of the way out. "Well, I suppose *that* didn't work." Her long, black hair tumbled down her back.

Watching her mother deftly wind her tresses around, pile them back in place, and pin them tight, Bea noticed that the white streak was more conspicuous than ever.

Nem ventured out from behind the chaise and stood nose-to-nose with Madam Daark. "There's a better way."

Bea held her breath. Where did this guy get his nerve?

"A better way?" Madam raised an eyebrow. "To get what to work?"

"To get that book open. Ooziss has a plan. That's why I'm here. But if you'd rather figure it out on your own . . ."

Madam Daark morphed into her gracious self again. "Why, how rude of me, Nem. Let's sit down and you can tell us all about it over a nice cup of tea." She called for Jenkins, who soon returned with a silver tray service filled with cakes and tea.

"Warney Stokes is a sly, old fox." Nem slurped from his cup and then sloshed tea in the saucer. "I suspected he had that diary, but couldn't prove it. Then, just when I'm ready to look under rocks on the western side of the swamp, the old man slips it to the mayor's son, Gavin Goodfellow." He paused. "Oh, and just so you know, those pages aren't mildewed together."

Madam's eyes flashed. "They're not?"

Nem tossed a self-satisfied look in Bea's direction. "No. They're not. They were supernaturally, hermetically sealed."

Bea brushed granules of sand from her blonde mane and twisted it around her fingers. *Almost dry.* "Well, Mr. Know-it-all, how did you figure that out?"

"In a word? Ooziss." Nem hee-hawed in Bea's face, and his breath made her jerk backward in her seat. "Here's another juicy tidbit," he said. "Only Gavin Goodfellow can open the diary. According to Ooziss, Gavin's taking over the job as swamp guardian from his crazy old uncle."

"I told you there was something supernatural about that old man," Bea said.

"He has an aura—a big one," Nem said. "But forget him. Gavin's the one we need."

Bea watched Madam Daark close her eyes to meditate. After a moment or so, she opened them and seemed much more composed. "There's only one thing to do," she announced, a faintly eager look flashing across her face.

"What's that?" Bea couldn't imagine what her mother might suggest, given tonight's display.

Madam lowered her voice. "We have to abduct Gavin and force him to open the book for us."

"My plan exactly." Nem broke into an earsplitting bray of laughter.

Bea laughed, too—until she realized they were serious.

CHAPTER TWENTY-EIGHT

GAVIN

White Lies

By the time Gavin trudged up the stairs to his bedroom, he'd had enough. During their walk home, all Molly could talk about was that stupid book and how they were going to spend lots of time together so she could help him read the diary and see what this was all about. Diary or no diary, Gavin didn't want anything to do with reading. The more Molly talked, the more Gavin knew this was going to be a disaster.

That's when he decided he never wanted to look at or think about that old, musty book again. For all he cared, it could stay right there in his backpack and rot. Why not? After all, the *secret* diary hadn't seen the light of day in years. And as long as he kept it out of Bea's hands, no one would be the wiser. Except for Molly.

Just before drifting off to sleep, an idea came to him. If he could pull it off, this could be the ticket to keeping her out of it. He smiled. Yep, problem solved.

Gavin was not surprised to find Molly at the bus stop early the next morning, pacing around, probably ready to quiz him again.

"Hey, Gavin!" She beamed. "Did you get the diary open again? What did it say? Do you know who wrote it? Do you have it with you? Can I see it?"

He was ready for her. "Sorry, Molly." He pinched his fingers together and ran them over his mouth in a zipping motion. "My lips are sealed."

"But—"

"But nothing. You know it's a secret diary, and I've been given a—" He searched his bank of "Mollyisms" for the right phrase. "A sacred charge. Even Uncle Warney can't get it open anymore." He gave her a wink. "If I find anything in it you need to know about, I'll let you know."

"Gee, thanks." Molly snapped her mouth shut.

Gavin couldn't believe she actually bought his story. But then, it was true . . . sort of. The diary still held its secrets, and Gavin couldn't tell them.

"Don't be surprised if you misinterpret something and wind up responsible for who-knows-what." She waved her arms dramatically. "After what we saw yesterday, I shudder to think what could happen if you misread the diary's instructions."

If you misread the diary's instructions. Molly's words troubled Gavin the rest of the morning. He couldn't help it if he had dyslexia.

Could his handicap make him responsible for a catastrophe? What if the swamp exploded like a volcano, consuming all of Ashboro, and he could have prevented it if he'd only opened the book?

By second period, Gavin could wait no longer. It was time to open the diary. If there were no dire warnings of impending doom, he could have some peace of mind.

Unzipping his backpack, he slipped his fingers into the pocket. Ice cold fear dropped like lead in his stomach.

The diary was gone!

But that wasn't possible. It *had* to be there! Gavin dug deeper, tracing the seams inside the bag, around the back, and even the front compartment where the book couldn't possibly fit. But if it was magic— Nothing.

"Gavin, is something wrong?" Dexter whispered from behind him.

"Yes, Gavin. Is something wrong?"

Gavin looked up, startled to see Mrs. Bullock standing by his desk, looking down at him. "Huh?" His standard stall tactic sounded lame, even to him.

What could he say? *I lost the secret diary Uncle Warney gave me and now who knows what could happen to Burnt Swamp? Maybe even the world?* He felt the blood rush to his face. "Um . . ." He fixated on a little heart someone had carved in his desk with the initials *K & W.*

"Gavin, look at me." His teacher sounded more concerned than mad. "Are you okay? You look flushed."

"Uh, yeah. I'm fine. Just couldn't find my, uh, pencil."

"Here. Use mine," Dexter said, handing Gavin one of his own.

"Oh, um. Thanks." Gavin felt his face growing hotter.

Dexter had to know he had lied about the lost pencil. And judging from the snickers that erupted all over the room as Mrs. Bullock returned to the chalkboard, everybody else knew, too. A few familiar and uncomplimentary names reached Gavin's now-burning ears.

Slumping in his seat, Gavin found it impossible to pay attention. What good would social studies be if Ashboro was destroyed because he lost a dumb book? He focused with all his brain power, mentally retracing the steps.

When did he see the diary last? At Uncle Warney's. He had it in his backpack on the porch when they heard the scream.

Bea? Nah, she was in quicksand, and the backpack was on the bush. Besides, there's no way she could have known it was there.

His Mom couldn't have found it in his room because she never snooped around his things.

His Dad? Maybe. He'd searched his room before. But he would have stuck it in Gavin's face and demanded an explanation.

Could it have fallen out of his backpack on the way to school? Impossible. The zipper was still zipped.

The book opened and closed when it wanted. What if it could move on its own? What if it decided he wasn't supposed to have it, after all?

"For homework . . ." The rise in Mrs. Bullock's voice penetrated Gavin's thoughts, snatching him from his ponderings. "Read pages 10 through 15 in your textbook."

Gavin jotted down the assignment. For once, reading didn't sound so bad—better than stewing over the missing diary. If it was meant to be, the book would turn up. If not, he'd just have to avoid Uncle Warney. He'd already taken care of Molly. If Widow Woebe cornered him, he'd just tell her he'd taken it to Uncle Warney, which wasn't a lie. He *had* taken it there.

Other than having to make up a lie about what was wrong and ditch Dexter when he quizzed him at lunch, the remainder of the day went well. Molly didn't bring up the diary at all, and Gavin managed to avoid Widow Woebe altogether. Even Bea kept her distance, occupying herself with Eric and her circle of new admirers.

Gavin spent Saturday in his room, determined to finish his homework for once without crawling to his mother for help. But he couldn't concentrate. Thoughts of the missing diary kept intruding. Gavin slammed his textbook shut. It *had* to be here somewhere.

He dug through and under his desk, pulled out every drawer in his dresser, and rifled through the clothes his mother had folded with care. Slinging hangers right and left, he checked from the highest shelf to the lowest shoebox on the closet floor.

"I hate—I hate—" Unable to hate God but needing to hate somebody or something, he flopped onto a pile of dirty clothes that he'd dragged out from under his bed and moaned, "Why me?"

"Gavin?" His mother rattled the knob of his bedroom door, giving him a start. "Are you okay? Open up. I need to know what you're doing in there."

Gavin scrambled to his feet and unlocked the door. "I'm fine . . . just . . ." He looked at his topsy-turvy room. "Fine."

"What's this?" She clutched her neck as if his stinky socks had jumped up to strangle her. "Are you cleaning your room?"

Gavin smiled. That sounded good to him. "Yeah. Like you say, 'it always looks worse before it gets better.' I was sorting through my stuff."

"Oh, Gavin." His mom hugged him. Ordinarily he'd have savored a hug from his mom, but he stiffened, unable to bring himself to hug her back. Besides, he was getting too old for hugs.

"Forgive me for thinking the worst. You just seem distracted lately." She touched his chin. "But I know you, dear heart. You're such a good boy, and you would never deceive your mother."

His mom was always apologizing for something, but what did she mean, *thinking the worst?* Gavin caught his breath. She couldn't possibly know—

"Want some help?" She surveyed the room.

Think quick. Grabbing a pile of clothes, he shoved them toward her. "Sure. These are dirty. Wash them for me, please?"

"Gavin Goodfellow," his mother chided, "if you keep this up, I'm going to have to get you your own hamper." With a wink, she turned, humming her way toward the laundry room.

You would never deceive your mother. The words hammered in Gavin's conscience. He was a coward and a liar. At that moment, he could think of no one he *hadn't* deceived.

Why did he have to go and lie to Dexter—the one kid in the whole world who could be a true friend? The pain he had seen in Dexter's eyes earlier that day registered all over again. It was the same look Uncle Warney used when he saw through him. *I'm a failure.*

CHAPTER TWENTY-NINE

GAVIN

Kidnapped

The church service ended, and Gavin ducked past the minister without having to shake his hand. He couldn't stand to listen to Pastor Fred say one more word about the *chosen* and the *faithful*. And he especially didn't want to hear any more about *cowards* and *liars*, even if it was in the Bible.

"Hey, Gavin," Molly said, sidling up to him. "Want to come by for dinner?

The cheery horn of his mom's white Honda Civic saved him from having to think up an excuse. Molly's invitation only made the nagging voice of Gavin's conscience shout louder. Today he couldn't tolerate being around someone who never did anything wrong.

"Sorry, Molly. Gotta go."

Just as Gavin turned to run down the steps, Molly executed a perfect block and reached his mom before he did. Eight seconds later, he arrived at the car door to hear his mother's reply.

"Of course, Molly." She leaned out the window. "That's fine, Gavin, but you be home before dark, or your dad will have a conniption."

She drove away, leaving Gavin standing there, Bible in hand. "What'd you do?"

"I told her we were having fried chicken and you were invited."

"And I told you *no! Nicely.*"

"But you ought to know by now that you can't blow me off that easily."

"Just what I had in mind for a nice Sunday afternoon—" Gavin said, his voice dripping with sarcasm.

"All right, then." Molly's braid whipped around, barely missing his nose. "I just thought you might want to talk about you-know-what. But if now's not convenient, then we'll take you home."

"No way. I'll walk."

"Come on, Gavin." Molly opened her car door. "It's two miles."

"Stop telling me what to do."

Gavin stomped off down the sidewalk. He could feel his nostrils flaring like mini-trumpets. Forcing a half-hearted wave to the Paces when Molly's car drove past, he didn't calm down until he was well out of town and where the wildflowers grew. Stopping to catch his breath, he picked a clump of goldenrods that reminded him of happier times when he and Grandma Jibbers collected bouquets of Queen Anne's lace and held buttercups under their chins. How anything as pretty as clover and field daisies could grow in all this swamp smoke he didn't know, but there sure were plenty of them.

His favorite was the Black-Eyed Susan. A vision of a black-eyed Molly came to mind, making him chuckle. A few minutes ago, he probably could have given her a good one, he'd been so furious.

Pastor Fred's words about cowards and liars sharing the same fate as murderers and witches kept going 'round and 'round in Gavin's mind.

Tossing the goldenrod aside, he felt the rhythmic thud, thud, thud of something coming. Then came the sound. The thunder of hooves and rumble of wheels made the hair on Gavin's arms prickle the way it sometimes did in an electrical storm.

But this was modern times. *It couldn't be horses*, common sense told him as he turned to see what was coming up behind him. Yet it was. Giant horses galloped toward him, pulling an antique carriage at full speed that sent sparks flying on the asphalt.

For a minute, he thought it might be Uncle Warney and his Clydesdales, but Uncle Warney never drove Candy and Drew faster than a high-stepping trot. His *babies*, as Uncle Warney called them, were built for strength and show, not speed. These horses were being pushed so hard that froth flew from their noses.

But it sure looked like Uncle Warney's team. Nobody else had a matching pair of Clydesdales. They must have been stolen! The idea froze Gavin to the spot. He squinted to see who was driving. Two people—one large, one small.

As the horses bore down on him, he saw that they had black hoods over their heads!

What could he do? If Candy and Drew had been stolen, then he had to *do* something. Gavin half-stepped off the road, crushing a patch of goldenrods as the mass of muscle, forelegs, and white-feathered fetlocks thundered toward him.

"Whoa," the larger one hollered, pulling on the reins.

Bewildered, Gavin watched the carriage slow, pitching dangerously to one side before it stopped in front of him. He knew he should run, but his feet weren't paying attention to his head.

"This is a p-p-prank, right?" he stammered as the hooded figures leapt down from the coach.

Gavin turned to run, but not fast enough.

A blanket went over his head, and a rope drew tight, pinning his arms to his side. In less than the time it took for Gavin to yell, "Help," they tied his hands. Gavin struggled, but the cold fear that started icing in his veins mocked him. Who was he kidding? What chance did he have against these thugs?

The next thing he knew, he was inside the carriage, curled up in a fetal position on the hard leather seat. What did they want with him? Where were they taking him? *Why* were they taking him? He certainly couldn't identify them. They had hoods!

No answers, just the rhythmic sway of the carriage. He sneezed, his nose irritated by the wool of the blanket over his head and the scent of horses and barn straw.

Why hadn't he gone with Molly like she wanted? Maybe they were horse thieves. No one else had horses like Uncle Warney's Clydesdales. But what did they want with him? Horse thieves *and* kidnappers in Ashboro? What were the chances of that? His heart flip-flopped.

A whimper started low in his throat and grew in pitch until it turned into a full-fledged scream, bringing with it waves of tremors that shook him uncontrollably. If only he could pray, maybe that would calm him down.

Please, God, the thought formed in his mind; his throat was too tight to make the words come. *Get me out of this.*

A tiny spark of something warm flared up inside him, making him feel safe, but not for long. Fear regained its grip and gnawed at his gut. No angels surrounded the carriage. No voice from heaven spoke words of comfort. He decided to try again.

"Dear Lord," he whispered beneath the blanket. "It's me. Gavin." His eyes burned. "But I guess You know that. I guess You know everything, huh?"

The carriage jolted Gavin's body almost off the seat, but he caught his balance and rolled back, recovering his focus. "And You know I won't be any good to You if these goons kill me, right?" What a dumb prayer. Couldn't he do anything right?

"Okay, Lord." He sucked in the stale air, trying his best to be sincere. A hot tear trickled down his cheek. He smothered a sob. "If You get me out of this, I promise I'll do anything You want me to. If You get me home safe and help me find that diary, I'll—" He gulped. "I'll read it and . . ."

But if he got out of this alive and found the diary, could he keep his word to Jesus? Even if he managed to read the words, could he make sense out of them?

A fresh wave of despair washed over him, followed by one of sheer terror of the unknown. His teeth chattered, and a million goosebumps teased his arms and legs. He let the tears come, releasing all effort to hold them back. Somewhere in the recesses of his mind he heard his dad saying, "Suck it up, soldier." But he didn't want to be a soldier right now. He wanted to be a little boy again, cuddled up in a blanket on his mother's lap.

"Mom. Mommy," he choked. Quiet sobs wracked his body and he hugged himself, knowing she couldn't help.

Maybe he deserved whatever was coming. An anguished sob shook him to the core, then another and another. But nobody deserved to be kidnapped.

After a while, there were no tears left. His body was too spent to resist the side-to-side sway of the carriage. Unable to think of any convincing words to pray, especially if God was punishing him, Gavin listened to the clippity-clop of the horses' hooves. Soon, somewhere between fear and confusion, a childhood prayer he hadn't thought of in years worked its way back to him. The words came in time with the horses' hoofbeats.

"Now I lay me
down to sleep
I pray the Lord
my soul to keep
if I should die . . ."

CHAPTER THIRTY

GAVIN

The "Aha!" Factor

"Gavin. Hey, Gavin." A gentle hand shook him by the shoulder.

Too groggy to realize what was going on, Gavin wondered where his pillow was and why his mom put such a heavy blanket on his bed. Then someone pulled him upright, and it all came rushing back—confusion, shame, exhaustion . . . but mostly fear.

While the blanket was being removed, Gavin trembled, afraid to open his eyes.

"It's okay," a familiar voice coaxed.

Sweaty and disoriented, Gavin forced his eyelids open and stared into the faces of . . .

"Uncle Warney? Dexter?"

Relief washed over Gavin like a spring shower. He leaned into Uncle Warney's open arms. "How'd you find me? Who were those guys? What'd they want with me? Did you catch them?" Gavin took a quick breath and looked from left to right, then back at Uncle Warney's serene face. "I can't believe you're here. I was never so scared in my whole life!"

"Slow down a mite there, Gavin," Uncle Warney said. "Young Dexter here and me, we got some explainin' to do."

Gavin had never seen his great-uncle's fingers shake quite so much. "Explaining? Like what?"

"I hope we didn't hurt you," Dexter said.

Gavin brushed off his Sunday pants as Dexter's words registered. "Hurt me? What do you mean? There were kidnappers . . . "

Uncle Warney and Dexter exchanged a knowing look.

"Ya figured out yet where we brung ya?" Uncle Warney gestured toward the tall weeds and abandoned mansion, complete with paint-chipped columns.

"Yeah, the Stokes place," Gavin said in a soft voice. To him, the decaying homestead was almost as spooky as the Lodge and in worse shape. It dropped loose shingles like a dying tree sheds leaves.

And then it hit him. "*You?* Where *you* brought me? *You* were the jerks that kidnapped me?" Blood pounded against Gavin's eardrums making his head throb. "How *could* you?" he demanded with a rage he didn't know he possessed. "And why? Never mind! I don't want to know. I just want to go home."

Gavin's knees buckled when he jumped down from the carriage step, but fury bounced him upright. "You really put me through it, you know. I thought I was going to be killed! I never want to see either of you ever, ever again. I'm through. I'm done. I'm out of here!"

Then, as if his outburst had taken all of his strength, Gavin's knees buckled again.

Dexter reached out to steady him.

"Don't touch me, you, you . . ." Words failed Gavin. He longed to sling an adequately painful name at Dexter. "You traitor."

"Now, Gavin," Uncle Warney cajoled gently. "Don't be sayin' nothin' you'll regret."

As Gavin stomped the ground, his *Infiltrators* game wiggled out of his pocket and dropped at Uncle Warney's feet.

"Ah, now, ain't that timely?" Warney reached down and picked up the game. "Here's the truth of it. Jest as sure as there's wisdom in this here plaything, I could tell ya weren't on board with the diary. And, sure enough, the good Lord woke me up in the middle of the night on muh birthday and showed me the book surrounded by darkness."

Gavin gulped hard. None of this made any sense. "The diary?" He glanced from Uncle Warney to Dexter. "The *secret* diary? And I suppose Dexter knows all about that, too?"

"Let me finish," Uncle Warney said. "When I seen the book in darkness instead of in your hands where it belonged, I had to do somethin' drastic to git yer attention. So I prayed, and God give me a plan that included Dexter."

"Yeah," Dexter said. "God had to do something to shock you to your senses. You should be glad He got *us* to shake you up."

"How'd you know I'd be walking home from church today?"

Uncle Warney hobbled over to the Clydesdales. He stroked Drew's mane, gave Candy a pat on the nose, and made soothing sounds before answering Gavin's question. "Let's jest say the Lord's got some mighty mysterious ways."

Dexter chuckled. "And you might be interested to know that, when we harnessed up the team and waited behind the church today, we thought it was going to be a practice run, not the real thing. We knew *what* to do, just not *when*."

Uncle Warney tapped the carriage with his walking stick. "Had to dust this old thing off to see if them wheels still turned. But all of a sudden, there ya were, walkin' by yer lonesome—"

"And we had everything set, so off we went, and here we are," Dexter finished.

"Now, fer the real reason we brung ya here. If'n ya think we give ya a ride you'll never fergit," Uncle Warney smiled, "jest wait 'til ya see what surprises God's got in store fer ya up yonder." He pointed to the top floor.

"The attic?" Gavin's gaze followed Uncle Warney's finger and then turned to the weathered sign surrounded by weeds:

Condemned Property

No Trespassing

Except by Caretaker

By Order of the Town of Ashboro

"Last time I went somewhere that said *No Trespassing*, I wound up doing community service. Besides, it doesn't look safe." Any excuse would do as long as it kept Gavin from having to face more of Uncle Warney's surprises.

"It says 'except by caretaker,' and that's me. It's safe." Uncle Warney had an answer for everything. "The place might look like it's in shambles, but it was built to last. The attic's where I first met God, and He'll meet ya there, too, Gavin, if ya give Him a chance."

296

"Wait till you see the ceremony we've got planned," Dexter beamed. "You're not going to believe it."

Gavin looked up at the attic windows, apprehension stabbing his every nerve. Deep inside, he felt a slight tug to do as Uncle Warney said, but he resisted. "This isn't fair, you know." He stared at the ground. There must be a way out of this.

"Yer choice," Uncle Warney said. "We mighta grabbed ya and brung ya here, but God don't force nobody to worship Him. Ya can go up with us to see whatcha see in the attic, or we can take ya home. The reins are yers."

"Wait a minute." Dexter climbed up to the carriage's rickety bench and sat down. "Aren't you going to tell him what we know? After all the trouble we went to for him?" His bottom lip puffed out in a pout that made Gavin think this kid might not be so perfect, after all. "You're just going to let him go?"

"If that's the way he wants it," Uncle Warney said, checking the traces on the carriage. "Mighty heavy stuff if a body's tryin' to outrun God."

"I'm not trying to outrun God." Why did Gavin's words ring so hollow? Struggling to steady himself on legs that had somehow forgotten what they were there for, his mind returned to Uncle Warney's words. "What heavy stuff?" He had to admit he was curious, not to mention tired of always being on the outside. Turning to Dexter he added, "And what did you mean by 'tell him what we know'?"

Uncle Warney cleared his throat. "Yer right. It's only fair to let ya in on what ya'd be gettin' yerself into."

A cloud crossed Dexter's face. "We figure Bea Daark and her mother and Hee-Haw Downes are up to their elbows in the occult. God wants to use you to sound the alarm. When you do—and God will show you how—Ashboro will be set free!"

Not that again. Gavin looked to Uncle Warney. "But—"

"Hear me out," Uncle Warney interrupted. He placed his hands on Gavin's shoulders and pulled him in close, nose-to-nose, eyeball-to-eyeball. "The Daarks have the diary." With a disgusted snort, he straightened. "The Lord showed me in a dream on the night of muh birthday. No sooner did ya get Bea outta the quicksand than she stole it from yer bag."

Gavin stumbled backward as if punched in the stomach. "Bea?" He barely had breath to say her name. Questions gushed out of his mouth. "When? How? When was she near my—"

Warney held up his palm. "There's more. They need you to open the diary for them."

"I'd never do that!" Gavin's confidence quickly deflated. "Would I? Well not on purpose, but if . . . "

"They was workin' up some sorta trap fer ya to walk into, but we stopped 'em by kidnappin' ya first. So what they intended fer evil, God can use fer good."

The low rumble of Ugly Cat's irregular purr exploded so loud it hurt Gavin's ears. There was something strange about Ugly—besides how he looked. He seemed to show up every time Gavin messed up.

"You don't get it, do you?" Dexter hopped down from the carriage and landed between Gavin and Ugly. Gavin jumped, but the cat never flinched. "Gavin, it's time to give God your all."

"Well, maybe I already did . . . on the way here . . . when I thought I was going to die. I made God a promise—"

"Makin' a deal with God 'cause ya want outta somethin' ain't the same as confessin' 'cause you're yearnin' fer a clean heart," Warney said. "The best weapon ya got against anything the Daarks can throw at ya is truth. You'll be shootin' blanks if ya load yer gun with fibs."

Gavin shivered. "What if we just stay out of their way? The diary's no good to them if they can't open it."

"Dodgin' fiery darts don't guarantee safety." Warney's deep voice echoed in the waning afternoon light. Candy and Drew nickered softly, patting their huge hooves in the leaf-strewn ruts.

"I saw spooky things at the Lodge—sick stuff." Gavin never wanted to set foot in that place again. "If they're really into witchcraft and I stand up against it, won't they cast spells on me?"

"God's bigger than spells are." Dexter's voice was quiet, almost reverent. "Witchcraft is based on unholy alliances and lies."

There was that word again, *lies*. Whatever Uncle Warney said from that point on transformed into a hum of static-like white noise while Gavin processed his wayward ways. Then, like a trumpet blast, his great-uncle's words broke through loud and clear.

"Truth is everlastin', Gavin. Truth prevails even when things seem darkest. Ya have to believe this. That's why we brung ya here—to meet Truth, to meet Jesus."

"Do you think Jesus will help me get the diary back?" Gavin groaned.

"That diary'll find its way back to ya in due time," Uncle Warney said. "Truth is, first ya need to get honest with God."

A grin overtook Dexter's face. "Seek ye first the kingdom of God and His righteousness, and all these things shall be added unto you."

Gavin punched Dexter in the arm. "You've got a Bible verse for everything, don't you?" Then he sobered because the Scripture gave him a sense of comfort. "So you're saying if I seek God up there—" he pointed to the attic— "then I get the diary back?"

"Well, it ain't quite that simple, Gavin." Warney's eyes were gentle, understanding. "But it would behoove ya either way to git yerself a healthy dose of the fear of the Lord. Jesus is up thar waitin' fer ya."

Jesus is in the attic of the Stokes Mansion? Gavin couldn't wrap his thoughts around the concept, but he dipped his head slightly and said, "Okay, I'll give it a try—for you, Uncle Warney." Out of numb curiosity, Gavin allowed Uncle Warney and Dexter to lead him into the foyer. The door slammed shut behind them, bumping Gavin like he'd been spanked.

The only other time Gavin had ever been inside Stokes Mansion was when he was eight and his mom needed to pack up some dishes from the dining room. He had full run of the mansion and explored every room, from basement to attic. By the time his mom was ready to leave, he'd had his fill of dust, cobwebs, smoky black windows, and mothballs.

Despite the mansion's outward appearance, inside it was immaculate.

"Wow! You've been busy, Uncle Warney." The massive staircase and hardwood floors gleamed.

"Everything's ready fer ya, Gavin."

"Ready for . . . me?" He swallowed, trying to ease his uncertainty.

"Yep. Come on." Uncle Warney held out his hand.

Gavin stepped backward. His heart raced.

Uncle Warney and Dexter headed up the stairs. This was his last chance to turn and run. Instead, Gavin placed a foot on the bottom step and held on tight to the banister. He looked up—three flights.

With each step, Gavin noticed a shimmering, gold-edged, blue-white light around Uncle Warney. It pulsated like a living, loving force that made him look young. Gavin had never seen him look so happy.

Dexter had it, too. And when he skipped up the stairs to the first landing, the light exploded into a layer of gold glitter that fell on Gavin and everything around him. No fairy godmother's wand could make a person feel better than Gavin felt at that moment.

Even before Gavin reached the attic, God was doing something in him. He remembered his eat-the-book vision and how it felt to be loved—no strings attached, no expectations, no apologies.

"Come on," Uncle Warney urged.

By the time Gavin joined Uncle Warney on the first landing, Dexter had passed the second landing and stood on the top step. "Gavin, every day of your life—even your mistakes—has been preparation for this day." Turning his radiant face toward the attic, he stepped inside.

Gavin nodded but couldn't bring himself to speak. *I don't understand what You're up to, Lord, but I think I trust You. And this time*—he considered his promise in the carriage—*it's not because I need to. I want to. Yeah, I really want to.* His heart thumped harder as he put one foot in front of the other, moving closer to the attic entrance.

"Whatever You have for me, Lord," Gavin whispered. "I want it. I want it bad."

GAVIN
The Anointing

A wisp of fragrant smoke greeted Gavin on the third story landing. "Is something burning?"

"Candles and incense," Dexter grinned, holding the door open. "I just lit them. They represent the prayers of the saints."

The musical sound of Uncle Warney's chuckle was as bright as the rest of him. "Dexter wanted to set the mood."

Gavin listened, bewildered. All this spiritual stuff swirling around left him blank, amazed, and shaken. His desire of moments before fled. "I don't think I can do this."

"If a little boy asks fer a slice of pizza, does his daddy scare him by puttin' a live snake on his plate? If a little girl asks fer an egg, does he trick her with a spider? Your daddy wouldn't do that to you, would he? O' course not!" Uncle Warney said. "Don't ya think yer heavenly Father who loves ya even more would do right by ya?"

Gavin trembled. He hoped so but wasn't really sure.

"Jesus told me He's gonna meet ya right here, and He's fixin' ta give ya good things."

Questions bubbled up inside Gavin and spilled out. "But isn't Jesus up in heaven? How's He going to meet me here? Good things like what?"

"Number one, yes; number two, you'll find out; and number three, good things like the Holy Spirit."

Gavin tried to swallow. Not that there was anything to swallow with his mouth as dry as barn dust. "Is that what this is all about? Getting the Holy Spirit? But, I got baptized when I was a baby and joined the church last March. Didn't I get the Holy Spirit then?"

Warney enfolded Gavin's clammy hands into his warm, strong hands and held them as he gazed into Gavin's eyes. "Ya truly did, Gavin. Without the Holy Spirit, ya wouldn't be able to believe in Jesus at all. Them were—"

"Covenant moments," Dexter finished. "And today is another covenant moment."

"You want me to go where nuns live?" Gavin said.

"Not *convent*." Dexter grinned, but not like he was laughing at him. "Cov-e-nant—an unbreakable agreement between you and God."

Was Gavin's deal with God in the carriage a covenant? If so, God wasn't wasting any time holding him to his end of the bargain. He felt even more confused than before.

"So, if I got the Holy Spirit and all, what more do I need?"

"It's like gettin' a new pair of blue jeans and stickin' 'em in a drawer fer a special occasion. Purdy soon, ya fergit all about 'em and might never put 'em on. Ya got Jesus as yer *Savior*, but now ya need Him as yer *Lord* and yer *Friend*."

"Gavin?" Dexter moved in closer. "Have you been getting funny feelings these past few weeks? Have you kind of felt like you're supposed to do something and you don't know what or why?"

Gavin nodded his head, afraid to speak.

"That's the Holy Spirit nudging you."

"Yes, indeedy," Uncle Warney said.

"But why?" Gavin felt dumber than ever.

"Cause, God's right ready ta put ya to work, and ya need a Helper. Ya need the Holy Spirit to help strengthen ya, to give ya the right words when yer mind goes blank, and to help ya pray when ya don't feel like prayin' at all. Yer a David about ta face yer Goliath, and the Holy Spirit is yer smooth stone and slingshot. That's why."

"Oh." Gavin had no more questions, just decisions. He scanned the dimly lit landing, waiting but hearing nothing. Suddenly, deep in his midriff, he felt a tingling.

He opened the door and stepped through.

As Gavin entered the attic, the sun streamed through the dormer windows so brightly that he had to shield his eyes to look around. The room was bare except for a low table, prepared as an altar in the center of the room. The white, floor-length cloth had a cross embroidered on the front in gold metallic thread. The brown leather Bible, with its well-worn pages lying open, must have been in the Stokes family for centuries. Gavin hoped he wouldn't have to read it. A breeze from the open center window made the flames of three pillar candles on tall brass candlesticks flicker and dance as though happy to see him.

"Wow, Dexter! You did all this for me? Even after how I've been treating you lately?" An instant replay of the way Gavin had given Dexter the brush off at school made it impossible for him to look Dexter in the eye.

"You've got a lot on you right now," Dexter said. "I knew you didn't mean it. Besides, it's like your Uncle Warney told me—you need a friend you can trust, and I need to stick close to you whether you like it or not."

"If it'd been up to me," Uncle Warney said, "I'd a used a footlocker." He nodded to Dexter. "But our friend here insisted on the fancy stuff."

"Thanks." Gavin gestured toward the altar, a quick and disturbing uncertainty piercing his brain. "But what's gonna happen?"

"This is about your relationship with God," Dexter said. "Today's about relinquishing control."

"What kind of control?" The warm, fuzzy feeling of the glow was great, but control? What did he control? Between his parents and his teachers, he didn't have control over anything.

"This is about the impartation of the Holy Spirit and about the callin' on yer life," Uncle Warney said, leaning on his cane.

Gavin held up his hand. "Impartation?"

"It's about receiving what God has to give you," Dexter said.

"But ya have to want it, son."

"Think of it as a commissioning ceremony, like a soldier being given a special mission." Dexter moved to the back of the table and bent down. With the flip of a switch, instrumental strains of *How Great Thou Art* filled the air.

Although the melody was soothing, something in Gavin competed with the sacred atmosphere. He opened his mouth to voice his concern, but Uncle Warney pressed a finger to his lips.

"Ya sense it?" His words were barely audible. "The presence of the Holy One?" The incandescent glow around his uncle intensified.

"Uh, I think so," Gavin whispered. "It's all around *you*." Gavin felt like he needed a bath.

"He's here," Dexter said in hushed tones. "God of gods and Lord of lords, the great God, mighty and awesome."

"What should I do? Sh-sh-sh-should I kneel?" Gavin's tongue seemed to have a mind of its own.

No one answered. They didn't have to.

Lowering himself until his knees touched the floor, Gavin kept his posture rigid. "Now what?"

"Dexter and me, we're gonna lay our hands on yer head to pray." Uncle Warney stepped closer.

"What?" Now Gavin *knew* he would freak out.

"Relax," Dexter said. "This won't hurt. Close your eyes."

Although Gavin's lids fluttered, somehow he kept them shut. Two pair of hands gently touched his head and neck. *Relax?* How was he supposed to do that? He let his arms fall limp at his side, which didn't help a bit. But then Uncle Warney prayed, and the sound of his voice drew all the tension out of Gavin's shoulders.

"Lord, we come to help Gavin along on his faith journey, and I thank Ya for the path Ya mapped out fer him, datin' back since before the beginnin' of time. Help Gavin travel from this point back through

his life and open the eyes of his heart so he sees what Ya need him ta
see. Use this time fer healin' the rough spots and cleansin' him through
and through."

Gavin squeezed his eyes tighter. *Funny, Uncle Warney's breath
smells sweet, like clover.*

"Gavin," Uncle Warney said, "the good Lord's gonna help ya see yer
life through His eyes. Ready fer that?"

Gavin nodded.

"Okay, then. Think on the problem that's been weighin' ya down
most."

"My dyslexia?" A pang of indignation rose up in Gavin's heart, but
he remained still.

"Now, I don't want ya to do nothin' 'cept think on how bad it makes
ya feel."

Gavin grimaced. "That's easy. I do that all the time."

Dexter gave Gavin's head a light pat. "This time's different. Jesus
is standing right here beside you. Can you see Him in your mind? Can
you sense His concern?"

Gavin shifted his weight to his left knee. "Uh, no, not really."

"That's okay. He's here all right," Uncle Warney said. "Lord, I'm
askin' Ya to give Gavin a word so he'll know Yer in this with him."

For a long time, no one spoke.

At last, a sliver of a thought crept into Gavin's mind and lodged
itself there, refusing to budge. "I think I'm getting something. A word,
just one word."

"Go ahead, speak it out," Dexter coached. "What word?"

"Weakness. But I don't get it. My dad hates me being weak." Gavin opened his eyes long enough to see that his uncle's were still closed, so he shut them again.

Dexter laughed with joy. "You got Scriptures, Gavin, straight from above—My grace is sufficient for you, for My strength is made perfect in weakness. For when I am weak, then I am strong."

"Huh? That doesn't make sense."

"It means when yer beat down and cain't do nothin' on yer own, then ya have to count on the Lord's strength," Uncle Warney said. "Recognizin' yer weakness helps ya see how strong God is."

Gavin felt the corner of his mouth pull into a half-smile.

"Let's git on with yer journey. We're walkin' in the light of God's presence, and I'm askin' Him to show ya, step by step, anything that's standin' between you and Him. If yer willin', that is. Are ya still willin'?"

"Yes."

"Okay, then. Dexter, ya got the oil?"

"Right here. Frankincense and myrrh, straight from the Holy Land."

Gavin heard a lid twist open. "What's going on?" He couldn't help but peek and saw Dexter handing a small glass vial to Uncle Warney.

"Keep yer eyes closed, Gavin," Uncle Warney said. "Now, lift yer head up a mite."

Dexter's cinnamon breath mingled with the other aroma. "We're going to dab this oil on your forehead. Then we're going to leave you alone to pray."

"Ya okay with that, son?" Uncle Warney choked out the words like he was holding back tears.

"I guess so," Gavin said, hoping he meant it. "Where will you be?"

"Close by," Uncle Warney said. "Either downstairs or back at the stables."

Three times, Uncle Warney's finger dabbed oil on Gavin's forehead in the symbol of a cross. "I anoint you in the name of the Father . . . in the name of the Son . . . in the name of the Holy Spirit."

Gavin heard the shuffle of footsteps and the click of the door. He wished Uncle Warney and Dexter would stay, but the loneliness never came. Instead, a soft, loving Presence approached as if on kitten paws, making him feel loved like he did when his mother checked on him after she thought he was asleep.

The oil created a tingly sensation on his forehead. Happy memories swept through his mind—swinging so high at the playground he thought he might go over the bar; walking in the snow with his dad to find the perfect Christmas tree; coming home to fresh-baked cookies; laughing with Eric and Molly in their backyard when they were little.

"I have loved you with an everlasting love," a quiet Voice whispered to Gavin's innermost self. Somehow he knew this meant he should prepare himself for God to bring other, more painful, memories to the surface.

The image of his dad's angry face flashed in his mind, giving him second thoughts about whether he wanted to do this or not. Before he could retreat, the scene shifted to Bea's haughty smirk and Eric's betrayal. He saw ridiculing football players, report cards with mediocre grades, and the time he got caught cheating. White lies and half-truths seared his conscience. His eyes started to burn. Quiet tears worked their way down his cheeks.

"Hold out your hand," the Voice said. "I have something for you."

Gavin didn't know if he was awake or asleep, but he stretched out his hand and felt a slender object being placed on his palm. He closed his fingers around it.

"Hold fast to everything I have spoken to you, Gavin. We're going deeper."

Deeper than this? Gavin's pulse was already racing so fast he didn't know how much more he could take, but he took an unsteady breath and said, "Ready. I guess."

"The road is dusty," the Voice said. "You've been walking for days. It's hot. You've never been so tired."

Gavin felt a thick, supernatural mist engulf him. Immediately he became aware of a bundle, slung over his shoulder, that pressed into the middle of his back. He shifted under the weight, stood, and looked down at his feet. *Sandals? And a tunic?* He wore a knee-length linen garment, fastened at the waist by a leather girdle, with an outer garment of soft wool. *I'm in Bible times. How'd I get here?*

He looked up, and there ahead of him on the dirt path was Jesus, beaten and bruised. His clothing was in shreds. He limped along the road, barely able to carry His own weight.

"Let Me carry your load for you." Jesus extended His hand.

"No, that wouldn't be fair." Gavin's voice came out louder than he expected and startled him as much as the dream he was living. "You've

311

barely got enough strength as it is." He didn't want to watch the agony of the Man limping toward him, but he couldn't take his eyes off Him.

He wore a crown of thorns on His head, forced deep into His scalp and forehead. "This is the Via Dolorosa, *the way of suffering.* It is the path that led Me to Golgotha, where I was crucified for something I didn't do."

A light flashed, and suddenly a history film played in living color on the TV screen of Gavin's mind. Roman soldiers drove seven-inch spikes into Jesus' wrists. Then into His feet.

"Enough! I know. Please." Everything in Gavin screamed STOP. "Can't you at least take those briars off Your head? There aren't any soldiers here now."

Abruptly, the vision ceased, but Jesus still stood before him. Slowly, He turned and glanced toward the attic wall.

With tears streaming down his face, Gavin turned around and saw it for the first time. There, leaning against the wall, stood a life-size, rough-hewn wooden cross. It was old and—a shiver ran through him—with rust-colored stains running into the grooves.

Suddenly aware of the object in his clenched fist, Gavin unfolded his fingers and looked down to see an ancient nail. His other hand held a hammer. "But You already *did* that." Gavin began to shake uncontrollably. "What are these for?"

Silence blanked the room until . . . at last, Gavin was prepared to hear.

"The nail represents the baggage you've been carrying, Gavin. All your hurts and shortcomings, all your fears and oversights, all the wrongs that have been done to you and the wrongs you've done to others, all the sins you've ever committed or ever will. It's personal. I hung there for *you*. Now, use the hammer, and let's get on with it."

"What? You want me to hammer this nail? In that cross? Crucify You all over again? I . . . I can't. I won't!"

Jesus shook his head, smiling. "Not all over again, Gavin. I died once, for all people, from the beginning of time to the end. My crucifixion is over and complete."

Gavin could hear Uncle Warney quoting his favorite verse as clear as if he were still there in the room with him. *I have been crucified with Christ and I no longer live, but Christ lives in me.*

The hammer grew heavy in Gavin's hand. A knot tightened in the pit of his stomach. He didn't understand except that somehow his own sin belonged on that cross where Jesus died. He agonized over just where to place the nail. With his hand shaking, he positioned the nail at eye level and prepared to swing.

Past offenses, long forgotten, flowed across his memory . . . unkind words he'd spoken, acts he thought he'd gotten away with, and times when he'd faked belief in God. With each one, Gavin swung the hammer against the cross, tentatively tapping the nail at first, then harder and harder. Each blow tore the guilt and pain from his soul and placed it on that cross.

He hadn't realized just how far he was from God. After striking it one last time, Gavin crumpled into a heap.

"I'm sorry, so sorry," he sobbed. "I know You want to forgive me, but I've been a lot worse than I ever thought."

"No one deserves forgiveness," Jesus said gently. "It is a gift."

At once, Gavin tasted a bittersweet blend of dried apricots, apple slices, and 7-Up—bringing thoughts of the diary and what might be required of him. "The job's too big for me. Let someone else do it," he blurted out.

"You sound like Moses."

Fire shot through Gavin like sunburn from the inside out. He opened his eyes and found the attic ablaze with light. If this was a dream, it sure seemed real. He no longer wore the tunic and sandals but the same starched shirt, now rumpled, that he'd put on that morning for church. The Voice spoke—but the light was too bright for Gavin to look directly at Him.

"Moses complained about his speech problem. Your learning disability is not much different." The light grew larger, filling the room. "In the days to come, what you see as a problem will become an attribute. It will keep you humble and dependent on Me, not on yourself."

The light continued to expand, but the figure at the center stepped forward and enabled Gavin to see as he shielded his eyes. It was the risen Christ! Light beams exploded into a shower of stars that drenched the attic in crisscross flashes, causing him to drop to the floor.

For some odd reason, the minute his knees hit the floor, the image of Bea Daark intruded. The hair rose on his arms and the nape of his neck. He saw her and another person—Hee-Haw Downes—stumbling into trees and bushes as if they couldn't see them. Were they blind? And what was that in the background—Stokes Mansion?

How many visions can one person have?

Daark Doings

"Nem? Nem! Where are you?" Bea clung to the bark of the tree she'd just collided into. In spite of her determination to keep her dignity, she convulsed into unexpected sobs.

"Quit your blubbering," Hee-Haw said. "I'm right here."

A whiff of body odor assaulted her nose and served as a reality check for her disposition. She was no namby pamby. Wiping her eyes, she said the first thing that came to mind. "I'd appreciate it if you'd keep your armpits at a respectable distance. Didn't your mother ever teach you to bathe?"

"Nope. She gave it up as a lost cause the day she died."

"She died?"

"Three years ago in a train crash. She and my brother."

Bea felt herself softening toward the bloke. "Oh, you poor dear. I'm so sorry."

"I'm not. She was a pain. Don't be going all mushy on me." Hee-Haw said from an indistinguishable place too close for comfort. "I'm trying to summon Ooziss to get us out of this mess."

Bea's heart banged in her ears. They were blind—blinded by the light that burst from those wretched attic windows. Why, oh, why had she insisted that she and Nem could lure Gavin into the limo?

Hee-Haw recited a mantra. Well, that was fine. His spirit guide might be their only hope. After all, it wasn't like she could call for help. How would she ever explain that two wonky blokes driving a horse-drawn carriage had kidnapped Gavin before *she* could and that she had instructed her driver to follow them?

"If only I hadn't released Alvin to take the limo home," she said to Nem. "At *your* suggestion, thank you very much." Armpits would get no more sympathy from her.

"Look, Miss Priss," Nem muttered in a low voice. "Shut your trap. How do you expect Ooziss to hear me with all your baby-whining?"

"First my shoes are ruined by horse excrement. Now we're *blind*." She could hear hysteria creeping into her voice. "If Ooziss can't restore our sight, can he at least get us out of this *dreadful* place?"

"This dreadful place." Downes mocked her accent. "I get it. You don't know how to shut up."

Bea fumed. If not for those hooded fools throwing a spanner into the works, she'd be back at the Lodge with Gavin under her control. And if she hadn't been distracted by Nem, she would have seen the hideous light coming before it blinded her.

Something wailed and hissed near Bea, jolting her already frayed nerves.

Tree branches rustled, and Nem swore under his breath.

"Don't you know anything? It's a stupid cat!" Nem snarled. "Now be quiet so I can reach Ooziss."

"A cat?" Bea gave a shaky laugh. "Just a cat? Great."

She fumed for a few moments, waiting for Nem to say something else or to start his mantra again, but she heard nothing. "What about Ooziss?"

"I—I tried," Nem said after a long silence. "I don't know what's going on in my head. All I can see is this light behind my eyeballs."

"What do you mean light behind your eyeballs?" Bea inched toward his voice. Even being with Nem was better than being alone.

"It's like refracted light. Lucky for us I have this," he said.

"Have what? You say that like I can see what it is."

"Give me your hand." He rubbed her fingers against what felt like a rough stone.

"What is it?"

"Moldavite. It's dynamite green, really cool, if you could see."

"Moldavite?" Her heart pounded. "Real moldavite? That's one of my passions."

"Yep, one and the same, straight from the meteorite shower in the Moldau Valley of Czechoslovakia twenty million years ago," he said. "It's a talisman."

"I know. I've been begging Mum for years to get me one, but she won't hear of it. How'd you get this?" She could almost envision the stone's colorful light show.

"Borrowed it from Auntie Soshal," Nem said. "Hold it, and it'll ground you in the energies of the planet. This blindness is temporary. The moldavite will speed up our restoration by putting us in balance with the earth."

Bea grasped the stone, but all she felt was its cold, multi-faceted surface. "It's not working."

"Give it a minute."

Bea counted to a hundred and still felt nothing—saw nothing. "This is worthless." She tossed it aside with a mixture of anger and dismay. "It's probably not even real."

"What did you *do?*" Nem shouted so loud that Bea shrank away from him.

"I threw it away. It was a fake."

"Are you *nuts?*" Nem shoved her, causing her to stumble into a tree. "Just 'cause you didn't feel anything doesn't mean it isn't real. You have to have the knowledge to use it."

"And I suppose you do?"

"Does a bat have wings?"

"Then why didn't you?" Bea demanded, insulted that the fool could possibly think he knew more about the crystal than she did.

"I was being polite."

"Right. You don't have a polite bone in your body." Bea kept her uppity tone but wondered if he might be right.

"If I don't get it back to my aunt's shop, she'll kill me." Nem grunted.

"Yes, well, that's just ducky. As if I could believe you about anything. Don't you get it? We're blind!" Bea was on the verge of being out of control. She wanted to scream loud and long until she remembered that she didn't want anybody to know they were there. "What makes you think we'll get our sight back?"

"I just know. I don't like this any better than you, but I'd feel a whole lot better if I could find Auntie's rock. Come on. How about helping me out here?"

Bea could hear him slapping the earth with his hands. "You had that moldavite on you—a lot of good it did protecting you. What was that blasted light that got us, anyway?"

"Don't know."

"I can tell you this much." A shudder ran through her. "Bad things happen to me every time I come near that old man."

Nem snorted. "Let's find the moldavite and get out of here."

Bea got on her knees and started patting around. "It's so black." Fear threatened to overtake her. She breathed in shallow, quick gasps, fighting back tears she refused to shed. "I can feel the sun, but I can't see any light at all."

Nem didn't say a word.

"Nem?" Bea held out her arms, trying to relocate him. "Don't fool around like that. Where are you?"

"Here." His voice cracked. "I thought I might be able to try out-of-body travel, but no luck. Can't get my body to relax enough to reach the astral plane."

"Some help you—" A brain flash brought Clyccan to mind. "Of course!" Bea felt for the chain around her neck. "Why didn't I think of you sooner?"

The pendant felt cool to her touch. "We cannot see, dear Clyccan. Guide us back to the Lodge, now." The pen emitted a soft, high-pitched whistle, and Bea felt a flash of heat at her fingertips. "Ready?"

"Make it help me find the crystal before we go," Nem said. "Seems like the least you can do since you got us into this mess."

Bea wished he could see the anger on her face. "All you want is that *precious* moldavite back."

"Well, sure, wouldn't you?"

"Clyccan, find!" With those words, Bea's fear diminished. Although she still couldn't see anything but inky darkness, she had regained some semblance of control.

The pitch of Clyccan's whistle dropped to a lower tone and crackled with an occasional series of faint, high beeps.

"Sounds like a Geiger counter." Nem moved closer and brushed against Bea's shoulder. His voice was loud in her ear.

"Get back! You'll mess up the calibrations." Bea pushed him away. "Don't you ever brush your teeth?"

"I have more important things to do. So, what do you think? Can that thing of yours find my moldavite and get us back to the Lodge?"

"More important things? What's more important than getting our sight back?" Bea aimed Clyccan in various directions, crouching low to the ground and inching from right to left. "If we find it, would your Auntie Soshal sell it?"

"Sure! But it'll cost you," Nem said.

"Of course. All I have to do is convince Mum." Clyccan warmed in her hand, crackled louder, and issued a series of steady beeps. Bea felt around in the ashes and twigs. Her hand settled on a smooth, squarish rock. "Is this it?"

Nem brayed loud, but not long, the instant he took the moldavite in his hand. "At least that pen thing of yours is good for something."

That was as good an apology as she could expect from Donkey Boy.

"Clyccan, you're a gem!" Bea laughed and gave it a kiss. "Now, lead us to the Lodge."

Clutching the talisman, Bea felt like a child playing a game her nanny taught her years ago. "You're getting warm," Clyccan indicated. "No, that's cold. Yes, hot, hot, this way!" Between the sounds, her sense of touch, and halting steps, it took Bea and Nem more than an hour to return to the Lodge.

"Almost there," Bea said when her foot touched the fresh macadam of their recently paved driveway.

"Yeah, it's downhill from here, but we're just at the entrance, and your driveway's humongous."

Hot, dirty, thirsty, and blind, Bea didn't have the energy or inclination for further debate, so she trudged the rest of the way without comment. When Madam Daark's lingering scent reached Bea's nostrils, she knew they had reached the front steps and her mother must be standing in the doorway.

"Bea." Madam's cool, impersonal tone broke the stillness.

"Mum?" Bea fought back childish tears and the desire to throw herself into her arms.

"I see you and Mr. Downes found your way. I was about to send Alvin back for you. But you were so sure of yourselves, I decided I'd rather watch."

"Watch?" Bea felt like a bug that had crawled out from under a rock. "You've been watching us?"

"Of course. I consulted the Rosaline ball to track you as soon as Alvin returned. Quite amusing, really, to see you groping around." She took Bea by the hand. "Let's go in, and you can tell me just how you came to be blinded in the first place."

Nem plodded along after them, up the steps and through the door. "Know any charms to help us get our sight back?"

"I have everything prepared." Madam's otherworldly voice reverberated off the cathedral ceiling. "Right this way."

Bea couldn't see if the drawing room tapestries were drawn, but she could sense the velvet hush as she passed through the French doors. Even without her mother's hand pulling her toward the ceramic table, the strong fragrance of her perfume would have directed her there.

"I know where we are." Nem sounded chipper. "The room with all those books, paintings, and breakable stuff."

The moldavite safely tucked away in Nem's pocket briefly crossed Bea's mind, but it was likely a blooming fake. And, all she really wanted was to have her sight restored.

Bea lowered herself to a velvet cushion on the floor and bumped her knee on the leg of the scrolled-foot table. When the inquisition commenced, it didn't take long for her to realize that her mother's observation hadn't included the initial chase. How much to tell? She decided to skim over the details. "So Gavin's kidnappers were really his great-uncle and a schoolmate. We hid in the weeds behind one of the outbuildings, but Nem thought someone might spot the limo so I sent Alvin home. Nem and I were—"

Madam Daark pounded the table. "Stop! Did you say Gavin's great-uncle? Warnard Stokes is not to be trusted."

Nem let out a low donkey bray. "So you know a little something about Gavin's Uncle Warney, eh?"

Madam's voice was strained but controlled. "If Warnard Stokes was involved, the power that blinded you constitutes a religious curse straight from the enemy of our souls. We must move quickly. There's no guarantee I can restore your sight."

The French Gothic clock chimed four times, sending a flutter of panic through Bea's veins.

"But you *can* reverse it, right, Mum?" She choked back a sob and kicked her foot under the table, hoping to strike Nem. "And you said it was temporary! A lot you know, you fool!"

Madam rang a bell, and the doors whooshed open. "Jenkins," she commanded. "Gather the elements we discussed, and bring them with haste. Don't forget the saffron."

Bea heard Jenkins exit and the flutter of pages being turned, bringing a glimmer of hope. "Mum, is that your Book of Shadows?"

"Don't start your prying again, young lady. Just when I think I can *begin* to confide in you, you go and pull a stunt like this, putting us all in a bind."

Putting us in a bind? Bea bit her tongue. Her sight had been taken, and her mother was upset because it put *her* in a bind?

"I'm having second thoughts about ever sharing my recipes with you." Madam's voice raised an octave. "And you, young man, what do you think you're looking at?"

"Nothing. I can't see, remember?" Nem sounded amused, which only served to make Bea more miserable.

It seemed to take an hour for Madam Daark to mix up her brew. With the incantations spoken too softly for Bea to hear, she finally gave up trying to figure the whole thing out and began praying in the name of Laddrach for the concoction to work.

"Divine goddess," Madam Daark said, startling Bea by smearing a cold, gooey paste over her eyelids.

Oh, great. I've been praying to the wrong god. She tried to visualize healing energy in the form of white light flowing from the divine goddess into her body, but the smell of the paste distracted her. She recognized the aroma of mint and other fragrant spices, but the odor of swamp water was far too dominant for it to be pleasant. How was she supposed to relax in the middle of that stench? But she knew she must.

Her mother completed the ritual. "Don't move until the mud dries," she said. "Well, you may recline, but don't so much as twitch your eyelashes until I return."

No sooner had her mother left the room than Bea realized how thirsty she was. Why hadn't she thought to ask for something to drink? She stretched out on the floor and pulled her knees up to her chin. If the magick didn't work and she was cursed to go through life blind, she'd rather die of dehydration.

"Told you it was temporary!" Nem danced a gangly jig as soon as Madam Daark removed the dry mud-paste from his eyes.

Bea was too busy gulping water to answer the arrogant fool.

"Quit guzzling and come with me." Madam Daark beckoned with a red fingernail. "I have a backup plan."

Never had Bea enjoyed the décor of the Lodge more as they moved down the hallway, through the dining hall, past the commercial kitchen, and into Madam's private laboratory. She could see! Every Tiffany lamp was more colorful than Bea remembered. The dark paneling seemed richer, and the stainless steel more highly polished.

And there, in a high-backed chair against the far wall, sat . . . "Eric?"

Bea hurried to his side, chattering on about how surprised she was to see him, when she realized he wasn't responding. She waved her hand in front of his eyes, and he continued to stare.

"Mum, what's going on? Is he blind, too?"

"No, dear. I've been having a nice soothing chat with the lad. He was more susceptible than most."

"You put him under?" Nem said.

Bea bent down to study Eric's frozen expression.

"As I said," Madam Daark stepped in front of Bea and brushed Nem aside. "Plan B." She drew herself into a queenly posture and began to sway.

Bea felt a spirit enter the room.

"Eric Everett," Madam Daark said in a silky voice, "it is time to fulfill the command. On the count of three, you will find Gavin and lead him back here. Tell him Molly is in grave danger at the Lodge. You must convince Gavin to come and rescue her. You *must*. Without Gavin, Molly will die. Do you understand?"

Eric nodded ever so slowly, and Madam continued.

"One. Two . . ."

CHAPTER THIRTY-THREE

GAVIN

Battle-Ready

Gavin's whole body quaked as he flattened himself face-down on the floor in Christ's presence. Sweat dripped off his brow. He wanted to wipe it away, but his arms felt pinned to his side. He knew that it was the Spirit of the Lord that held him there, washing him and cleansing every cell in his body. His pulse pounded in his temples, shooting pins and needles through his limbs.

Scenes flashed through his mind like movie clips. The one of a blinded Bea and Hee-Haw, morphed into a cloud that became his dad's scowling face. When the image of Bruce Goodfellow spat out the familiar, *you'll never amount to anything,* Gavin was sure he had returned to his nightmare. He wanted to hide, but the Lord wouldn't let him.

"We deal in truth, Gavin."

"Wh-who is 'we'?"

"The Father, the Son, and Me. We are One."

The Holy Spirit. Gavin lifted his head and looked at Jesus. But the sight was too much, so he squeezed his eyes shut and pushed his chin into the cold, hard floor.

"Why does my dad act like that?" Gavin trembled, perplexed by the range of emotions assaulting him.

"Your earthly father has lessons of his own to learn. As much as you yearn for him to be proud of you, Gavin, you must be patient. Until then, know that Your heavenly Father loves you. His love is more than enough."

Gavin's head began to spin. He took three deep breaths. An odd sense of belonging wrapped him in an invisible cocoon. None of this made sense, but he didn't want it to end.

"Listen to the Master," the Holy Spirit said.

Gavin studied the figure of Christ before him. His face shone brighter than the sun. No amount of bleach could make a robe that white.

"Just as God gave Moses his staff—" the voice of Jesus made Gavin's insides quiver— "so I give you this armor. Stand up, son, and let Me dress you for the battle you will soon face."

Gavin gulped. Armor? What would he need armor for? Wasn't that for knights and castles? He clambered to unsteady feet. He closed his eyes, feeling silly, like a child waiting for his mommy to dress him for school.

"Open your eyes," Jesus said in a feather-soft command.

The instant he gazed into his Lord's loving expression, Gavin's inadequacies vanished. He felt something tighten around his waist. Venturing a glance down at a mysterious leather belt, he was nearly blinded by the reflection off its gold buckle.

"This is the belt of truth." As Jesus uttered the words, a burning, fiery, gliding, angelic being appeared with a hot coal in its hand and rested it on Gavin's lips. Oddly enough, it didn't hurt. A tingling sensation accompanied the angel-soft touch that traveled from his slightly opened mouth to the back of his tongue, leaving him with a fresh, clean feeling.

"Whom shall I send? Who will go for Us?" the Lord said.

"I'm here! Send me!" Gavin wondered where those words and the conviction to say them came from. But he meant it.

Then Jesus lowered a breastplate over Gavin's head. It came to rest on his shoulders with thick leather straps. Turning his head to look over his shoulder, he was surprised to find that it not only covered his chest but had a protective panel for his back, as well. It was heavy.

"Guard your heart," Christ said.

Next came the sandals. Gavin lifted his left foot off the floor and wobbled in stork-like fashion to be fitted by the Master's hand. Putting his foot down, he raised the right one for the same treatment. When both sandals were in place, a pervading sense of peace encircled him.

The Lord placed a shield in Gavin's left hand. It was large, four-cornered, the size of a small door. His legs bowed under the weight. But then Jesus lifted one corner off the floor. With His assistance, it was featherlight and stable, and Gavin marveled. Suddenly Gavin knew that with God nothing was impossible.

Stillness blanketed the room for an hour, a day, a lifetime—Gavin couldn't tell.

Then, in the distance, he heard a drum roll as the Lord encased Gavin's head with a helmet. Strains of music from the boom box broke the silence and swelled, adding to the fanfare. The ornate helmet weighed more than all the rest of the armor put together, but Gavin's knees didn't buckle, and his shoulders didn't droop. Standing tall and confident, his mind was clear as he peered through the protective slits in front of his eyes. It reminded him of the blinders the Clydesdales wore. He couldn't see to the right or to the left—only straight ahead.

"Follow Me," Jesus said and moved to the far side of the attic. They stopped by a footlocker where the Lord lifted the lid, withdrew a short sword, and presented it to him. As soon as Gavin's fingers touched the gleaming metal handle, he saw innumerable letters engraved in the blade, layer upon layer, hundreds of layers deep. *The Word of God!* He swallowed hard and bit back tears realizing that he could comprehend whole sentences without any effort—it wasn't that he read the words so much with his mind but with his soul.

"By faith you have received the armor of God. Learn well the lessons and properties of each piece. I have provided the armor, but you must put it on every day. You must choose to take it up, to put it on. Dexter will serve as your armor bearer. When it comes time for you to confront the evil in Burnt Swamp, he will help you wield the authority you have been given. The power to overcome is not in the armor, Gavin. It is in the spirit realm."

Gavin shook his arms and legs in an attempt to get the feel of his new equipment. In the distance, he heard trumpets—a faint crystalline sound coming straight from heaven.

"Many are called, Gavin. Few are chosen. My Father has chosen you to sound the trumpet for those who have ears to hear. Follow Me in the ways of truth, humility, faithfulness, and love, and see what I will do through you. Begin with the belt of truth. It will remind you to think before you speak."

Gavin's lips and tongue continued to tingle. Between the hot coal and the belt of truth, lying was no longer an option.

Jesus' eyes shone like summer lightning bolts. "Put your trust in Me. The armor is effective because I am your protector. Remember—" Jesus lifted his eyes toward heaven. "I am the Way, the Truth, and the Life."

The words Gavin heard registered in his spirit as well as in his ears.

"The battle is Mine," Jesus said. "You are the vessel I have chosen to work through in these challenging days. No one else has ever walked the path I have prepared for you; no one else ever will. You are uniquely Mine and will serve as an example to others as you put on your armor and follow Me."

Gavin's heart vaulted into somersaults. A question rose up in him that he couldn't bring himself to ask. *Follow You where?*

The answer came as quickly as the question formed in his mind.

"I will show you the way; I will reveal the truth; I will guard your life. Whether you succeed or fail will depend on the choices you make. Daily, you must decide who and what to trust. Choose wisely."

Somewhere in the background, a horse whinnied. Before Gavin could say a word, Jesus vanished.

Although lamplight and flickering candles remained, the sudden loss of divine light caused Gavin to blink as his eyes adjusted to the dimness. Had he fallen asleep? His forehead pulsed where Uncle Warney had placed the three oil images of the cross. As Gavin touched it, he spied the shadow of a giant cross on the wall, projected by the afternoon sunlight coming through the attic window. It moved toward him, stretching and growing, spreading across the floor until it touched his feet.

In that instant, as if riding on the sunbeam, a pure white dove flew in through the open center window of the attic. Circling once over Gavin's head, it continued in a straight path to perch on the vertical beam of the cross. There it opened its mouth to coo softly and dropped something that clattered to the floor. Giving Gavin what seemed like a significant look, the dove flew out.

Gavin's heart fluttered and skipped.

I must be dreaming. He patted his arms, his legs, and his chest to make certain he was awake. But when he touched his waist, his fingers felt something that wasn't there before he entered the attic— a fine leather belt with a solid gold buckle. The sun glinted off it. And upside down or not, he recognized it right away—an ornate "T" engraved in the buckle that looked remarkably like a cross.

"Truth," he whispered. It was no dream. It was his destiny.

He turned to the wall where Christ had stood and the dove had visited moments before. Bending to see what the object was that had dropped from the dove's mouth, he retrieved an antique nail that looked identical to the one Jesus had given him—the one he'd hammered into the cross. Couldn't be . . . could it?

CHAPTER THIRTY-FOUR

For Such a Time as This

"Don't ya just love it when a plan comes together?" Warney asked as he and Dexter smoothed the red-checkered cloth over the table in front of the dining room fireplace.

Gavin had been in the attic so long, Warney decided to go ahead and set up the picnic he'd brought for the celebration. Setting three places with paper plates and cups, the fanciest Warney could find at Fennemore's Dollar Store, he exhaled a long, contented sigh. This was an occasion Warney had been anticipating for a long time.

Just as they heaved the picnic basket onto the table, the sound of footfalls on the staircase caught Warney's ear. "He's comin' down."

Warney and Dexter moved quickly into the foyer where they had to shield their eyes to watch the radiant-faced Gavin descend the stairs.

"I knew it," Warney whispered. The foyer blazed from the intensity of Gavin's inner light. Every fixture dazzled with brilliance and emitted a shimmer of pure glory.

CANDY ABBOTT

Warney shadowed his eyes with his hand and squinted to get a better look. Even Gavin's smile looked different, more genuine.

"We done right to bring him here," Warney said as he watched Gavin move down the stairs and come to rest on the landing. Gavin's spirit had matured during the last hour. The presence of God was so strong and the intensity of Gavin's gaze so joyful that it made Warney feel giddy.

"I thought it was a dream but . . . but this . . ." Gavin held out the nail. "This is real."

Warney saw the nail, and his breath caught in his throat. It was identical to the one he'd found that gave him the far-fetched idea to kidnap Gavin and plan the attic ceremony. With a trembling hand, he reached into his pocket. It was still there. "I meant to give this to ya, Gavin," he said, holding it out for him to see, "but it slipped muh mind. The Lord Hisself give ya that nail as a symbol."

"The nail . . ." Gavin started to speak but looked perplexed. "What happened up there was . . . was . . ."

"Was impossible to comprehend, let alone explain," Dexter said. "Tell him what we saw from outside." He turned to Uncle Warney.

"Glory to God!" Warney's spirit stirred all over again at the recollection. "We was sittin' on the porch when we heard a great whooshing sound up thar on the top floor. Light beams come a-streamin' this way and that, like a crate of firecrackers gone haywire."

Dexter's eyes grew large. "You should have seen it! A huge—I mean *huge*—light surged over the whole mansion, growing brighter and brighter by the second, spreading like wildfire, setting every pane of glass on the top floor aglow." He became still. "Mama would have called it a 'mountaintop experience.'" Dexter lifted his wire rim glasses and wiped his eyes. "Not everybody gets that. Wish it could have been me," he mumbled as he shoved his glasses higher on the bridge of his nose where they rested, cockeyed.

Warney noticed that the expression on Gavin's face seemed to touch Dexter at a heart level as they gazed into one another's eyes—their souls connecting for sure. The glow that emanated from Gavin's face intensified. "It was the evil one who made you question why God did not protect your parents from the curse." Gavin's few words triggered a long-overdue release of pent up grief in Dexter.

"I've been blaming God and didn't even know it." Heart-wrenching sobs wracked Dexter's body. "I've been trying to figure out why God allowed my parents to die when who am I to comprehend His ways and His thoughts? I've just got to trust Him. I—I thought I did."

Warney felt God's power to heal come upon him. Placing his hand on Dexter's head as the boy crumpled in a heap on the floor, he said, "In the name of Jesus, Name above all names, be healed."

Gavin joined them and placed his hand on Dexter's shoulder. He didn't speak a word. He didn't have to. The power of God was present.

Dexter wept long and hard. Then, abruptly, as if flicking away a bumble bee that had left its stinger in him, he sniffed, wiped his eyes, and smiled. "Thanks. I needed that."

Gavin opened his mouth to speak again, and Warney held his breath. What other Christ-inspired wisdom would he utter?

"I feel like Superman!" Gavin puffed out his chest and grinned. "Like I could take on the swamp dragon and wring the stuffin's out of him."

Warney chuckled at the notion. Gavin was still all boy. "Let's not be gettin' carried away now. Ya might jest have to *do* that afore things are said and done." He caught a look of concern in Dexter's eyes and grew serious. "Gavin, right now yer as frisky as a newborn pup, but thar's something that's been weighin' on me ya gotta know."

"Lay it on me, Uncle Warney," Gavin beamed. "Today I feel like I can handle anything."

"Well," Warney said, "Bea and Madam Daark movin' into the Lodge weren't no mishap. They been sent to us with their glitter and riches to lure young uns away from God."

Warney watched a strange expression creep over Gavin's face, so he paused, expecting him to say something. When he didn't, Warney went on. "Gavin, when ya let Bea git her hands on that diary, ya done more than ya know fer their cause. That ain't no ordinary old book. It's got signs in it that point the way to restorin' or destroyin' the swamp."

"Like what?" Gavin's eyes were ablaze with interest.

"Clues, that's what—fer good or fer evil. Bea's mother'll be droolin' all over them pages if she's got that book in her clutches, providin' she can get it open. Gavin, if Burnt Swamp's to be saved, ya gotta git it back and go to work figurin' out them *good* clues b'fore Madam and Bea and that Downes' boy figure out the *bad* ones."

Gavin waved the nail in the air like a miniature sword. "I'm ready and willing, and I promise you, Uncle Warney, with Jesus' help I'll get it back."

Warney tapped his walking stick on the floor. "Yer goin' into spiritual battle, real and deadly, Gavin. Think yer ready? Ready to put on the armor of God?"

"I've already got it." Gavin's hand flew to his waistband. "I almost forgot." He felt for the leather belt and gasped. "It's gone!"

"What's gone?" Warney asked.

"The belt of truth Jesus gave me! It was leather with a gold buckle and it had a big 'T' engraved in it." His fingertips quivered at his waist searching for the missing belt. "But I can still feel it."

Uncle Warney chuckled. "It's still there, Gavin." He folded his hands together in a comfortable gesture. "Ya jest got a sneak peek into the spirit realm. The belt's a spiritual weapon, not physical."

"I know," Dexter said. "Just like when Elisha prayed for his servant to see a whole mountainside full of heavenly horses and chariots of fire!"

"So Uncle Warney's right?" Gavin continued to touch his waist. "My belt of truth is still there even though I can't see it?"

Dexter's face grew serious. "It's as real as your faith. But the belt's just one piece of God's armor, Gavin. You're going to need all six pieces to fight the battle with the Daarks."

"I have them all," Gavin said with a faraway look. "Jesus dressed me from head to toe. It's just that I saw the belt with my own eyes, like it was real."

"And so it is." Warney smiled. "All the pieces, whether ya can see 'em or not, are real. And I 'spect yer gonna have a chance right soon ta use that belt of truth."

"Although you might have to let it out a notch when you see all those sandwiches Uncle Warney packed for us," Dexter teased and pointed to the table in the next room.

"Great, I'm starved!" Gavin said.

"Think ya could eat some chicken salad sandwiches?" Warney asked as the threesome waltzed toward the humble spread. "Time ta celebrate!"

It did Warney's heart good to see the boys finish off two sandwiches each, along with the old-fashioned barrel pickles he'd been soaking in brine for the past four weeks. He was so filled with joy, he hardly did more than nibble on his own sardine and mustard sandwich.

"Save room for dessert," he said when they reached for more chips. Digging in the basket, he took out three Moon Pies, another of Gavin's favorites.

"Wow!" Gavin grabbed one. "Do you like Moon Pies, Dex?"

"I love them." Dexter mumbled through a mouth full of chips. "This is the best—"

"Gavin! Gavin!" someone yelled.

"Sounds like Eric." Gavin and Dexter jumped up and ran to the door.

Warney struggled to his feet and grabbed for his cane. "Sure does. And he sounds mighty agitated."

———

Eric stumbled up the walk, breathless.

"What's wrong? You been sleeping in your clothes?" Gavin tried to sound lighthearted while alarms rang inside his head.

Eric swayed and stumbled toward him but didn't answer.

Gavin dashed down the steps and caught Eric under the arms. "You look spazzed out; your eyes look funny. What's wrong with you?"

"He looks drunk," Dexter said, grabbing Eric's other arm to steady him.

With no warning, Eric's knees gave out, and Gavin caught him again.

"No. Waddaya think, I'm stupid?" Eric's tongue seemed to get hung up on his braces. "I'm an aaathlete. I don't drrink or do drrrugs."

"Then what's wrong with you?" Dexter asked.

"It's not . . . what's wrong . . . with me," Eric said in a monotone, all inflection gone out of his voice. "It's what's wrong . . . with Molly."

"Molly?" Uncle Warney pulled Eric to his feet. "What's wrong with Molly?"

"She's at . . . the Lodge," he continued in his robot voice. "Madam Daark . . ." Eric seemed puzzled, as though trying to remember something. "Molly is . . . at the Lodge . . . in trouble. Madam Daark said . . . Gavin has to come . . . now." He started to shake all over.

"Okay, Eric," Warney said. "You jest git yerself calmed down a bit. I'm gonna have a quick word with Gavin over yonder where I left muh walkin' stick. Dexter, you stay here and look after Eric."

Warney guided Gavin by the elbow to the hundred-year-old oak. "I see their game," he whispered in Gavin's ear.

"But Molly!" Gavin's heart thudded in his chest so hard he wasn't sure he'd heard anything right. "And what's wrong with Eric?"

"Hold yer horses thar, young fella. I see right through it. That Daark woman has drugged Eric or put him under some sort of spell to lure ya smack into their clutches. All they want is fer ya to open that thar diary Bea stole from ya. If fer one minute I thought thar was any truth to them havin' Molly, I'd be bustin' over thar muhself."

"So Eric's bait?" Gavin's skin ran hot, then cold, as a whole cluster of emotions collided inside him—confusion, fear, excitement.

"Not to worry," Warney said.

Gavin felt Uncle Warney's his eyes clinging to his and studying his face.

"Here's the plan." Uncle Warney held hs gaze. "You go along with Eric to the Lodge, and I'll follow after."

Fear surged to the top of Gavin's tangled feelings. "But you said it was a trap."

"And you got a secret weapon they don't know nothin' about," Warney reminded him. "If this had happened before today, you'd o' been their pawn. Difference is, yer fresh empowered from yer anointin', and the Lord's gonna send ya right out to try that belt of truth on fer size. No need fer ya to be afeared of 'em. Dexter and I'll be coverin' ya with prayer, and the Holy Spirit is right in thar." He tapped Gavin's chest over his pounding heart. "You pray, too—all the time—'bout everything. It's what makes yer armor work. But 'specially now!"

Gavin prayed, "Help me, God," with his eyes open, fingering the nail in his pocket, a symbol to remind him that all the power of God was at his disposal. Funny how such an ordinary thing could make him feel so brave. "Let's do it!"

He felt goosebumps as Uncle Warney gave his shoulder a firm squeeze.

"Dexter, how about callin' yer grandpap," Warney said. "Git him to come by the Lodge in the patrol car jest in case we need the law in on this. I feel it in muh bones you'll accomplish yer mission in the spirit realm, but it won't hurt to have Officer Charlie showin' up."

He turned to Gavin. "Yer about to find out what it means to be faithful and true on the front lines. Be strong and of good courage. The battle is the Lord's. Whatever words He gives ya, speak 'em out loud and clear. Stand firm. Stand firm no matter what!"

"My stomach's doing loop-de-loops, but I'm ready," Gavin said in a voice that didn't sound like his own. "After all, with Jesus, nothing can go wrong." He swallowed hard. "Can it?"

CHAPTER THIRTY-FIVE

GAVIN

Showdown at the Lodge

"Come *on*. What is *wrong* with you?" Gavin couldn't believe Eric would drag his feet on a mission to rescue his own twin. Eric scuffed along at a snail's pace. Instead of breaking into a run as he longed to do, Gavin had to steady his cousin to keep him from stumbling.

"Not much farther," Gavin said. "Tell me again how Molly wound up at the Lodge." Maybe this time he could get a little more out of him than the same broken record.

Eric didn't even sound like himself. Instead of rambling on about football or his study hall antics, he sounded like a computer voice. "Molly is at the Lodge. She's in trouble. Madam Daark says you have to come."

Nothing about Eric rang true. *Who was this? A clone? How did the Daarks get a hold of Eric? What did they do to him? What if Molly isn't there at all? Will I be walking into a trap? What if Molly is there? How do we get her out?*

It was just too risky, but as much as he hated the idea of returning to the Lodge, he had no choice. Had it been two months? It seemed like yesterday. Rounding the bend, the Lodge came into view. Gavin was amazed at how different everything looked. Better. Petunias and marigolds peeked through beds of red mulch. All traces of overgrown brush and scraggly limbs were gone, as if they'd never existed. Cheerful, green shutters replaced faded ones. The place almost looked normal, but Gavin knew better.

It was the inside that worried Gavin. Swallowing his fear, he walked down the long, freshly black-topped driveway toward the house with Eric in tow.

"Molly is at the Lodge . . ." Eric repeated.

"So you say." Frustration and fretfulness battled inside Gavin.

Before Gavin and Eric could walk up the front steps, a stocky, tuxedoed butler opened the door. He stood in the threshold like a gatekeeper, his false smile disarming. Gavin backed into Eric as the butler's crooked finger motioned them to follow. "This way, gentlemen."

"Hey, Gav!" Eric swung around and struck a bendable Gumby pose. "What are you doing here?" He grinned and winked.

"What's with you, Eric? One minute you're a zombie, and the next you're . . ."

Eric turned to the butler. "Where'd you hide her, your Excellency?"

"The name is Jenkins," the butler announced. "Hide who, sir?"

Eric's expression grew puzzled, like he'd forgotten he was here on a mission to find his sister. Gavin had stepped into Creepsville for sure and wanted nothing more than to grab Eric and sprint. But he remembered Uncle Warney's words.

Be strong and of good courage.

Jenkins' chest swelled, fit to pop his buttons. "Madam and Bea are expecting you. Follow me . . ."

The spring had returned to Eric's step, and he followed Jenkins like his old self. This time Gavin lagged behind, trying his best to think like a soldier. *Hut-two-three-four.*

Down the winding hallway and around sharp corners they went. When they approached the great room, Gavin noticed the stuffed ram's head still mounted and wondered what they had done with the petrified buzzard. With each step, his legs felt heavier.

At least his dad couldn't say he was lazy and worthless now. His mom would have a heart attack if she knew what he was up to. *If they really kidnapped Molly and she's in there, maybe locked in a closet or . . . worse . . . somebody's gotta save her.* Gavin pushed out images of Molly's hands tied behind her back while a bare lightbulb dangled overhead.

"The great room," Jenkins announced, but Gavin recognized it as the former ceremony room.

When Jenkins ushered them in, three faces swung Gavin's way. A hint of a smile played on Bea's lips as she stood by the fireplace next to a tall woman whose expression was unreadable. Madam Daark. If she just had a long cigarette holder, she could be *Cruella DeVil.* But it was the tall kid, seated in a straight-back chair in the corner, which caught Gavin's attention. Even in the shadows, the look of contempt on his face was undeniable. Hee-Haw Downes.

"Like I said, 'I . . . got . . . your . . . number.'"

The chill in Hee-Haw's voice sent shivers through every nerve in Gavin's body and reminded him that he stood in the room with the candle drippings. Quickly, he scouted for wax on the floor but couldn't recognize the spot because of the Oriental rugs. The full force of his nervous energy blurted out in two words. "Where's Molly?"

"Now, now," Madam Daark said in a soothing voice that had the opposite effect on Gavin. "Molly? Molly who? There's no Molly here." Standing at her full, intimidating height, she pursed her lips and glared at Gavin with upraised eyebrows.

Gavin scowled back. "My cousin, Molly, that's who. Eric said she was in trouble."

Bea smoothed her hair with her hand and arranged the blonde tresses over her shoulder. "There must be some misunderstanding, Gavin. Molly's not here—never has been." Glancing at her mother, Bea's eyes danced. "We have a little something of yours we need to talk about though," she said as she circled to Gavin's left.

"Oh?" Gavin couldn't believe this was happening.

Madam Daark drew something out from beneath the folds of her flowing skirt.

The diary!

Biting his lip so hard he could taste blood, Gavin slipped his hand to his waist. *Yes, still there.* But without faith, his belt of truth wouldn't activate. *I believe. I believe. Lord, help me believe!*

With Bea inching closer, Madam Daark glaring at him, and Hee-Haw perching in the chair ready to pounce, Gavin felt like a fly in a web with three spiders competing for the first bite.

And there in the middle of the web with him was his dumb cousin who was—what? Surrounded by all this ritzy stuff, there stood Eric in a world of his own, scratching himself like he was in a locker room. Gavin elbowed his cousin.

"What!" Eric exclaimed, clueless.

"Boys, boys." Madam Daark glided toward them in a cloud of ankle-length fabric that would have tripped a normal person. But something told Gavin that *Cruella* was anything but normal. She approached him, as cunningly as a snake, with her head up, measuring him with a cold gaze. Gavin didn't even want to think why.

"Enough nonsense." Her voice couldn't have been louder if she held a megaphone to her lips. "You're here because of this." She held the diary in both hands and stroked the cover with her thumbs.

Gavin wanted to push her down, grab the diary, and hotfoot it out of there, but he held his ground. "That's mine, you know."

"Yes, well." The velvet in Madam's voice took on a razor edge. "I know you *think* it's yours, but there is some question about rightful ownership. We hold it in *our* possession now, don't we?" She sat on the chaise lounge and patted the cushion. "Here. Sit with me, Gavin."

"I'd rather stand." Gavin 's heartbeat hammered the words *stand firm, stand firm, stand firm* into his brain.

"As you wish." Madam placed the book on her lap and motioned to the shadows. "You've made Nem Downes' acquaintance, I presume?"

Gavin glanced in Hee-Haw's direction, then back to Madam Daark. He didn't know which one made him feel more squeamish. "Didn't know his name was Nem."

"You can call me Clever," Hee-Haw said, a burst of laughter reverberating through his nose. He tossed Bea a wink that sent a shiver up Gavin's back. Now there was a pair that deserved each other.

"I've been watching you and your strange old uncle," Hee-Haw said. "And I know you have what it takes to open the diary."

"Oh, do hush up!" Bea's mother stomped her foot, her harsh tone turning once again to sugar. "I will handle this."

"Better get out of her way, Nem." Bea's lips twisted into a cynical smile. "This is her show."

Uncle Warney was right. No Molly. Gavin had been lured there for the sole purpose of opening the diary. He didn't know if he felt more relieved or terrified.

With a smile that raised goosebumps on both of his arms, Madam extended her hand and offered him the diary.

Gavin couldn't believe that she would just hand it over. It must be another trick.

"Go ahead." Bea's delight was unmistakable. "Mum trusts you."

Yeah, said the spider to the fly. Gavin hesitated. He swallowed hard and squared his shoulders. The moment he touched it, all three of them would probably pounce on him and do only heaven knew what.

Stand firm. Stand firm. Stand firm.

Bracing himself with a deep breath, Gavin clutched the book—and nothing happened. At least, nothing he could see or feel other than the tingle that came into his fingertips. The diary was his once more!

Madam Daark reclined in the chaise lounge and tilted her face toward the chandelier, but Gavin wasn't fooled. She was watching him through slanted eyes, like a cat waiting to unsheathe its claws on unsuspecting prey.

"Go ahead, young man. Open it up. All I ask before you go is that you read a passage to me. Any passage will do."

He wasn't falling for that line. "No, thank you, ma'am. I'm not into reading. I think I'll just be on my way."

No sooner were the words out of his mouth when something outside the window caught Gavin's eye. Thick, gnarly vines and briars grew up the side of the Lodge like a fast-forward, time-lapsed Disney movie. He blinked, sure that it was an illusion. But no! In a matter of seconds, a third of the window was covered with vegetation that was climbing up to the stained glass half moon.

"What's that?" he ran to the window and pressed his nose to the pane.

"Whoa," Eric said, joining him. "What's happening?"

Gavin swiveled around and stared at the woman behind all this madness.

"Oh, just a little something to ensure your cooperation, boys." Madam sat up straight, no longer smiling at Gavin. "You will open the book. Now! Or those treelings will work their way in here and around your stubborn neck . . . and his." She pointed to Eric.

"Gavin?" Eric looked alarmed.

Truth. Truth. Gavin knew he had to tell the truth. *Truth is, I'm not paralyzed with terror.* The thought jolted him.

"Gavin?" Eric repeated as he crept up closer to him. "What's going on?"

Bea answered. "Do as Mum says, Gavin, and there will be no trouble."

"Don't, and them trees'll hang you both." Hee-Haw sneered and then his face relaxed as he began to chant strange-sounding vowels and syllables. "Ooziss," he said, "come now in power and persuade this young fool to do as he's told."

"Not on your life." Gavin gripped the invisible belt at his waist. Was there a speck of truth that could help him now?

Clever lies wormed their way to the surface of his mind. He was tempted to say he didn't know anything about the book, but when he opened his mouth, he blurted out, "Truth is, Officer Charlie's on his way."

"Is that so?" Madam Daark seemed genuinely amused. "But he's not here yet, is he?" Her eyes bored holes in his. "Open the book!"

The diary felt hot in his hand. Maybe he could plead ignorance from his dyslexia. No. He must tell the truth, no matter how much it ticked her off.

"Truth is," Gavin realized in spite of the taunting, "God is with me—" *And Eric, too.* Whatever drug or spell they'd had over him had worn off completely.

"Okay, Eric," Gavin said, pocketing the diary and taking a chance. "This would be a good time for you to flex those muscles and get us out of here."

"Huh? Oh, right!" Eric lunged for the door, but Jenkins blocked his path. Bending down like a fullback, Eric rammed his head into Jenkins' stomach, which only served as a trampoline to bounce Eric back where he started.

Gavin ran to Eric, but Bea and Hee-Haw grabbed Gavin's arms and pulled him aside.

"Ooziss has you now," Hee-Haw hissed, tightening his grip on Gavin's arm.

"*Enough!*" Madam Daark shouted. "Ooziss Naturus, allow me the pleasure. This battle is mine."

Gavin broke loose and spun in time to see the crimson-faced witch rise from her chaise. *Uh-oh, this doesn't look good.*

In a flash, the crazed woman leapt to the fireplace, grabbed a poker, and aimed it at Eric. A stream of angry gibberish spewed from her mouth.

Eric dropped his head and whimpered.

Gavin bit his lip until it throbbed like his pulse and touched the diary to be sure it was safe in his pocket. If he did what they wanted, he could save Eric. But he couldn't, or he would betray Uncle Warney and God. *Stand firm. Stand firm no matter what.* Even as he thought the words, warmth spread from his pocket. *The nail!* The nail Jesus had given him was in his pocket.

Gavin wrapped his fingers around it. The moment he touched the pointed edge, heat spread up his arm, releasing energy in Gavin he had never felt before. In that instant, with the infusion of courage and strength, he knew what to do. The nail was smaller, much smaller, than her poker, but the power of the Holy Spirit flowed through him, and *that* she didn't have.

He brandished the nail at Madam Daark. Rushing between the priestess and his re-zombiefied cousin, Gavin raised the nail against the poker. The two metals converged in an eerie *claaaaannng*, opposites clashing, good versus evil, David and Goliath. Madam Daark met Gavin's gaze across their locked weapons. Time suspended as they stood frozen, glaring at one another.

"The power of the Lord flows through this nail." Gavin had never known such boldness.

"Ha!" In spite of the disbelief in her voice, Madam backed off, breaking contact. "Terribly amusing." She maneuvered side-to-side in her beaded jacket and flowing skirt while Gavin hopped around in his red and black Nikes, wielding his nail. "That may be so, but *you're* just an ordinary boy and no match for me, child. You are obviously untrained in the art of fencing."

Fencing? Was that what he was doing? That's what they did in *The Three Musketeers.* Doubt intruded into his mind. God was strong, but Gavin Goodfellow wasn't. *Jesus, Jesus, help me, Jesus!* Even as the words formed in his mind, Gavin became more confident.

Gavin circled Madam, who stood rooted to her spot, staring into his eyes. "Put down that silly nail, and let's get back to the diary, shall we?"

"Nem!" Bea said from somewhere in the periphery of Gavin's vision. "Toss me the moldavite."

Distracted, Madam Daark glanced her daughter's way. "What moldavite?"

"This!" With a flourish, Hee-Haw tossed a bottle-green crystal to Bea. "You know how to use it?"

"Of course." The way Bea caressed the gem gave Gavin the willies. "It's my passion, remember? Moldavite's extraterrestrial properties enhance human evolution."

"I didn't ask for a history lesson," Hee-Haw said. "So do you know how to use it, or not?"

"I was getting to that," Bea quipped. "When placed on the third eye, moldavite establishes a cosmic connection."

"Rubbish." Madam scowled and tucked the poker under her arm. "That's an old wives' tale. My ways are more effective."

"Is that so?" Bea challenged. "Then how come he stopped you with a rusty, old nail?"

"He didn't stop me." With a patronizing sniff, Madam Daark returned the poker to its place in the rack by the fireplace. "But, for the sake of argument, tell Mum what you two have been learning—" her voice became a hiss "—*behind my back.*"

"Watch, I'll commune and show you." Bea held the rock to her temple and closed her eyes. "While I'm recruiting allies, Nem, why don't you explain how it works? I've been waiting years for this."

Madam Daark raised an eyebrow. "Yes, Mr. Downes, tell us."

Was this the answer to Gavin's prayer? In their longing to out-voodoo each other, had they all but forgotten about him and the diary? Gavin clenched his fist around the nail and shoved it back into his pocket.

"There are countless souls from Sirius, Orion, and other systems," Hee-Haw said, grabbing center stage. "For our earth to fully heal itself, we need new races with a more cosmic view of existence. These souls, incarnating for the first time on our planet, must be grounded in the energies of earth. Moldavite is our way of connecting with them."

Gavin edged slowly toward the dazed Eric.

"So, what are you saying?" Gavin hoped he could build on the distraction. "You think people came from rocks that got zapped, and if you grow a third eye and rub it with that broken glass some aliens will pop out and . . . do what?"

"Let me have that." Madam Daark snatched the rock out of Bea's hand. "I told you, no moldavite! I'll have no aliens interfering with my plans."

Snapping out of her meditative mode, Bea shot her mother a look of alarm and confusion. "No!"

Cupping the stone in both hands, Madam uttered an incantation and squeezed. *Poof!* The moldavite crumbled into dust.

Bea's face grew beet red. Scalded by the glare of her mother's superiority and withering inside from the crushing defeat, Bea turned downcast eyes in Hee-Haw's direction. "I guess it wasn't meant for me to have moldavite, after all."

Hee-Haw turned paler than the dust Madam Daark brushed from her hands. "Either she's got more power than the stone or Auntie was peddling a fake. How am I gonna explain—"

The distant sound of approaching sirens cut him off.

Grabbing Eric with one hand, Gavin dragged him toward the door. Like a quick-draw gunslinger, he yanked the nail from his pocket and raised it at Jenkins.

Whether from the power of the Holy Spirit, the sirens, or both, Jenkins moved aside and let them pass.

"Not so fast." Madam Daark cast a black look toward the window, which prompted the jungle of thorny greens and twisting brown branches to quadruple in size, bursting through the glass and throwing shards deep into the room.

"You think you can just walk away with that diary?" Madam shouted above the clatter of the fast-growing branches.

Angry vines lunged past Eric, straight at Gavin, wrapping their tendrils around his ankles. Knocking him to the floor like a sack of concrete, thistles and treelings engulfed him, sending thorny tentacles up his torso and around his throat.

CHAPTER THIRTY-SIX

GAVIN

Power Struggle

Gasping for air and bleeding from the thorns, Gavin clawed at the vines to rip them away before they could choke him. That gave the creeping plant a new target—his wrists. Panic surged when leaves sprouted next to his mouth and crept toward his nose.

Completely pinned, Gavin's ears began to ring. In the distance, he heard voices but couldn't tell whether they were cheering his opponent on or calling the battle off. Completely exhausted in the tangled mess, he resigned himself to the bleak truth and stopped struggling.

He felt a tickling sensation as the thistles and vines released their grip. But, in a flash, he realized the ivy shoots weren't releasing him, but just working their way toward his pocket—and the diary.

Drawing strength from the nail he still clutched in his fist, Gavin blurted out, "When I am weak, then I am strong!" The horror on Madam Daark's face, coupled with his surprising utterance—words he didn't know he knew—gave him courage. He forced his hand to move.

"That's mine!" he yelled and jabbed the tip of the nail into a wiry stalk that had plunged into his pocket.

Shrieks erupted from the plants like a room full of wounded cats. The sound assaulted Gavin's ears, but he felt instant relief as the tangled mess retreated from his body. The vines and treelings stood, agitated. Slowly, they converged on Madam Daark. Gavin watched in a mixture of glee and terror as they pounced on her.

When Bea, Hee-Haw, and Jenkins rushed to Madam's aid, Gavin saw his chance and helped his cousin to his feet. "This way, Eric."

"Cool." Eric was still out of it, but at least he followed directions. "Cool plants. Are we in a terrarium?"

Gavin braced his shoulder under Eric's armpit, hoisted him up by the waist, and led the way down the twisting hall. Moving as fast as he could with Eric leaning on him, Gavin hobbled around corners, bumping knickknacks off end tables in the process. He didn't want to think about what was happening to Madam Daark, but it was her own fault. At last, they reached the front door.

Stuck!

"Help me push it open, Eric."

Gavin shoved against the massive door with all his might; it gave way so easily that Gavin nearly fell onto the porch. He recovered his balance, but Eric wasn't so lucky and sprawled into a flower bed where he convulsed into waves of laughter.

Expecting to see a jungle of vines and briars covering the Lodge, Gavin couldn't believe they were gone! His own wounds had vanished, too, with the exception of his lip that was swollen and bleeding from all his chewing. The only thing that seemed real to Gavin at that moment was the fresh air, sunshine, and Officer Charlie's patrol car fishtailing to a stop in the driveway.

Relief surged in his chest. Leaving Eric to his flowers and giggle fit, Gavin raced down the porch steps toward Officer Charlie and Dexter, eager to tell them all about Madam Daark, when the sight of his dad and Molly climbing out of the back seat knocked the wind out of him. Bruce Goodfellow wore his familiar what-kind-of-trouble-do-we-have-here expression.

But this time, Gavin felt he could face him with confidence. After all, he'd been heroic, and God was on his side.

"Dad!" he called out.

"Gavin, what's going on? Are you okay?" For once, Bruce Goodfellow rushed to him with open arms.

Gavin's hopes shot sky high. His dad believed in him! "You gotta come inside and see, Dad—you, too, Officer Charlie. They're . . . they're . . ."

Gavin couldn't think of a single thing to say that would come close to describing the danger he'd so narrowly escaped. "They pretended to kidnap Molly, but she's not there and—"

"Of course, I'm not there—I'm here," Molly said.

"We just had fried chicken with Molly," his dad said, "and your mother was worried sick over why you weren't there and where you'd wandered off to after church. We were about to file a missing person's report when Officer Charlie told us he was on his way here—that Dexter said you were in some kind of danger."

"Yeah, I'll say!" Gripped by a frantic urgency to make his dad understand, Gavin nearly swooned with excitement. "That Daark woman is some sort of witch. She grew vines all over the windows to lock us in and went after Eric with a poker, but I fought her off with my nail. Then Hee-Haw gave Bea a stone, and she tried to call on aliens from outer space, but Madam Daark crushed it and—"

The more he rambled, the harder his father's expression grew. Gavin knew it sounded far-fetched, but he also knew it was the truth.

"Now, Gavin," Officer Charlie began in a condescending tone.

"Tell them, Eric!" Gavin turned to his cousin, but Eric just stared at him, still in a stupor.

"See? He's under their spell."

"I'm just tired," Eric said. Plucking petunias from his hair, he zigzagged to the patrol car where he flopped into the back seat.

Desperate, Gavin turned to Dexter. "You believe me, right?"

"I believe you've had a long, eventful day, Gavin." Dexter winked.

Gavin couldn't have been more wounded if he'd been kicked in the chest by both of Uncle Warney's Clydesdales. *Some friend!*

Officer Charlie nodded. "I think we owe it to Gavin to have a quick look around—"

"And say a neighborly hello to the Daarks," Gavin's dad interrupted. He straightened his tie, very much the mayor now. "Pretty tall tale you've tossed at us," he said. "From the ruckus Dexter raised, we thought you were in trouble, but you look fine to me. Hope you haven't upset the Daarks. They're bringing a lot of jobs to this community. You're a budding reporter, Molly. Come on."

Molly grabbed her pad and pen and followed the mayor in while glaring at Gavin over her shoulder.

Gavin slumped, the fight gone out of him. So much for his dad being an ally. Seeing was believing, and Gavin had nothing to show. There was no way his dad would believe him without proof.

"Come on, Gavin, time to do damage control." At least Officer Charlie still had a smile in him.

"I . . . uh . . . yes, sir. Would it be okay if I stayed out here with Dexter while you go in?"

"Sure, Bud," Officer Charlie nodded and went into the house.

"Why don't we wait by the well?" Dexter said after the door closed. "I'm sure there's some shred of evidence they've overlooked that will vindicate you. I believe you." He winked again.

"Why? Nobody else does. And what's with the winking and 'you've had a long day' crack?"

"Cut the pity party, Gavin. I didn't think you'd want to spill the beans about what went on in the attic, and I could tell your dad couldn't get a handle on what you'd just been through."

"No kidding."

"You've got to remember, Gavin, it was only a few hours ago that you encountered the Holy Spirit, and the Lord saw fit to take you straight into battle. This is no Monopoly game—*Do not pass go, do not collect $200.* This is the real thing. You had your first taste of spiritual warfare in there, and I want to know every little detail. Did you see the diary?"

"Did I ever! Had to fight for it, but I got it back." Gavin felt both relieved and concerned. "What about him?" He pointed toward the patrol car where Eric lay curled up on the seat, resting his head against the window. "He saw it, too. Now *he* knows about the diary."

"If he even remembers." Dexter shrugged. "He seems kind of out of it. We'll cross that bridge later."

Dexter and Gavin leaned against the hard, cold stones of the old well. A gust of cold air swirled up from the depths, nipping at Gavin's neck. Was it all for nothing? His courage in the face of danger?

Dexter pointed to Uncle Warney who was limping toward them. "Now you can tell both of us what happened."

Gavin slipped his hand into his pocket to touch the nail and the diary. *Still there.* At least, Uncle Warney would believe.

"Ya ain't diggin' fer a penny to put in that wishin' well, are ya?" Uncle Warney smiled as he approached.

Gavin shook his head.

"Ya been through the wringer today, ain't ya, son?" Uncle Warney wheezed. His shaved head, ruddy cheeks, and rigid posture had never looked so good. Resting his cane against the well, Uncle Warney wrapped his arm around Gavin's shoulder in a good, long squeeze. "The Lord's had me prayin' up a storm fer ya, every step of the way here. But I see ya made it out safe 'n sound. Tell us all about it."

Gavin recounted his tale, from saving Eric from being zapped by the poker, to the strange duel with Madam Daark, to the fast-growing and house-engulfing vines, to his narrow escape. "And through it all, I just kept thinking, *stand firm, stand firm, stand firm.* I was so scared, but my mind didn't go blank. I could feel the power through the nail . . . and through me. It was awesome."

Gavin glanced at the Lodge which appeared to be as pristine as a summer cottage, free of life-threatening vines. All evidence of the magic inside was probably gone, too.

"But when I told the truth," he choked back disappointment, "Dad didn't believe me. He thinks I'm a bigger liar than ever."

"But we know better, don't we? He'll come 'round in due time," Warney said. "Yer dad's a hard man, but not too hard fer God."

"Yeah," Gavin nodded and turned toward the Lodge. "Things could be worse. I could live in there."

"Hey." Dexter snapped his gum, releasing a hint of cinnamon. "I know, let's pretend this is a military debriefing and see what we can learn from it."

"Yep, that's a good way ta put it." Warney's eyes took on a faraway look. "Ya know, Gavin, even Jesus got mocked. Fact is, folks made fun of Him for speakin' the truth. That's why yer mighty special to Him, 'cause He knows jest how yer feelin' right now—heart hurtin' and all."

A fresh wave of divine affirmation washed over Gavin. He felt cleansing streams of living water trickle their way into his thoughts and emotions, soothing him from the inside out.

"Ya know," Warney said, "it don't always show whether or not we're winnin' or losin', least not right away. But 'member this: the battle is the Lord's. And in the end, when it's all said 'n done and the dust settles, the good Book says God wins!"

Dexter's smile was so broad Gavin could see most all of his pearly whites. "I'll bet Father God's up there saying, 'Well done, thou good and faithful servant.'"

A trace of sadness lingered in Gavin. If only he could hear words like that from his earthly dad.

"You accepted the call of God today, Gavin," Dexter said. "You even had a chance to try your belt of truth on for size, and you came through with flying colors."

"Now, here's a question fer ya." Uncle Warney coughed. "Whar's the diary?"

Gavin smacked his head with his palm, then dug into his pocket and produced the leather-bound treasure. "Ta-da! Safe and sound, Uncle Warney!"

"Well, I'll be a horseshoe fly's saddle, ya got it back." The old man's smile widened. "That's plenty fer one day, don't ya think?"

Gavin caressed the frayed leather. "Wish I'd kept my mouth shut and just let Dad think everything was fine."

"But that wouldn't a been truthful, now, would it?" Uncle Warney scratched the stubble on his chin. "It takes wisdom to know when to speak and when to zip yer lip. That'll come in time. Yer jest gettin' started on yer journey."

Although goosebumps scrambled on Gavin's skin, his insides were warm enough to grill hamburgers. In a small but sincere voice, feeling a sense of triumph that nearly lifted him off his feet, he uttered words he would remember the rest of his days. "No matter how foolish it makes me look, from now on, I vow to tell the truth, the whole truth, and nothing but the truth, so help me, God."

The front door opened, and there stood Madam Daark, the image of poise, as Officer Charlie and his dad said their goodbyes. Bea and Molly looked pretty chummy. Maybe it had something to do with the pretty blue sweater Molly had over her arm.

Bruce Goodfellow's campaign smile faded the second he met Gavin's expectant gaze. "Gavin, front and center. Now!"

Gavin took a deep breath, stood up, and braced himself.

"These two lovely ladies," he gestured toward them, "were hosting a tea party with cakes and silver service, entertaining Nem Downes, of all people, when you barged in with Eric, uninvited and rude! They were completely baffled by your behavior as am I!"

Gavin's dad's eyes bulged. "There is no excuse for this, young man. Once again, you have put me in an embarrassing position. Do you hear me? No excuse! What do you have to say for yourself?"

"Well, I . . ." The wheels of Gavin's mind turned, looking in all the old places for a lie to smooth things over, but Uncle Warney gave him a look, and he felt the belt cinch his waist. "I told you the truth, Dad. They're witches. Maybe Madam Daark used her magic or something to cover up, but—".

Bruce Goodfellow threw his hands in the air. "Warney. It seems you're always somewhere nearby when Gavin has a creative tale to spin. Did you put him up to this? What kind of crazy ideas have you been putting in his head?"

When Uncle Warney didn't answer, Gavin watched his dad's face do its red balloon thing.

"All right." Bruce heaved a sigh of exasperation. "Everybody in the car." He glared at Uncle Warney. "Except you. You can walk back the same way you came."

"Yes sirree." Warney nodded as pleasantly as if talking with a close friend. "Walkin' keeps the cricks outta muh bones."

Gavin held his hand out to Uncle Warney but received a bear hug instead of a handshake. The old man pulled him close and whispered in Gavin's ear, "Yer father loves ya. He jest don't know how ta show it yet."

CANDY ABBOTT

"Keep your hands off my boy! You hear me?" Bruce Goodfellow shouted, then turned on his heel toward Gavin. "In the car. Now! I'll deal with you when we get home." He held the front door open for Molly who slid into the vehicle without a word.

As Gavin climbed into the back seat with Dexter and a now-dozing Eric, Officer Charlie poked his head through the open window.

"Dexter, I'm not very happy with you either, so you can quit trying to look so innocent. I know you're up to your eyeglasses in this, and I'm going to get to the bottom of it."

Gavin saw the same apprehension on Dexter's face as he felt in his gut about what punishment awaited them. But in spite of it all, Gavin felt good inside. He was different. He had stood firm in the face of evil. Even better, he had resisted the urge to lie to his father.

The battle was over—for today, at least. Heaven only knew what the diary would require of him, if and when it opened up. With all those pages still sealed, the battle for good and evil over Burnt Swamp had just begun.

Get Gavinized!

You are cordially invited
to join
Gavin's goodfellows
online
at
www.GavinGoodfellow.com
to share your Gavinesque moments,
thoughts, and opinions
with the Mollyites, the Ericdotes,
the Dextereans,
and friends.

Uncle Warney says,
"Stop by anytime, day or night!"

Special Thanks

- To the Holy Spirit who called me to write Gavin even when I kept saying, "But, Lord . . . but, Lord . . . "

- To my husband, Drew, who is unwavering in his conviction that "we can do this," especially when it became evident that God's plans for my writing were going in a different direction than I had anticipated. No wife has ever been so blessed.

- To my grandchildren: Natalie and Trevor who inspired the characters and to Kade and Saige who serve as strong motivators for me to do my part in equipping the next generation with godly fiction.

- To Marlene Bagnull who has been my writing mentor since the early 1990s and whose Greater Philadelphia and Colorado Christian Writers Conferences, and related resources, continue to equip me with the tools and networking I need to pursue my call to write. It was Marlene's attention to detail in the final editing that polished more rough edges than I knew existed.

- To Diane Cook who was the first to catch my vision for Gavin and has been coaching me ever since—not only in plot, setting, character development, and dialogue but as my managing editor, marketing consultant, and trusted sister in Christ.

- To Linda Windsor who not only line-edited my rough beginnings but labored in love with Diane to help me map out the subplots and, in general, bring the Gavin Goodfellow series to life.

- To Nancy Rue who not only took this beginning novelist under her wing to mentor on the fine points of fiction but claimed me as her adopted godmother and connected me with the "Writeen Crue" (Pam Halter, Joyce Moccero, Rosemarie DiCristo, Dawn Moore, Floss Craig, Dr. Dale McElhinney, Brenda Ulman, Vivian Dippold, Winnie Kutchukian, and Tim Shoemaker), critique and prayer partners.

- To Gwen Ellis and Natasha Sperling who put me through the paces of royalty publishing which refined the manuscript and provided clarity for the project that I would surely have missed otherwise.

- To the members of Delmarva Christian Writers' Fellowship who have been cheering Gavin on since the beginning. Special thanks to my proofreaders: Wilma Caraway, Betsey Farlow, Barbara Foster, Marianne Leavitt, and Floydie Sabo. And to my writer-friend encouragers and prayer partners: Betty, Jean, Dee, Judi, Donna, Lori, Linda, Connie, Lois, Eva, Karen, Kris, Rhona, Leslie, Patty, David, Cindy, Stephen, the "Nangie" crew, and so many others . . . I had to stop somewhere.

- To Pastor Mike Williams and my Georgetown Presbyterian Church family who provided a safe launching pad and biblical springboard. And to Linda Wolfe and the choir whose anthems kept me focused.

- To our daughters Kim and Dana and their husbands, Wyatt and John, who treat Gavin like a member of the family. To our son Troy, who has taught us victory in spiritual warfare. To my brothers Mike and Jim, their wives Mary and Shelly, and their families. To my in-laws, Howard and Kelly, Tim and Myrna, and Dean.

- To the intercessors who prayed Gavin into existence: Malorie Derby, Lois Theofiles, Chris Ann Waters, Lin Zornig, Linda Hostelley, Joyce Thomas, Floydie Sabo, Pat Atkins, Wilmetta Stevens, Joyce Sessoms, Margie Biosotto, Betty McKinley, Marilyn Kirk, Tom and Laura Lagana, Dan and Ruth Hayne, my Emmaus group, Barbara and Randy Walter, and four hundred-plus e-mail prayer warriors.

- To the members of the Fruitbearer Publishing Marketing Team: Diane Cook, marketing consultant; Bart Fennemore, web designer; Karen Gritton, event planner; and Ashley Theis, publicist, who are making sure Gavin gets a chance to make a whole lot of new friends.

- To Laura Pritchett, who graciously and enthusiastically stepped forward when I realized that an artistic map was not optional but necessary. Calmly and efficiently, using her artistic genius, she created the "Burnt Swamp map" within days of going to press.

- To all who have reminded me in one way or another that "faith is the substance of things hoped for, the evidence of things not seen" (Hebrews 11:1). This day, my faithful co-workers for the Kingdom, hope has not disappointed us. Let's see what God will do with Gavin now that he is on the move!

Meet the Author

When God calls, you either obey or run away. In Candy Abbott's case, the call to write came more than twenty years ago while she was working as an executive secretary at a local community college. After her initial response of, "Who, me? Write a book?", Candy accepted God's call and embarked on a remarkable journey that rivals the adventures Gavin is facing in her first young adult novel.

Her non-fiction book *Fruitbearer, What Can I Do For You, Lord?*, is now in its third edition and is blessing others with the story of how she found a personal relationship with the Holy Spirit.

The Lord challenged Candy to write the Gavin Goodfellow series in 2000. During the seven years it took to produce book one, God not only equipped her with all the tools she needed, but brought her husband, Drew, and many friends and professionals alongside to mentor her through the process. Like Gavin, Candy's encounter with the Holy Spirit reshaped her life.

Her fervent prayer is that Gavin's story will entertain and inspire young and old alike to search out truth and make wise choices that lead to an intimate relationship with our Lord Jesus Christ; to confess without apology, "As for me and my household, we shall serve the Lord."

Candy is a wife, mother, grandmother, Sunday school teacher, author, and publisher. Her inspirational stories appear in numerous anthologies, including *Chicken Soup for the Christian Woman's Soul*. In her role as founder and director of Delmarva Christian Writers' Fellowship, and president of Fruitbearer Publishing, she has earned a respected voice in Christian publishing circles. A CLASServices speaker, Candy's inspirational messages are heard throughout the Delmarva Peninsula and beyond. In addition to serving in the Presbyterian Church as an ordained elder and deacon, she co-founded Sisters in Christ, an inter-denominational women's prayer ministry that has been encouraging believers for more than twenty years.

Looking ahead—

Watch for the further adventures
of Gavin Goodfellow.

In *The Gathering at Burnt Swamp,*
Gavin's newfound faith moves to the next level
when evil forces align to overtake
the school, the town, and the swamp.

Check our Web site for updates:
www.GavinGoodfellow.com